Endorsements for *Queering Health: Critical challenges to normative health and healthcare*

This is an excellent addition to the literature and body of evidence on the complex issues that still challenge members of our society in their access and experiences of healthcare. Not only have the authors captured the essence of the book in its title but they have focused their writings, evidence base and knowledge on key issues and pivotal issues that have a direct impact on the equality of care expected by all. In my view the authors have bravely decided to explore issues that some may find uncomfortable: age, mental health, lesbian narratives, and user perspectives. The queer theory that frames this book provides a rigorous approach to the critical understanding of the issues addressed.

There is no doubt in my mind that this book is a must-read for all health and social care practitioners. It will challenge, stimulate, provide understanding and insight into the wider needs of society and the role that practitioners can play. For those looking to provide insight into equality and diversity in their programmes and curricula, then this book does just that in a way that will inspire.

**Professor Brian J Webster, Assistant Dean, Faculty of Health, Life & Social Sciences, Edinburgh Napier University**

This engaging, troubling, and beautifully written book dives into the assumptions and paradoxes that shape our experiences of healthcare. It challenges systems of classification that attempt to reduce human complexity to a label by recognizing the fluid, hybrid nature of contemporary identities. Thus, it expands our understanding of queer theory and queer practice that aim to 'undo normativity'. The integration of theory and narrative is masterful, and the book's messages are both timely and timeless. *Queering Health* insists (despite the hegemony of the market) that kindness, dignity, and compassion are more relevant today than ever. I can't wait to share this work with my colleagues and students. Its stories and exquisitely clear theoretical presentations support anti-oppressive practice in a variety of fields, inspiring the reader to re-imagine systems of care. This important new work will inform, and perhaps more important, open up the discourse on healthcare and health policy to new questions and perspectives.

**Amanda Barusch, Professor of Social Work, University of Otago and University of Utah**

# Queering Health:
# Critical challenges to normative health and healthcare

Edited by
Dr Laetitia Zeeman
Dr Kay Aranda
Dr Alec Grant

*PCCS Books*
Ross-on-Wye

First published 2014

PCCS BOOKS
2 Cropper Row
Alton Road
Ross-on-Wye
Herefordshire
HR9 5LA
UK
Tel +44 (0)1989 763900
contact@pccs-books.co.uk
www.pccs-books.co.uk

**Queering Health: Critical challenges to normative health and healthcare**

British Library Cataloguing in Publication data.
A catalogue record for this book is available from the British Library.

ISBN 978 1 906254 71 1

We gratefully acknowledge the kind permission of the Queensland Art Gallery, Gallery of Modern Art to use their image for the cover of this book.

Ah Xian. 'Metaphysica' series (detail) 2007. Bronze and brass. 36 sculptures: dimensions variable.

Works from Ah Xian's 'Metaphysica' series 2007 in 'The China Project' at GOMA.

With the generosity of Tim Fairfax, AM, a group of six of the sculptures was acquired for the Queensland Art GalleryCollection.

Photograph by Natasha Harth, QAGOMA.

Cover designed in the UK by Old Dog Graphics
Printed in the UK by Imprint Digital, Exeter

# Dedications

**Laetitia Zeeman**
To my family in Africa, for their love has endured over time. A kind of love that takes on many different forms, that I have been defined by, guided by and inspired by.

**Kay Aranda**
For our young ones who live near and across the pond, Richard, Kathryn, Amelia, Fiona and Isabella.

**Alec Grant**
For Charlotte.

# contents

# Acknowledgements

This book would not have been possible without the unstinting support of Heather Allan and her colleagues at PCCS Books. Thank you all for believing in its value and supporting us in its construction and delivery. We are also grateful to Professors Ian Parker, Gillian Bendelow, Amanda Barusch and Brian Webster for writing the forewords and blurbs, and to all the contributing authors who brought a rich variety of queer and critical theoretical-informed empirical and experiential wisdom to the project. Our combined experience in healthcare tells us that a critical and queer turn is constantly needed for patients, clients, carers and others who find themselves at the mercy of often discriminatory, marginalising and assaultive normative healthcare practices. We acknowledge you and your experiences as *the* central driver to this book.

# foreword

## – professor gillian bendelow –

Health and illness are multifaceted concepts which span a range of disciplines and have varied meanings in different societies. Since the nineteenth century we have witnessed dramatic advances in the understanding and cure of disease with an unprecedented extension of both quality and length of life (albeit confined to so-called *developed* countries). Yet even as medical science has progressed, the dominance of the biomedical model with its narrow philosophical grounding has been under constant challenge from the social sciences, and from within medicine itself. Social sciences associated with medicine, such as medical sociology, medical humanities, bioethics and health psychology, have made major contributions to shaping modern ideas about health and illness. In particular, critiques of the limitations of the mind/body divide with biomedicine and the emphasis on high-technology, cure and have developed hand in hand with the decline of high mortality rates from infectious diseases.

In richer industrialised 'western' countries, mortality from infectious disease tends to be largely replaced by degenerative illnesses such as cancer and cardiovascular disease, and the burden of chronic illness is a global phenomenon. Furthermore, contemporary morbidity patterns are increasingly dominated by illnesses associated with increased life expectancy and by complex chronic conditions closely associated with 'lifestyle', such as diabetes, arthritis, and a range of conditions associated with anxiety and depression. In the twentieth and twenty-first centuries, the role of the 'social' and the critiques of medicalisation and healthism within contemporary healthcare have gained increasing importance together with the decline of faith in biomedicine alongside major public scandals, litigation and government regulation.

Thus, both biomedicine and medical social sciences have been challenged by a host of illnesses or conditions with multifactorial aetiologies and complex mind–body relationships, which require traditional categories, formulations and management strategies to be re-evaluated. In particular, the role of emotion and stress in contemporary patterns of health and illness demands considerable rethinking across the traditional divisions between mental and physical conditions, in order to transcend not just the split between mind and body, but the mind/body/society divide. In turn, these insights inform social theories of embodiment in illness disability, alongside the growth of lay knowledge and user movements, aided by public understandings of science and knowledge, especially through new information technology.

Whilst scientific progress continues to be vital in understanding these phenomena, it is equally important to advance understanding of the social and socioeconomic factors that play a part in the promotion and maintenance of health, the prevention and causation of disease, and of the relationship between these and the broader social structure; in other words, as many others have urged, to develop values-based practice alongside evidence-based medicine.

As this volume emphasises, a critical approach to the propensity for medicine and healthcare to be an agent of social control *against* the backdrop of the potential for increased surveillance and social manipulation is essential to challenge the normative, alienating, even damaging and iatrogenic assumptions that are perpetuated in modern healthcare. Empirical research into health inequalities has persistently provided evidence of the association between poor health and socioeconomic status, which is cross cut by gender, ethnicity, sexuality and disability. The need for rich qualitative research on 'lived experience' to complement the wider positivist studies is much needed, hence the theoretical insights derived from queer theory to help analyse these narrative accounts is to be welcomed.

This volume addresses the challenge of the need for this *rapprochement* between social and biological models of health and illness, which include the political dimensions of the relationship between individuals and the wider social structure. We may not be able to find universally valid, comprehensive and agreed definitions of health and illness because of variability between cultures, historical periods and individuals, but instead of remaining embedded in debates between biological and cultural determinism, the sophisticated theory-driven empirical research described in these chapters provides an example of how to embrace these complexities.

Gillian Bendelow, November 2013

# foreword

## – professor ian parker –

This book provides an overview of and intervention into the world of health and healthcare, disturbing, 'queering' we might say, the assumptions that govern that world.

One way into a different perspective on that world is to explore what impact 'queer' has on our practice, that is, on our political practice first and then on our clinical practice. While the writers in *Queering Health* concern themselves with more diverse areas of health, healthcare and critical theory, for the purposes of this foreword I have chosen to focus on psychoanalysis, specifically Lacanian psychoanalysis. I have done so because psychoanalysis is a 'health practice', a 'talking cure' that has been a crucial resource for the work of Judith Butler and, implicitly if not explicitly, in the work of other queer theorists.

My starting point is the argument that this psychoanalysis is always already profoundly political (Parker, 2011). Even if we are to conceptualise clinical space as an arena in which politically correct modes of behaviour and experience are interrogated as a problem, even as an arena where our assumptions about politics as such can be bracketed, that definition of the space operates in relation to social relations, interpersonal relations and intrapersonal relations that are politically invested. The relation between analyst and analysand, for example, is a relation of power even if that peculiar relation permits the unravelling of power as such.

Because power relations in heteropatriarchal capitalism are suffused with what we think we know about gender, with what we think we know about the nature of men and women, the power relations between an analyst of whatever sex and an analysand of whatever sex is structured in such a way that feminist critique must be relevant to us. This much has been recognised by psychoanalysts in traditions other than Lacanian, even by post-Jungian writers who one might otherwise think of as mired in deep-grained universal mythology about what is male and what is female (Samuels, 2009). Recognition of this facilitates a *rapprochement* with socialist feminist arguments about the way the domain of the 'personal' under capitalism is political (Rowbotham et al, 2013). This means that the crucial distinction we must make between political space and clinical space is itself inhabited by a certain kind of politics.

First, political space is the domain in which collective action comes up against the capitalist state, even if the mobilisation is first of all as a demand for representation of the oppressed, of the right to speak and act, to challenge, for example, power relations in the family that inhibit that collective action and sabotage the self-organisation of the working class. Feminist demands are just one example here, and we need to include anti-racist and other kinds of politics that address the forms of division that are part of the necessary structure of contemporary neoliberal capitalism.

Second, clinical space is the domain in which personal reflection is made public in a peculiar, limited but transformative kind of action: speech. It entails a demand for representation which cuts across the normative representation of what is private and what is public, what is inside and what is outside. The very separation of clinical space from political space enables the crystallisation of political identity around the figure of the 'individual' – the bourgeois individual, we might say – to be broken open so that what speaks in analysis is the 'subject'. Here are some of the stakes of the conceptual-historical distinction between psychoanalysis that aims to strengthen the ego and that which facilitates subversion of the subject. Lacanian psychoanalysis, it should be noted, does not even pretend to strengthen the subject instead of strengthening the ego; it subverts the subject so that individual and collective action are themselves the places where a different relation to what we take to be 'individual' and 'collective' can be forged.

This is why it is sometimes claimed that 'Queer theory debunks any simple notion of the subject on the basis of the problematics of discourse, power, identity, agency, history and the materiality of the individual' (Giffney & Watson, forthcoming), that psychoanalysis is a process through which this potential may be realised, and that Lacanian psychoanalysis has a privileged role in this game (Watson, 2009). More on Lacan in a moment, but let us step back a bit first and untangle some different elements of queer, and what is important about it for us as psychoanalysts who think of our clinical space as necessarily outwith but intertwined with political space. I hope this will serve as a brief introduction to queer; this is 'queer for Lacanians'. I will undertake this exercise by distinguishing between three different elements that are crucial to queer, but which are often confused in psychoanalysis; the three elements are femininity, feminism and feminisation.

Queer first of all disturbs 'femininity', and it disturbs what psychoanalysis has to say about femininity. It is, perhaps, inimical to queer theory to anchor it in the contributions of specific authors. In this, queer has something in common with feminism, which is a political movement defined by what it does rather than who named it; and it unfortunately differs, it should be said, from Marxism, which is too often traced to individuals (usually men), who founded or then at different points in its history re-founded it. That is, queer departs from a stereotypically masculinist way of configuring the political field, and it disturbs masculinity as much as it disturbs femininity. Anyway, that said, I want to note, with reference to this queer disturbance of femininity, the work of Judith Butler (1990, 1993). Butler kick-started queer theory and queer politics with, among other things, a critique of the way 'femininity' is treated as the defining essence of what it is to be a woman. She makes use of some distinctions that Freud makes, but takes them further and she undercuts some assumptions made about femininity in psychoanalysis after Freud.

Freud (1905) drew a subtle differentiation between biological difference (between males and females), social role (that defined the position of men and women) and personal identity defined by one's masculinity or femininity. The logic of this triple-layered differentiation of human sexual relationships was that sexuality as such could conceivably be reconfigured outside the binary operations that most forms of patriarchy were predicated upon. Freud hints at this possibility and then draws back from it; at one moment the infant is described as 'polymorphously perverse' and at another as 'constitutionally bisexual', and the trajectory that the growing child must follow in order to enter the adult world of compulsory heterosexuality is thereby questioned but then reaffirmed (Freud, 1905; cf. Worthington, 2008). For Butler, 'femininity' is performed by those who come under the signifier 'woman', and this performance reiterates what we presume to correspond to this social role and reiterates what we take to be biological difference. Butler is actually very psychoanalytic here, but she refuses the appeal to underlying 'femininity' in psychoanalysis, for that appeal does women few favours. A recent very friendly interview with two Lacanians reveals that she is in three-times-a-week analysis with an International Psychoanalytic Association (IPA) analyst (Butler, 2010).

The appeal to underlying femininity reiterates a presumed category, and there are then many consequences for those who refuse to reiterate it. We all, Freud (1905, p. 145) says, make a homosexual object-choice in our unconscious, and fantasy is itself, of necessity, perverse. While normal neuroses of various kinds come to organise suffering in consciousness – to some degree conscious, and in a relationship between consciousness and the unconscious marked by repression – the perversions organise a relationship to sexuality that is not necessarily ever conscious at all. French psychoanalysis has routinely filled this formal definition of perversion with normative content, content defined by the reiteration of categories of masculinity and femininity, the most notorious being Chasseguet-Smirgel's (1985) insistence that perverts flout distinctions between genders and between generations, usually both at the same time so that the homosexual is also quite likely to be prone to paedophilia. Lacan (1960–1961) also fills the oedipal structure with a particular content, insisting that homosexuality was as perverse in ancient Greece as it is in modern France, if marked by a different 'quality of objects' in the two cultures. Lacan was not against homosexuals coming to psychoanalysis and he did not aim to 'cure' them, but even so his position on perverse clinical structure resulted in claims by some analysts that those with such a structure ruled themselves out of analysis whether they liked it or not (Roudinesco, 2002; cf. Sauvagnat, 2007).

This brings us to feminism, a political movement with which Butler is allied. She is a feminist, and much queer theory is also explicitly feminist, and with respect to psychoanalysis both queer theory and feminism make the point that while Freud described forms of subjectivity under patriarchy, he did not prescribe them (Mitchell, 1974). Here the distinction between feminism and femininity is crucial, for this feminist argument about the value of Freud's description relies on a refusal to buy into the idea that feminism will appeal to, celebrate, defend or retrieve any kind of hidden 'feminine' essence. There are forms of feminism that do argue for universal unchanging differences between men and women, and there are even forms of feminism that value what is 'feminine'. However, the feminism I am concerned with here treats the feminine as a construction, not as a given; it is something to be transcended not something to be affirmed. Here a relevant queer theorist is Eve Kosofsky Sedgwick (1990), whose ground-breaking book *The Epistemology of the Closet* unravelled the appeal to something hidden under the surface that would then seem to define the truth of individual subjects, those subject to normative social categories.

Sedgwick's examination of the way that sexual categories constitute another hidden dimension of experience that then seems to clamour for expression is also actually quite Lacanian. Her account reminds us of the way repression operates not on some pre-existing material that simmers away in the unconscious but charges what is shut away with a force that is produced by the very process of shutting away. Sedgwick shows how homosexuality, for example, is given definition as something hidden, inside the 'closet', so that those who could only be visible as marked by that category have to 'pass' within other dominant legitimate categories. In this way, processes by which 'homosocial' bonds are maintained also produce the sense that there is another, obscured, secretly 'homosexual' aspect which is not acknowledged as such. The argument here is, again, in line with a feminist critique of the way 'femininity' is mobilised to define what woman is, to name her and define her; and also, of course, it is in line with the critique of the way feminists are labelled as those who are not sufficiently in touch with their own 'femininity'. The 'epistemology of the closet' argument is also very relevant to the way we understand the place of psychoanalysis in culture, the way psychoanalysis not only functions as a clinical practice but also circulates as a tantalising representation of what it pretends to reveal to those who repress, disavow or foreclose its truth.

The third key concept, one that must be differentiated from 'femininity' and 'feminism', is 'feminisation'. This term does refer in some psychiatric and psychological accounts to the process by which an individual is turned into something 'feminine', but that understanding of feminisation already colludes with the assumption that 'feminine' and 'masculine' are underlying essences. Instead, we should see 'feminisation' as a process which constitutes subjects within historically determined categories. Today, in neoliberal capitalism there is a feminisation of the workplace, for example, in which stereotypically feminine qualities are harnessed to make the service sector run more smoothly. Women are employed because they are already trained to perform 'emotional labour' in the family, and they show sensitivity to the needs of customers that men typically do not. Then men are also trained to perform in this way, sometimes even to display stereotypically feminine modes of relating that enable them to maintain their power. Feminisation does not necessarily benefit women, and feminist demands are undermined by this exploitation of 'femininity' (Hochschild, 1983).

Feminisation also bears on the way that men and women are encouraged to share their feelings, and psychotherapy becomes one of the cultural domains in which 'feminisation' of social relations takes place. This brings us to what is called the 'antisocial turn' in queer studies, which is a refusal of an appeal to nurturing capacities of women, a refusal of any underlying femininity (Halberstam, 2008). This antisocial turn also makes explicit the refusal of queer to conform to stereotypical feminised representations of gay men, refusal of the assumption that when a man departs from essential underlying masculinity they must necessarily slide closer to essential underlying femininity. This queer critique, in the work of Judith Halberstam, for example, then pits itself against the feminisation of social and sexual relations, against any appeal to the feminine as an ideal. In one recent formulation, to give you a flavour of this line of argument, there is a refusal of idealisation of women and children, of what has been called 'the fascism of the baby's face' (Edelman, 2004).

There is, then, little sympathy for the kinds of psychoanalysis that reduce themselves to the psychotherapeutic search for the needy inner child. If there is space for Lacanian psychoanalysis in this queer antisocial turn it would be as a practice that did indeed turn signifiers of 'femininity' into nonsense, and we could view this as part of a genuinely feminist refusal of the ideological feminisation of contemporary society that reinforces patriarchy while giving capitalism a new lease of life (Zavos et al, 2005).

That is a question not only for politics, but for our 'mental health' as a political question, and then for health generally, which this book so successfully addresses. I have belaboured psychoanalysis generally, and Lacanian psychoanalysis in particular, here in this foreword because psychoanalysis is a 'health practice', a 'talking cure' that has been a crucial resource for the work of Judith Butler and, implicitly if not explicitly, in the work of other queer theorists. This book builds on those arguments and takes them forward in the domain of practice.

# References

Butler, J (1990) *Gender Trouble: Feminism and the subversion of identity.* London and New York: Routledge.

Butler, J (1993) Bodies That Matter: On the discursive limits of 'sex'. London and New York: Routledge.

Butler, J (2010) Interview by Nassia and Réginald Blanchet for Hurly-Burly. *Hurly-Burly: The International Lacanian Journal of Psychoanalysis, 3,* 111–123.

Chasseguet-Smirgel, J (1985) *Creativity and Perversion.* London: Free Association Books.

Edelman, L (2004) *No Future: Queer theory and the death drive.* Durham, NC: Duke University Press.

Freud, S (1905) Three essays on the theory of sexuality. In S Freud (1966–1974) *The Standard Edition of the Complete Psychological Works of Sigmund Freud* (Trans. J Strachey). London: Vintage, the Hogarth Press and the Institute of Psycho-Analysis, Vol. VII.

Giffney, N & Watson, E (Eds) (forthcoming) *Clinical Encounters: Psychoanalytic practice and queer theory.* London: Routledge.

Halberstam, J (2008) The anti-social turn in queer studies. *Graduate Journal of Social Science, 5*(2), 140–156.

Hochschild, A (1983) *The Managed Heart: Commercialisation of human feeling.* Berkeley, CA: University of California Press.

Lacan, J (1960–1961) *The Seminar of Jacques Lacan, Book VIII: Transference* (Trans. C Gallagher from unedited French manuscripts).

Mitchell, J (1974) *Psychoanalysis and Feminism.* Harmondsworth: Penguin.

Parker, I (2011) *Lacanian Psychoanalysis: Revolutions in subjectivity.* London: Routledge.

Roudinesco, E (2002) Homosexualities today: A challenge for psychoanalysis? (Interview). *Journal of European Psychoanalysis, 15.* Available from http://www.psychomedia.it/jep/number15/roudinesco.htm [accessed 5 September 2009].

Rowbotham, S, Segal, L & Wainwright, H (2013) *Beyond the Fragments: Feminism and the making of socialism* (2nd edition). London: Merlin.

Samuels, A (2009) Carnal critiques: Promiscuity, politics, imagination, spirituality and hypocrisy. *Psychotherapy and Politics International, 7*(1), 4–17.

Sauvagnat, F (2007) A few thoughts about the Lacanian movement's position on the gay question. *JCFAR: The Journal of the Centre for Freudian Analysis and Research, 17,* 29–37.

Sedgwick, EK (1990) *The Epistemology of the Closet.* Los Angeles: University of California Press.

Watson, E (2009) Queering psychoanalysis/psychoanalysing queer. *Annual Review of Critical Psychology, 7*, 114–139.

Worthington, A (2008) Freud's young female homosexual: A clinical exemplar of the three essays? *JCFAR: The Journal of the Centre for Freudian Analysis and Research, 18,* 43–68.

Zavos, A, Biglia, B, Clark, J & Motzkau, J (Eds) (2005) Feminisms and activisms, Special Issue. *Annual Review of Critical Psychology, 5.*

# 1

# introduction

## – laetitia zeeman, kay aranda and alec grant –

These are challenging times for western healthcare. In common with many other formal and publicly funded healthcare systems in the global north, the British National Health Service (NHS) is currently experiencing profound questions over its purpose, practice and place in delivering safe, affordable and effective health services and care. In addition, broader global, demographic and sociocultural changes are creating many anticipated but equally unprecedented demands and expectations within systems which continue to be shaped by neoliberal and neoconservative political and economic philosophies (Taylor-Gooby, 2013; George & Wilding, 2002). Furthermore, research continues to show how dominant the biomedical model is, in intent and effect. In combination with neoliberalism, these forces crucially shape the practices and structures of healthcare, actively produce and reproduce health and illness identities, constitute and construct healthcare subjects, and produce bodies that do and do not matter (Butler, 1993; Fish, 2008, 2009; Reczek & Umberson, 2012).

Thus, the aim of this book is to undo or trouble these neoliberal healthcare practices and systems and the dominant biomedical scientific norms operating in every sphere of healthcare, be that hospital, clinic or home. The chapters in this book represent a deliberate and diverse set of interventions into the myriad ways in which experiences, identities and struggles are produced and reproduced, but equally resisted and changed. Our aim is to create a space to continue to contest the hegemony of the often unexamined normative healthcare assumptions underpinning healthcare relations, structures and practices.

Overall, our hope for the book is that it will engage and encourage our students and colleagues to think again about health and healthcare and make a small but valuable contribution to developing inclusive, participatory and ethically accountable healthcare practices, and to furthering an agenda of social justice.

In this introduction we first outline the key challenges to healthcare posed by global, international and national trends. We set the scene and introduce readers to the broader context of political, economic and social challenges and changes shaping the organisation and delivery of healthcare across the global north, and especially in those mid- to high-income countries with developed, formal healthcare systems. We then introduce our shared understandings of critical and queer theory, and why and how such perspectives potentially provide significant challenges to conventional accounts of health and healthcare in contemporary times. We suggest that these viewpoints, both together and alone, offer unique theoretical tools with which to re-examine, interrogate and re-imagine both familiar and ordinary concerns related to health and illness, and concerns often rendered invisible or marginal.

In each of the chapters that follow authors have discussed the challenges these perspectives provide either theoretically and/or empirically. Though the examples are mainly those impacting upon health and healthcare in the United Kingdom (UK), we hope our readers find these resonate with and are useful for interrogating issues and concerns relevant to their own health settings.

## Global challenges to health

Undoubtedly, one major achievement of modern western societies, with their respective welfare states, has been the rise in life expectancy and living standards. People now live longer, are wealthier and arguably lead much healthier lives. These are trends that look likely to continue even with the economic downturn in the UK, USA and Europe. Yet paradoxically, these unprecedented levels of personal wealth, economic growth and material comfort have failed to translate into greater levels of happiness: indeed, the very opposite is occurring (Wilkinson & Pickett, 2009). Growing prosperity has led to greater disparities and inequalities in income and the distribution of wealth. This relative gap is known to generate social inequalities that in turn manifest as damaging levels of ill-health, producing different forms of suffering, ranging from increased emotional distress, anxiety and depression, to rising levels of stress-related behaviours, witnessed in increased smoking, excessive alcohol intake and over- or under-eating (Wilkinson & Pickett, 2009; World Health Organization, 2000; Marmot, 2010). And, whilst rising longevity is partly a success of formal or publicly provided and funded healthcare systems, together with overall improvements in standards of living, those living longer are now doing so with higher levels of disability and complex, multiple, long-term conditions (Denny & Earle, 2009).

## Neoliberalism

Western healthcare systems additionally share a common challenge in that they have been shaped and are increasingly influenced by the expansion of neoconservative and neoliberal economic ideologies. These forces have for the last 30 years or more underlined the use of markets, reinforced competition and insisted on individual freedom of choice and consumption (Taylor-Gooby, 2013). This trend towards privatisation of health and illness is rather surprisingly occurring at a time when the global or collective and socially determined nature of health and inequality is increasingly recognised (World Health Organization & CSDH, 2008). The resulting shifting pattern of illness, disability and mortality, across class, gender, race, age and sexuality, means inequalities are growing in relatively rich-income countries with well-developed welfare states. Moreover, this inequality is spreading as global capitalism increases its reach and a double burden of illness is appearing in low- to middle-income countries (World Health Organization & CSDH, 2008). Infectious diseases, like tuberculosis, malaria or HIV and AIDs now regularly appear alongside higher levels of chronic illness and disability as the expansion of capitalism and consumerism generates higher levels of affluence within emerging economies. Moreover, mass movements and migration of people triggered by unemployment, war and famine, or through fear of violence, torture, exploitation or trafficking, has meant health providers face the challenges of attending to individuals and families with vastly differing and diverse cultural histories, identities, experiences, struggles and needs (Labonte, 2008).

These unparalleled demands might imply a continuing need and support for publicly funded healthcare, but the overall neoliberal welfare ethos means there is instead a culture of restricting needs and declining support. Individual personal responsibilities are reinforced, justifying further retrenchment of the state to collectively provide what is increasingly becoming residual welfare provision. Moreover, here in the UK, continuing questions over what constitutes acceptable levels of public spending have acquired further impetus with the global economic downturn. At the time of writing, measures are currently underway to address an entrenched recession in the UK. The loss of jobs and rising unemployment, together with austerity measures intended to cut public expenditure, are known to be severely affecting women and children more so, and to greatly damage the lives of those who are poor, disadvantaged and vulnerable (Fawcett Society, 2012). These measures and damaging impacts are highly visible in the continuing disputes over who is deemed eligible or less eligible for access to and continuation of welfare support (Denny & Earle, 2009; Scambler & Scambler, 2010). In the National Health Service, these measures and neoliberal ideologies have more recently produced further significant changes to the structures and relationships in the NHS, local government, and in community and public health, where a whole series of reforms have radically altered the shape of the NHS and further embedded private market principles, practice and provision (Department of Health, 2012a).

## Patient and public involvement

Alongside growing inequality there has been a further important challenge posed by the stories of personal suffering resulting from intolerable systemic failures in care. Scandals in both the British NHS and in private healthcare have once again exposed unacceptable levels of abuse, increased public scepticism over professional authority or expertise, and raised serious concerns regarding the moral values underpinning healthcare (Francis, 2010; Department of Health, 2012b). The level of public and political concern over questions of kindness, dignity, compassion, recognition and respect suggests there is again an urgent need to deliberate more fully the type of care that ought to take precedence in contemporary healthcare. And though probably long overdue, these failures in care can be seen as part of a greater backdrop of critique arising from a much longer history of struggles and survivorship in health and social care (Davies et al, 2006). In the UK, a significant, discernible outcome or response to these challenges of inappropriate or poor or inadequate care has been the active promotion of public participation, patient involvement and engagement in healthcare. Though often in danger of being tokenistic, the primacy now given to patient and public experience has nevertheless become central to government health policy (Beresford, 2013). The British government's slogan of 'No decision about me, without me' is now enshrined in law under the auspices of the recent Health and Social Care Act 2012 for England (Department of Health, 2012a). This has imposed a legal duty upon commissioners of healthcare to consult, engage and involve patients and the public, meaning that involvement, engagement and participation are slowly and increasingly becoming seen as the norm.

Politically, involvement has become one main mechanism for achieving inclusion and for ensuring relevant, acceptable and affirming forms of healthcare. Converging with this participatory ethos has been a further emerging trend and focus on people's own strengths or capacities and capabilities. Such shifts have facilitated the use of asset-based or solution-focused approaches in community healthcare especially, and these trends are seen as a welcome corrective to the common biomedical models of pathology or deficit approaches dominant and central to much healthcare and welfare provision (Labonte & Laverack, 2001; Nussbaum, 2011; Abel & Frohlich, 2012; Grant & Zeeman, 2012).

## Troubling social justice

More profoundly, the aforementioned political, economic and social challenges represent a further troubling of the fundamental relationship between governments and their subjects over questions of equality and social justice in health and welfare. The increasing diversity of people's experiences and identities, and the different patterns of living, loving, caring and dying together, suggest challenges to healthcare will constantly emerge. The need to interrogate rather than assume what it means to live well, in sickness or in health, is therefore vital, as is the need to start from a position of uncertainty and listen, rather than being sure or fixed about what is needed in order to enable healthcare systems that no longer marginalise, oppress or exclude.

Troubling neoliberalism is critical to this task as its scope is extensive. Economic market values are known to influence not only the organisation and relationships of healthcare, but also reach in and shape the very subjectivities and identities of subjects, as patients, clients or workers (Halford & Leonard, 1999, 2006; Coffey, 2004). These forces construct the subject of healthcare as an individual with rights to health and to care, but with accompanying responsibilities. These responsibilities include becoming active, reflexive, entrepreneurial selves, consuming health to improve, fix or care for the self. Individuals must take charge of their health through attention to risky or excessive attitudes, beliefs or lifestyle behaviours known to increase risk factors for illness and disability, such as high blood pressure, smoking, excessive alcohol intake, obesity and low levels of physical activity or exercise (Baum, 2008; Nettleton, 2013). Moreover, the competition, privatisation and rational choice inherent to neoliberal philosophy come to shape how individuals define or see themselves in health and in illness. Neoliberal values are therefore internalised, felt privately, individually and psychosocially; they shape a subject's sense of self, their subjectivity or identity. This self-governance is said to represent a new form of regulation and control, and with the entry of economic principles into social life, in policy and practice, the notion of individual choice is said to become a new morality (Rose, 2007). These forms of self-governance and regulation underpin contemporary western healthcare and are principles reinforced by the dominant trends of consumerism and materialism. To consume or purchase goods or services, including health and healthcare, is now seen to be the main means of self-expression, personal fulfilment and gain, and is argued to perpetuate little meaningful connection to collective forms of living or community life (Lupton, 1995; Yeatman et al, 2009; Daly, 2011).

## Queer and critical challenges to health

Critical and queer theory provide necessary tools with which to explore and to further understand the specificities of these global, national and local challenges as they impact on people's lives. These challenges shape people's identities, experiences and their struggles over health and wellbeing, during illness, or when vulnerable and disadvantaged, invisible or excluded. And whilst we wish to respect and endorse open, diverse, fluid understandings of each perspective, in this section we nevertheless outline what are some of the defining and often shared characteristics of each. In each chapter that follows, author(s) have developed their own understandings, use or critique of these perspectives.

As editors, our shared starting point is that critical and queer theories constitute complex, overlapping perspectives that are multiple, fluid and diverse, rather than being universal, fixed or unified. Critical and queer theory therefore collectively seeks to destabilise, deconstruct, challenge or re-imagine dominant binaries, discourses, normative categories or moral ideals, structures, relations and practices in health and healthcare. The strength of these perspectives is to critique the increasing power of biomedical sciences and norms regulating the subjects of health and healthcare, in order to contribute to inclusive, participatory and ethically accountable healthcare systems and practices. In the remainder of this introduction we outline the complex, entangled nature of critical and queer theory, as we explore what it is that is distinctive, and what each can do – to queer and to critique are actions that challenge, undo and trouble the many inherent assumptions governing understandings of health, illness and care.

## Critical theory

Critical social theories are those commonly associated with an intention to not only understand or theorise the world, but to change it. Classical accounts trace the development of Marxism in the twentieth century through the work of the Frankfurt school and the intellectual endeavours of scholars such as Adorno, Horkheimer, Marcuse and Habermas. In those accounts, critical theory starts from a premise of conflict, assumes latent material structures, processes and relationships, and seeks to expose implicated oppressive forces or ideologies, in order to develop theory that can be used in the service of human emancipation.

This is theory utilised as a moral critique and a force for social change. In its development in the UK, it brought together cultural with social analyses of oppression, exclusion and marginalisation, driven by a growing identity politics and demands for inclusion and equality. The theorising of inequality and invisibility has been correspondingly evident in the expansion of social movements, such as those of feminism, antiracism, lesbian and gay studies, disability activism and, latterly, green politics and environmental politics (Seidman, 2004; Hall et al, 2013). This focus on identities and the politics of difference continued to relate subjective concerns to social interests, power relations and cultural life. It meant that concepts such as hegemony, or the representation of interests of dominant groups in society as being the interests of everyone, came to encapsulate a rethinking of modern day Marxism (Gramsci, 1995). But there was also an important and subtle shift in scholarly interest, no longer focused on the established concepts of division of labour or class, with the rise of cultural studies, interest focused on issues of meaning and fluid, hybrid identities and subjectivities. A related feature of this shift was the emerging need to question the historically androcentric and ethnocentric human subject at the centre of modern social theories.

The subsequent 'turn to culture', with its focus on linguistic and discursive formations was given further impetus through the critical works of key European poststructural thinkers such as Foucault, Derrida and Lyotard. Their work was central to critical interrogation of the grand narratives of modernity, along with their attendant notions of universalism, reason, power, progress and emancipation. A rapidly changing world became evident in phenomena like globalisation, new forms of technology and new allegiances based on identities rather than formal party political systems. Further, the increasing loss of faith in religious and political institutions, the rise of fundamentalism, mass movements, migration of peoples around the globe and debates over multiculturalism were manifestations of a new social order that required different forms of theorising.

This impacted on poststructural revisions of critical theory, which came to assume subjectivities inscribed within discourse rather than coherent individuals and societal groups struggling for emancipation against a backdrop of historical oppression (Calhoun & Karaganis, 2001; Kincheloe & McLaren, 2005). A key and influential figure in this regard is Michel Foucault, who challenged central principles of modernity and modern thought. He critiqued the project that gave rise to the totalising theories of Enlightenment thinking, with its desire to liberate humanity by uncovering essential structures or laws of social order and change (McNay, 1992). His writing called instead for a focus on local, specific, provisional and contingent mechanisms and understanding of power and politics: this constituted a form of knowledge without secure foundations which he called genealogy (Seidman, 2004; Lloyd, 2007). The aim of this was to disrupt and disturb the normalising role of dominant discourses, and to understand the social effects of particular forms of knowledge and how these come together with power.

The popularity of Foucault's work in health and healthcare studies has been enormous and serves to illustrate the challenges to health this book seeks to explore. Drawing on *The Birth of the Clinic* (Foucault, 1976), and *Madness and Civilization* (Foucault, 1971) in particular, he showed how knowledge functions as a regime of truth to produce and control the object of its gaze. This includes the regulated and disciplined healthy or unhealthy subject, produced via key institutions of the family, the hospital and therapeutic institutions. Such biomedical or health-related discourses can then appear to be totalising in their ability to define 'what can be said, by whom, when and in what form' (Seidman, 2004, p. 181). This is a view of a disciplinary society where there is no central authority in control, but rather technologies of confinement, surveillance, separation and classification, and the normalising social behaviours that maintain order. Social forces become heterogeneous and, simultaneously, productive and repressive and regulatory, as seen in the self-surveillance involved in maintaining a healthy lifestyle. In the institutions of healthcare and medicine, the dominant biomedical discourse focuses on regulating bodies, desires, identities and behaviours, revealing how disciplinary power is exercised and how particular discourses constitute subjectivities and identities (Chouliaraki & Fairclough, 1999; White, 2004; Mancini & Rogers, 2007; Powers, 2007; Zeeman & Simons, 2011). These may repress or regulate and control subjects, but equally these same subjects may actively take up particular discursive positions and resist and subvert dominant stories of health, ill-health and healthcare.

## Queer theory

Queer theory originally emerged as a radical critique of the cultural norms of gender, sex and sexuality, complementing the broader agenda of critical theoretical approaches seeking to challenge and deconstruct taken-for-granted normative assumptions about social life. Queer, in turn, brings to light the processes by which the normal and natural is produced:

> Queer is by definition whatever is at odds with the normal, the legitimate, the dominant. There is nothing in particular to which it necessarily refers. It is an identity without an essence. 'Queer' then, demarcates not a positivity but a positionality vis-à-vis the normative.
> (Halperin, 1997, p. 62)

Queer is resistant to any form of demarcation, as the field contains many intersecting strands across disciplines that are loosely connected via a radical critique of the categories of identity and an awareness of the non-normative. In terms of its location in sexual identity politics, queer theorists challenge the view of sexuality as a natural feature with biological origins, proposing instead that sexuality is a constructed category of experience with historical, social and cultural roots. The biological base of sex is discounted and replaced by the discursive construction of sexuality that takes place in the realms of the social and cultural, and through language. These domains become spaces where power relations are acted out.

A range of scholars from diverse academic disciplines in the arts, humanities, feminist studies, lesbian and gay studies, gender studies, cultural studies, geography, and health make use of queer theory, as it accommodates different theoretical positions. As an emergent and vibrant interdisciplinary field, queer theory has gained credence since the early 1990s and is informed by, complements and is often in critical dialogue with poststructural, postmodern, postcolonial and feminist theorising, research and texts.

## Queer politics

Queer theorists are brought together in an ever-expanding field by a kind of politics that advocates subversion. The politics contests the assumed naturalness of heterosexuality by questioning the norms and values that support and have sustained heterosexuality, as well as problematising sexual and gender categories and identities in general. Queer activism rejected the politics of civil rights in favour of a politics of transgression, parody, of deconstruction and decentring, and of anti-assimilation. In *Gender Trouble,* a seminal queer text, Judith Butler (1990) destabilises the categories of sex, gender and sexuality, and rejects theories of gender that suggest gender is an expression of sex. Instead, queer thinking suggests that gender gains shape in the process of repeated practices, gestures, movements and declarations over time. *Performativity* shapes and constitutes gender as a process. Gendered identity comes about as a result of 'doing gender'. Sex is an effect of gender and follows on from gender, rather than being one of the determinants of gender. The politics of performative acts, where gendered identity gains shape over time, is a disruptive politics. This politics is dependent upon a reformulation of current gendered identities and suggestions for how a different kind of gender reality could be. Subversion becomes possible in the radical act of repeatedly challenging the inflexible dichotomies, such as heterosexuality/homosexuality, which serve to regulate sexuality.

## Binary oppositions sustain the heteronormative gender order

The implications of queer politics accompanied by queer activism have impacted on many sectors of society. In health and healthcare where scientific discourses are prominent, the assumed biological foundations of sex are contested by queer thinking – and this leads to questioning practices which, for example, segregate subjects based on male/female, heterosexual/homosexual, masculine/feminine dichotomies. Queer theory resists these binaries and the reproduction of normative models of gender, sex and sexuality which facilitate and enable the regulation of subjects. Heterosexuality is considered central to the reproduction of gender and sexual inequality, as seen through the establishment of heterosexuality as a norm. In turn, institutional and disciplinary discourses construct categories like homosexuality via regimes of truth that produce 'the homosexual' as a distinct person with a particular nature (Foucault, 1979, 1986). In other words, the discourse of sexuality constitutes sexuality itself and troubles any essence or essential nature. This brings into question the norms that support the heterosexual matrix. The prevalence and assumed naturalness of heterosexuality is contested. The book will illuminate how the normative comes about and will expose the binaries that sustain these norms. The aim of queer politics is to subvert or to create opportunities and spaces where non-normativity can flourish, and though this often refers to sexuality or to LBGT concerns and struggles, to queer is to undo normativity more generally.

## Why is queer theory relevant to health?

The persistence of queer theory in advancing the question of sexual difference is potentially relevant to a range of areas.

> The philosopher Luce Irigaray has claimed that the question of sexual difference is the question of our time. This privileging of sexual difference implies not only that sexual difference should be understood as more fundamental than other forms of difference, but that other forms of difference might be derived from sexual difference.
> (Butler, 1993, p. 167)

Queer scholarship is not only interested in sexual difference, but embodies a form of resistance to all forms of minoritising logic that lead to exclusion. In this pursuit, the queer field represents a firm opposition to any system that supports and upholds the normal or natural. Queer politics gains its critical edge, by defining itself not only against the heterosexual, but also against the systems and processes that sustain the normal. Drawing on the vision of Judith Butler, such a critical and queer critique of the processes that sustain the normal contributes to inclusive, participatory and ethically accountable systems and practices. This fulfils the social justice aim of widening the scope for inclusion and citizenship.

Therefore, from its original location of radical critique of gender, sex and sexuality, and in combination with critical theoretical principles, queer theory can contest other forms of normative and oppressive identity practices that mediate social and cultural relationships and reveal the dynamics of exclusion.

## So why queer and critical challenges to health?

The starting point for this book was the potential of critical and queer theory for rethinking sexual and gender non-conformity and other forms of difference, in ways that would not reproduce the margin. As we outline below, it is the plea for the interrogation of all conventional categorisations and analyses that makes queer theory potentially productive for exploring health and healthcare alongside more familiar, established critical theoretical accounts and deconstructionist critiques. In its insistence on the interrogation of areas not normally considered sexual, to conduct 'queer readings' of hetero and what might be seen as non-sexualised concerns, issues or texts, means we can explore overlaps, tensions and potentially productive relations. From queer and critical scholarship, we therefore see potential to explore and trouble individual and collective spaces, places, relations and structures embedded in and shaping the experience of health, illness and healthcare.

The chapters that follow address our encounters with the broader fabric of healthcare in its daily practices, relations and organisational structures. This text is written from a position of solidarity with queer and critical politics to challenge oppressive identity accounts and the hegemony of normative and restrictive healthcare assumptions and related practices. In this context, identities are explored beyond the gendered and sexual in order to address the intersecting axes of difference, of disability, age, class, race, gender and sexuality that cross and profoundly shape experiences of illness and mental difficulties.

## Queer and critical challenges to health and healthcare

The contributions in this book create a set of creative dialogues and critical conversations about the landscape of contemporary western healthcare more generally, and specifically of the UK. The collection signposts current and emerging concerns and issues facing not only those who use, need or rely on services, but equally those who work to provide, manage or commission healthcare. In organising the collection, the chapters undertake three tasks to meet the challenges outlined, and they are the guiding themes for the book. Critical work is needed to: 1) *disrupt* knowledge and understanding by addressing gaps in our understanding; 2) *trouble* known concerns or re-explore familiar issues, such as evidence-based practice, or resilience or recovery; and 3) *re-imagine* or rethink healthcare identities, structures, relationships and processes so that these might come to be underpinned by more inclusive forms of knowledge.

The chapters aim to contribute to broadening the critical healthcare dialogue and, together, share some common themes. Scientific bio-medicine, as the most prominent healthcare discourse, has done much to provide systems whereby disease can be accurately assessed, diagnosed and treated but its biomedical norms have also served to marginalise and 'other' those considered different. The chapters demonstrate how critical and queer theory provide the theoretical tools to disrupt and challenge biomedical normativity, to indicate how marginalisation occurs, and reveal the normative truths about how healthcare systems classify those who differ from the norm as 'ill' or 'disordered'. A further shared assumption found in these chapters, and commonly endorsed by critical and queer theorists, is the importance of the subject and questions of identity. Here questions of language, discourse and power are vital to understandings and the constitution of subjects, but so too is the recognition of the importance of language and the contingency of meaning. Labels such as lesbian, gay, bisexual, trans and queer descriptors may serve as visible markers of collective action, but may equally and unintentionally buy into the prevailing system of classification whereby dominant norms such as heterosexuality are left undisturbed, naturalised and maintained. So, whilst progressive social movements have relied upon the solidarity of unified identity labels and language to bring about transformational change for women, black and ethnic minority groups, and gay, lesbian, bisexual and trans people, queer theory (more than critical theory), both troubles and refuses and yet can also be complicit with, or strategically adopt, collective identity delineations.

A number of chapters deal directly with these tensions or challenges of shared or essentialist notions of identities. In their chapter, **Jane Traies and Sally Munt** make visible the social and material realities of lives lived at the intersections of identities to provide an account of the complexity of lives beyond labels. They interrogate **the social realities and health narratives of older lesbians** in order to give an account of their life histories. The narratives show the specificity of lesbian identity whilst accommodating the queer flexibility of sexual orientation. Readers are encouraged to think beyond lesbian categorisation in popular discourse where lesbianism does not take precedence over other social identities, whilst acknowledging the specificity of health needs where identities intersect. By bringing the lives of older lesbians into focus, the chapter aims to challenge restrictive norms in order to create opportunities, spaces and health practices where the non-normative might thrive. In his chapter on **older gay men**, Lee Price focuses on this group as a relatively hidden, silent and poorly understood sub-group of society for whom multiple discriminations associated with sexuality, age and gender may intersect (Age Concern, 2002; European Commission, 2007; Heaphy, 2007). Queer theory is employed to provide a radical contemporary critique of heterosexual normative perspectives of UK health and social care specific to older gay men.

Discussions of queer can often omit bisexuality, despite the theoretical overlaps that have been noted by bi theorists. Queer theorists' examinations of sexual and gender binaries have forced a reconsideration of the normalisation and regulation of sexual identities within binaries of heterosexuality/homosexuality. In their chapter, **Kath Browne, Leela Bakshi and Georgina Voss** reconsider **bi identities, desires and practices** as the means to disrupt the binaries of heterosexual/homosexual. Using the Count Me In Too data, a participatory research project where LGBT people worked with service providers and others to develop data that sought to progress positive social change for LGBT people, they focus on sexual health. Bi people 'queer' sexual health provision by moving between the provisions for straight/gay people. Yet it also challenges queer erasures of identities where naming bi identities offers practical support needed for service provision. The chapter augments discussions of queering healthcare, which could be reduced to the needs of lesbians and gay men, and also contests queer deconstructions that can fail to acknowledge the importance of identities in the provision of services.

Other chapters return to familiar concepts governing debates in healthcare practice, such as evidence-based practice, the body, resilience, biographical writing and recovery. In their chapter, 'Queer challenges to evidence-based mental healthcare', Laetitia Zeeman, Kay Aranda and Alec Grant trouble the concepts of evidence, knowledge and mental illness. They explore how discourses of health inform the evidence-based movement that emerged within biomedicine and dominates healthcare. The biomedical notion of 'evidence' has been critiqued extensively, and is seen as exclusive and limiting. Even though social constructionism attempts to challenge the authority of biomedicine, to legitimate what constitutes acceptable evidence or knowledge for those experiencing mental illness, biomedical notions of evidence appear to remain relatively intact. Queer theory offers theoretical tools to disrupt biomedical norms, and challenges biomedical normativity to indicate how marginalisation occurs. A Deleuzian notion of the rhizome is used as a botanical metaphor to suggest a relational approach to knowledge that does away with either/or positions in either biomedical or queer knowledge to arrive at a both/and position where the biomedical, constructionist and queer are interrelated and entangled in needing the other for their own evolution. However, queer does not ask for assimilation but celebrates difference by remaining outside to disrupt that which is easily overlooked, assumed to be natural, or represented as the norm in health.

The amalgam of queer with critical theoretical principles is utilised in **Alec Grant and Helen Leigh-Phippard**'s chapter 'Troubling the normative mental health recovery project: The silent resistance of a disappearing doctor'. This deconstructs the normative category of the 'recovering patient' in mental health policy and professional discourses. On the basis of Leigh-Phippard's years of distressing experiences as a psychiatric patient, the chapter utilises dialogue as a progressive qualitative device to resist the colonising representational practices of institutional psychiatry. In this context, rescuing 'difference' from the pathologising tendencies of institutional psychiatry represents a commitment to social justice and emancipation. Further, the chapter hopefully contributes to the developing body of contemporary, open-ended and emerging narrative explorations of what 'recovery' might signify.

The relationship between descriptive practices and institutional discursive language and power in mental health is critiqued in a somewhat different but complementary way by **Alec Grant** in his chapter 'Breaking the grip: A critical insider account of representational practices in cognitive behavioural psychotherapy and mental health nursing'. Writing as a critically reflexive insider, in a style governed by integrated meta-autoethnographic, poststructural and critical principles, he draws on his own published work and related texts in a story that critically exposes abusive representational practices in cognitive behavioural psychotherapy and mental health nursing.

His aim in writing the chapter is that his biographical positioning in over 30 years of practice, in mental health nursing and cognitive behavioural psychotherapy, should prove useful in challenging the normative hegemonic representational practice of each discipline.

In community health, research and policy interest in resilience has increased enormously during the last decade. Resilience is now considered to be a valuable asset or resource with which to promote health and well-being and forms part of a broader trend towards strength-based as opposed to deficit models of health. In their chapter, **Kay Aranda and Laetitia Zeeman** re-examine the subject within two established **narratives of resilience**, as 'found' and 'made', and then use queer feminism to explore the potential of a third narrative, that of resilience 'unfinished'. This latter story considers what it means to undo the resilient subject, and explores further questions of the body, identity and subjectivity in contemporary public health.

In the chapter 'The body queered', **Kay Aranda** explores the familiar yet often silent or invisible but ever present topic of the body in health and social care. Drawing on queer theory's tangled, productive and ongoing relations with feminist theory (Jagose, 2009), the chapter explores whether queer and feminist theory help interrogate this lack of recognition and how more exactly this occurs within the dominant biomedical normative paradigm, where the body is perceived as the object and where its physicality and need for regulation are central. Queer and feminist poststructural theorising will be shown to reveal a gendered subject of healthcare whose body is marked by difference; is desirable but excessive; is cared for and worked upon; but is, at the same time, managed and controlled (Butler, 1993; McNay 1994; Shildrick, 2002; Twigg, 2006). This governance reveals healthcare bodies to be inscribed or marked with particular meanings of difference (Shildrick, 2002), often seen as unacceptable bodies, or as bodies that fail to achieve contemporary corporeal or ethical norms, and which frequently become abject or unthinkable. Using the example of the fat body and public health concern with the obesity epidemic, the chapter explores how the fat body is both excluded and abject, but highly visible, included and present in public health discourse, where it becomes both monstrous and vulnerable.

Finally, in '**Queer teeth**', **Olu Jenzen** highlights the 'messy' nature of trauma by examining the Vipeholm Archive in Sweden, to give an account of the sugar experiments that mental health inpatients were subjected to from the 1940s to 1950s, and she examines enforced sterilisations of transgender people. The text explores the potential of queer responses to a medical archive as an archive of feelings where the non-pathologising ethos of queer culture is bound up with other feelings, including those relating to desire and pleasure. In an attempt to politicise trauma, she moves away from an individualising perspective, insisting that the individual's lived experience is tied to 'structural social injustice, discrimination and violence'. The chapter makes visible gestures of resistance imprinted on archive material, as well as a refusal to map the sugar experiments and enforced sterilisation of transgender people as a contained moment in time, and thereby questions the taken-for-granted notion that healthcare systems protect vulnerable citizens. Queer theorisation adds to health discourses, policies and practices that 'serve as a resource for a demedicalised and depatholigised model of trauma'.

As an introduction for those new to critical and queer theory, and for those readers highly conversant with the debates, we hope this book encourages dialogue of what it means to be the same or different in any healthcare setting. Our ultimate aspirations for the book are for it to engage, disturb and possibly transform our everyday understandings or taken-for-granted views of healthcare education, research or practice. The following questions act as a guide to that engagement, disturbance and transformation for the reader.

- How might we critique health discourses, policy and practice through queer and critical theoretical lenses?

- What is the interrelationship between disciplinary knowledge, power, sexuality, normativity and difference?

- How do certain types of knowledge shape health practices and traditions?

- What are the material effects that are produced as a result of these ways of knowing?

- What is the impact on being and doing and feeling?

- How are these practices inscribed on the body by means of guidelines, medical procedures and regimes of care?

- How do we expose and resist commonly accepted forms of truth which create a unifying 'other' as healthcare subjects?

- How would queer and critical approaches to health and healthcare repoliticise and reinvigorate debates about health, wellbeing and social justice?

These questions originally represented the book's intentions and focus, but we hope they provide you the reader with a useful map with which to navigate and evaluate the rich landscape of writing present in this book.

# References

Abel, T & Frohlich, K (2012) Capitals and capabilities: Linking structure and agency to reduce health inequalities. *Social Science & Medicine*, *74*(2), 236–244.

Age Concern (2002) *Issues Facing Older Lesbians, Gay Men and Bisexuals.* London: Age Concern.

Baum, F (2008) The commission on the social determinants of health: Reinventing health promotion for the twenty-first century? *Critical Public Health*, *18*(4), 457–466.

Beresford, P (2013) *Beyond the Usual Suspects*. London: Shaping Our Lives.

Butler, J (1990) *Gender Trouble*. New York: Routledge.

Butler, J (1993) *Bodies that Matter: On the discursive limits of sex.* London: Routledge.

Calhoun, C & Karaganis J (2001) Critical theory. In G Ritzer & B Smart (Eds) *Handbook of Social Theory* (pp. 179–200). London: Sage Publications.

Chouliaraki, L & Fairclough, N (1999) *Discourse in Late Modernity: Rethinking critical discourse analysis.* Edinburgh: Edinburgh University Press.

Coffey, A (2004) *Reconceptualizing Social Policy: Sociological perspectives on contemporary social policy.* Maidenhead: Open University Press.

Daly, M (2011) *Welfare.* Cambridge: Polity Press.

Davies, C, Wetherell, M & Barnett, E (2006) *Citizens at the Centre: Deliberative participation in healthcare decisions.* Bristol: Policy Press.

Denny, E & Earle, S (Eds) (2009) *The Sociology of Long Term Conditions and Nursing Practice.* Basingstoke: Palgrave Macmillan.

Department of Health (2012a) The Health and Social Care Act. Available from http://www.legislation.gov.uk/ukpga/2012/7/contents/enacted [accessed 19 February 2013].

Department of Health (2012b) *Transforming Care: A national response to Winterbourne View Hospital – Department of Health review: Final report.* Available from https://www.Gov.Uk/government/uploads/system/uploads/attachment_data/file/127310/final-report.pdf [accessed 27 June 2013].

European Commission (2007) *Tackling Multiple Discrimination: Practices, policies and laws.* Luxembourg: Office of Official Publications of the European Communities.

Fawcett Society (2012) *The Impact of Austerity on Women: Fawcett society policy briefing, March 2012.* London: Fawcett Society.

Fish, J (2008) Navigating queer street: Researching the intersections of lesbian, gay, bisexual and trans (LGBT) identities in health research. *Sociological Research Online*, *13*(1), 12. Available from http://www.socresonline.org.uk/13/1/12.html [accessed 27 June 2013].

Fish, J (2009) Our health, our say: Towards a feminist perspective of lesbian health psychology. *Feminism and Psychology*, *19*(4), 437–453.

Foucault, M (1971) *Madness and Civilization: A history of insanity in the age of reason*. London: Routledge.

Foucault, M (1976) *The Birth of the Clinic*. London: Routledge.

Foucault, M (1979) *The History of Sexuality, Volume One: An introduction*. Harmondsworth: Penguin.

Foucault, M (1986) *The History of Sexuality, Volume Two: The use of pleasure*. Harmondsworth: Penguin.

Francis, R, QC (2010) *Independent Inquiry Into Care Provided by Mid Staffordshire NHS Foundation Trust January 2005 – March 2009 (Volume I and II)*. London: Stationery Office.

George, V & Wilding, P (2002) *Globalization and Human Welfare*. Basingstoke: Palgrave.

Gramsci, A (1995) *Selections from the Prison Notebooks of Antonio Gramsci* (Eds. Q Hoare & G Nowell Smith). New York: International Publishers.

Grant, A & Zeeman, L (2012) Whose story is it? An autoethnography concerning narrative identity. *The Qualitative Report*, *17*(72), 1–12.

Halford, S & Leonard, P (1999) New identities? Professionalism, managerialism and the construction of the self. In M Exworthy & S Halford (Eds) *Professionals and the New Managerialism in the Public Sector* (pp. 102–120). Buckingham: Open University Press.

Halford, S & Leonard, P (2006) *Negotiating Gendered Identities at Work: Place, space and time*. Basingstoke: Palgrave Macmillan.

Hall, D, Jagose, A, Bebell, A & Potter, S (2013) *The Routledge Queer Studies Reader*. London: Routledge.

Halperin, D (1997) *Saint Foucault: Towards a gay hagiography*. Oxford: Oxford University Press.

Heaphy, B (2007) Sexualities, gender and ageing: Resources and social change. *Current Sociology*, *55*, 193–210.

Jagose, A (2009) Feminism's queer theory. *Feminism and Psychology*, *19*(2), 157–174.

Kincheloe, J & McLaren, P (2005) Rethinking critical theory and qualitative research. In NK Denzin & YS Lincoln (Eds) *The SAGE Handbook of Qualitative Research* (3rd ed) (pp. 303–342). Thousand Oaks: Sage Publications.

Labonte, R (2008) Global health in public policy: Finding the right frame? *Critical Public Health*, *18*(4), 467–482.

Labonte, R & Laverack, G (2001) Capacity building in health promotion, part 1: For whom? And for what purpose? *Critical Public Health*, *11*(2), 111–127.

Lloyd, M (2007) *Judith Butler: From norms to politics*. Cambridge: Polity Press.

Lupton, D (1995) *The Imperative of Health: Public health and the regulated body*. London: Sage Publications.

Mancini, M & Rogers, R (2007) Narratives of recovery from serious psychiatric disabilities: A critical discourse analysis. *Critical Approaches to Discourse Analysis across Disciplines*, *1*(2), 35–50.

Marmot, M (2010) *Fair Societies, Healthy Lives: Marmot Review final report*. Available from http://www.instituteofhealthequity.org/projects/fair-society-healthy-lives-the-marmot-review [accessed 10 February 2012].

McNay, L (1994) *Foucault and Feminism: Power, gender and the self*. Cambridge: Polity Press.

Nettleton, S (2013) *The Sociology of Health and Illness* (3rd ed). Cambridge: Polity Press.

Nussbaum, M (2011) *Creating Capabilities: The human development approach*. London: Harvard University Press.

Powers, P (2007) The philosophical foundations of Foucaultian discourse analysis. *Critical Approaches to Discourse Analysis across Disciplines*, *1*(2), 18–34.

Reczek, C & Umberson, D (2012) Gender, health behavior, and intimate relationships: Lesbian, gay, and straight contexts. *Social Science and Medicine*, *74*(11), 1783–90.

Rose, N (2007) *The Politics of Life Itself: Biomedicine, power and subjectivity in the twenty-first century*. Oxford: Princeton University Press.

Scambler, G & Scambler, S (Eds) (2010) *New Directions in the Sociology of Chronic and Disabling Conditions: Assaults on the lifeworld*. Basingstoke: Palgrave Macmillan.

Seidman, S (2004) *Contested Knowledge: Social theory today* (3rd ed). Oxford: Blackwell.

Shildrick, M (2002) *Embodying the Monster: Encounters with the vulnerable self*. London: Sage Publications.

Taylor-Gooby, P (2013) *The Double Crisis of the Welfare State and What We Can Do About It*. Basingstoke: Palgrave Macmillan.

Twigg, J (2006) *The Body in Health and Social Care*. Basingstoke: Palgrave Macmillan.

White, R. (2004) Discourse analysis and social constructionism. *Nurse Researcher*, *12*(2), 7–16.

Wilkinson, RG & Pickett, KE (2009) *The Spirit Level: Why equality is better for everyone.* London: Penguin.

World Health Organization (2000) *Obesity: Preventing and managing the world epidemic: Report of a World Health Organization consultation* (WHO Technical Report Series 894). Geneva: World Health Organization.

World Health Organization & Commission on Social Determinants of Health (2008) *Closing the Gap in a Generation: Health equality through action on the social determinants of health.* Geneva: World Health Organization. Available from http://whqlibdoc.who.int/publications/2008/9789241563703_eng. pdf [accessed 2 January 2014].

Yeatman, A, Dowsett, M, Fine, M & Guransky, D (Eds) (2009) *Individualization and the Delivery of Welfare Services: Contestation and complexity.* London: Palgrave.

Zeeman, L & Simons, L (2011) An analysis of discourses shaping mental health practitioners. *Journal of Psychiatric & Mental Health Nursing*, *18*(8), 712–720.

# 2

# life histories and health narratives of older british lesbians

## – jane traies and sally r munt –

### Older lesbian invisibility

There is now a small but steady growth of interest in lesbian, gay, bisexual, trans and queer (LGBTQ) ageing in the UK (Heaphy et al, 2003; River, 2006; 'Gay and Grey in Dorset', 2006; Guasp, 2011). In practice, the particular experiences of trans people (Bailey, 2012) and those who identify as bisexual (Jones & Ward, 2010) have received comparatively little attention, and most of the research focuses on lesbians and gay men. However, gay men are significantly more likely to be the subject of such work than lesbians (Berger 1990; Heaphy et al, 2003). One reason for this under-representation of women includes the difficulty researchers have experienced in recruiting older lesbians to a study: in their major survey of LGBT people over 50 in the UK, Heaphy and his colleagues originally intended to have an equal gender balance in their sample, but ultimately recruited only half as many women as men, and only three of those women were over 70 years of age (Heaphy et al, 2003). These researchers suggested that 'older lesbians may have particular concerns about "going public" about their sexuality, and experience greater pressures to conceal their sexual identities' than gay men do (2003, p. 6). The result is a typical dearth of broad-based empirical data about older lesbians on which to build theory, policy and practice for older people, whether in healthcare or in other social services. In order to counter such stories of invisibility, in 2010 Jane Traies set up a national project: Women Like That: The lives of British lesbians over 60 survey (WLT). The study, which was doctoral research commenced under the supervision of this article's second author, Sally R Munt, aimed to raise awareness of the lives and experiences of older lesbians and so in some way help to counter their continued near-invisibility in academic literature.

There are no reliable statistics for the number of lesbians and gay men in the UK. The first official attempt to quantify this demographic, the UK Integrated Household Survey (Office for National Statistics, 2011a), identified 1.5 per cent of the population (726,000 people) as lesbian, gay or bisexual. This data was obtained through face-to-face research which asked people to self-identify, which we know from previous methodological critiques is problematic for a number of reasons, including the reluctance to disclose sexual orientation to complete strangers. While 1.5 per cent of people identified as lesbian or gay, nearly twice as many refused to answer the question; it seems reasonable to assume that the actual number of lesbians and gay men is higher than the 1.5 per cent that this survey suggests.

Currently there are 7.5 million women over 60 in the UK (Office for National Statistics, 2011b). Even using the Integrated Household Survey's figure of 1.5 per cent, well over 100,000 of them can be assumed to identify as lesbian or bisexual (although the true number is probably much higher). The UK parliamentary LGBTQ-lobbying group Stonewall estimates that there are 'one million lesbian, gay and bisexual people in Britain over the age of 55' (Stonewall, 2012); at least half of them (probably more, since women live longer than men) would be lesbians or bisexual women. By the Stonewall estimate, then, there could be at least half a million older lesbians in the UK. In sum: there are hundreds of thousands of older women in the UK who currently identify as lesbian. (The word 'lesbian' is used here, as it was in the survey, as a convenient umbrella term which was recognised by the respondents, although only two-thirds of them would habitually use it to describe themselves; 40 per cent of respondents said that they prefer to call themselves 'gay' or 'gay woman'.) Research has shown that older LGBT people are more likely than their heterosexual peers to be childless, to be single and to be estranged from their families (Guasp, 2011). In consequence, they may have disproportionate need of health services and social care services for older people. However, current evidence suggests that the sexual identity and specific needs of older lesbians in particular largely go unrecognised by those care services (River, 2011).

## The Women Like That study

'Women Like That: The Lives of British Lesbians over 60' was the largest study of older lesbians to be carried out in the UK. This three-year research project, which ran from 2010 to 2013, collected a combination of quanti-tative data from a large-scale online questionnaire, together with qualitative biographical data garnered from face-to-face and telephone interviews, and life-history narratives. More than 400 lesbians aged between 60 and 90 took part in the research. A total of 372 women completed the questionnaire; 45 of them were aged 70 or over, and nine were over 80. Respondents self-identified as 'lesbian' by filling in the questionnaire; 5 per cent also described themselves as bisexual and 4 per cent as queer. Four of the respondents were born male, and one intersex; two now identify as 'trans' and two as 'genderless'. In addition, 44 women contributed their life-stories, either through interview or by autobiography. Geographically, research participants came from all over the UK, from towns and cities, suburbs and rural areas. In terms of occupation, respondents had a wide variety of jobs and careers. Although the large majority (83 per cent) now describe themselves as 'middle-class', nearly half were born into working-class families. Just over half of respondents had been married; four out of ten had had children. In these ways, the participants could be said to be fairly representative of the lesbian community and also of the population at large. However, they were less representative in two respects: that of ethnicity – they were almost all white – and that respondents benefited from higher-than-average levels of educational achievement.

The project used a 'whole life' approach to data collection, intending to harvest information from a range of categories. Health was not an explicit focus or planned subcategory of the research; nevertheless, the data provided us with useful insights into the physical and emotional wellbeing of this neglected population, as well as enabling us to gather new information regarding participants' attitudes to health service provision. Methodologically, the quantitative data was processed using the analysis tools of Bristol Online Surveys; the interviews and life-writing were analysed with the help of NVivo software.

The rest of the chapter will now outline our findings.

## Older lesbians' attitudes to health services

The invisibility of older lesbians in the healthcare system has had two main causes: the unexamined cultural assumptions of many healthcare professionals (Traies, 2012) and the unwillingness of many lesbians to reveal their sexual orientation in a healthcare setting. Only 58 per cent of women in the survey have 'come out' to their doctors. This figure is similar to those from comparable studies; River (2011) found that 60 per cent of older LGB people in London had disclosed that they were lesbian, gay or bisexual to their primary healthcare provider (GP); Hunt and Fish (2008) report rather startlingly that only half of lesbian and bisexual women of all ages have come out to their GP. The idea that older LGBT people are more likely than younger ones to have come out to their doctors is supported by Browne and Lim (2009) who found that 69 per cent of LGBT people over 55 had disclosed their sexual orientation to their doctors, compared with only 38 per cent of younger people. However, the fact remains that over a third of older LGBT people (42 per cent of women in our study) have not revealed this key aspect of their identity to their doctors.

These results appear to be typical; other health professionals are no more likely to be trusted. Only about a third of respondents reported that they were out to 'most' health professionals, with another third saying they were out to 'some'. But 22 per cent said that they had not revealed their sexual orientation to any health service worker or volunteer, and four in ten claimed that they had never felt able to discuss sexual matters with a health practitioner.

In answer to the question 'Who would you turn to for help if sick or disabled?' half of our survey respondents said they would look to a partner or family member first for help; fewer than two in ten said they would expect to rely on health services. Lesbian gerontologist Monika Kehoe (1988), who published an American study of 100 lesbians over 60 years of age, noted a similar reliance on partners and friends among her respondents. This reluctance to trust 'representatives of the state', or to accept help from 'outsiders', may stem from years of concealment, from negative experiences in the past, or from both.

Turning now to the data: Lindsay River (founder of Age of Diversity), interviewed about *Appropriate Treatment* (2011), Age of Diversity's report on older LGBT experiences of the health service, recalled that,

> [...] one woman in the survey said, 'I didn't want the doctors to know I was a lesbian because I had to do everything I could to make sure that no-one was ever going to take my child away from me.'
>
> (Interview, 24 November 2011)

One of our interviewees, Monica, sought the help and understanding of her family doctor just once, when she was young and 'desperate'. At 23 she fell in love with a woman for the first time:

I finally told her my real feelings and she was quite shattered – 'I do love you, but not like that,' was how she put it. I was desperate, and sure I was doomed to that sort of rejection. I [...] told my doctor, who didn't really understand.

(Monica, born 1922, interviewed 28 April 2011)

She never came out in public again, keeping her lesbian life a close secret whilst privately building a strong network of lesbian friends.

To understand older lesbians' attitudes to public sector services, it is necessary to recall their life histories. In the 1940s and 1950s, homosexuality in the West was generally interpreted according to a medical model of illness or through models of social deviance (Bullough, 1994). Interviewee Merle's first negative experience of the health service happened whilst she was still at school. She wanted to apply to college to train as a P.E. teacher. The nature of her schoolgirl friendships had already drawn the attention of her teachers, and her best friend had been expelled for kissing another girl.

Merle: I think they were trying to stop me from going to become a teacher, because I had to go and have a medical; not just an ordinary medical, but a full medical [laughs].

Interviewer: Who had made this decision?

Merle: I don't know! Just, one day I was told, 'Here's a letter. You've got to go and have a full medical.' So I had to go to this other school, and there was a doctor there, a female doctor, I might add [...]. So she asked me to take my clothes off, you see. She said, 'You take all your clothes off.' So I took all my clothes off and she was examining me – nothing abusive, just an examination – and that was that. Anyway, no more was said about it, and I got into college, and then when I was in college, I said, 'Wasn't that medical awful that we had before we came here?' So they said, 'What medical?' [laughs] And then I realised that I'd actually been subjected to something to try to find out – I don't know what, whether they thought I was a hermaphrodite or something like that, or what...

Interviewer: So they examined you sexually?

Merle: Yes, just to see – because I was completely naked. Yeah.

(Merle, born 1945, interviewed 20 November 2010)

Experiences such as Merle's can have a lifelong effect on attitudes to doctors and health services. Ward et al (2012) emphasised the value to developing health and social care best practice of embracing biographical approaches; they argued that life narratives serve as a means to better respond to the specific needs of service users.

Barriers to trust are not all rooted in the past. There is substantial evidence to suggest that many older lesbians are dissatisfied with the treatment they are currently receiving from health services: for instance, Heaphy et al (2003) report that their participants generally believed health and care service providers operated according to heterosexist assumptions (p. 12). If healthcare practitioners routinely assume that a patient is heterosexual, the patient will not always receive appropriate advice (Hunt & Fish, 2008, p. 15). Further, River (2011) found that older lesbians and gay men often recounted experiences of hostility, differential treatment and a generalised lack of understanding by health professionals. She also found that lesbians reported much higher levels of dissatisfaction with primary care providers on grounds of their sexual orientation than gay men. The effect of this invisibility can be wearing: even though half of River's participants reported positive experiences of being treated supportively as an LGBT person by a general practice worker at some point, River concluded that '[m]any older lesbians were exhausted and irritated at being routinely assumed to be heterosexual' (2011, p. 9).

Of course, because our identities are intersectional (Cronin & King, 2010) the experience of a lesbian woman interacting with health services can be multi-layered: she might at different times respond principally according to her ethnicity, cultural or social capital or dis/ability. Edwards and van Roekel (2009), working with same-sex attracted women in rural Australia, suggested that sexuality is not the only criterion women use to evaluate healthcare. Some do use a framework based on sexuality, in which good healthcare is associated with how the practitioner deals with same-sex attraction. However, some evaluated general practitioners by how well they treated women's bodies, whereas some evaluated standards of care chiefly on the basis of clinicians' perceived medical knowledge. Edwards and van Roekel argued that these women do not define themselves in a unitary way in relation to gender or sexuality, but that they selectively and strategically employ discourses of gender, sexuality and embodiment to structure and evaluate their healthcare.

## Participants' perceptions of their own physical health

Three-quarters of the Women Like That (WLT) survey respondents rated their own physical health as good or excellent, and only 4 per cent said that their health was poor, even though 35 per cent had a physical problem or illness that seriously affected their health or restricted their activity (most commonly arthritis, followed by chronic back pain and lung disease). The charity Age UK (2012) estimated that 40 per cent of all people aged 65 or over have a limiting long-standing illness. The Gay and Grey in Dorset study of older gay men and lesbians (2006, p. 28) found a similar situation: 95.7 per cent of older lesbians and gay men in their survey indicated satisfactory to excellent health, although 47.3 per cent said they had a long-term illness. Hunt and Fish (2008, p. 13) found that lesbian and bisexual women of all ages are slightly more likely than women in general to think their health is good or very good.

The determination to make the best of long-term difficulties is exemplified by interviewees like Fran:

> Yes, well I'm really lucky, you know, because I'm 75 and I'm reasonably fit – although I've now got chronic obstructive lung disease from all those years of smoking [laugh]. Which I do not regret. And I'd much rather be drinking a glass of red wine and have a fag than anything, still!
>
> (Fran, born 1935, interviewed 16 November 2010)

But many participants, such as Chris, reported trying to protect their health through exercise:

> What I'm trying to do at the moment is to keep myself as active as I am now, because that is only going to benefit me in later years. I enjoy gardening, which is a good form of exercise, I use the Wii – bash a few things round on the old Wii – I do try and keep myself as active as I can. [...] I'm not on any medication, although I have been called a chronic back pain sufferer – that happened when I was about 15, anyway, out in Africa – I hit a series of waves, and cracked the coccyx. I had a lump removed the size of an egg at the base of my spine. And I've also twisted the back. But that's been going on for years, so I've just learnt how to cope around it. Oh, and [laughs] I dropped the motorcycle on my foot!
>
> (Chris, born 1946, interviewed 17 August 2011)

Survey results show that the large majority of older lesbians remain physically active. Age UK (2012) found that for those older people in the UK who do take exercise, recreational walking was the most popular activity, and was done by 10 per cent of people over 65 years of age. In WLT, 70 per cent named walking as a regular feature of their leisure time, and around 80 per cent of women in the survey said they take vigorous exercise (such as a long walk, heavy gardening, or going to the gym) at least once a week, half doing so more than once a week. These data support Guasp's finding (2011, p. 17) that older lesbian, gay and bisexual people are more likely to take regular exercise than heterosexual people of the same age. The interview data also suggests that sport has been an important element in the lives of many older lesbians: three out of ten women are still involved in some form of active sport.

## Public health and mood-altering substances

Our findings suggest that some older lesbians are less likely to smoke, but more likely to drink alcohol and take drugs, than the general population. The survey's data on cigarette smoking runs counter to previous research on smoking by lesbians and by older LGB people (Hunt & Fish, 2009; Browne & Lim, 2009; Guasp, 2011). Only one in ten of our respondents smoked – most of those smoking fewer than ten cigarettes a day. This is a considerably lower percentage than the 17 per cent of the general population who smoke (Kenny, 2012). By contrast, Hunt and Fish found that '[m]ore than a quarter of lesbian and bisexual women currently smoke' (2009, p. 6), and Guasp (2011) found that there were no significant differences between the smoking habits of LGB and heterosexual older people. Since the incidence of smoking is related to socioeconomic class, this discrepancy might be accounted for by the atypical predominance of highly educated middle-class women who answered the WLT survey. The survey data also contradicted previous research in respect of the smoking habits of single and partnered lesbians. Guasp (2011) found that older people who are single, regardless of whether they are LGB or heterosexual, are nearly twice as likely to smoke as those who are in a relationship. By contrast, our participants showed no significant difference between the smoking habits of single and partnered older lesbians.

Alcohol consumption has historically been part of lesbian culture, both public and private; it is therefore not surprising that a quarter of all lesbians believe lesbian and bisexual women drink more than heterosexual women

(Hunt & Fish, 2009). In Guasp's (2011) study, older lesbian, gay and bisexual people drank alcohol more often than older heterosexual people. Of the WLT survey respondents, 88 per cent reported drinking alcohol in some measure, a proportion which is slightly higher than the figure for lesbians of all ages (Hunt & Fish, 2009). Thirty-one per cent said that they drink 'occasionally'; 25 per cent said that they drink alcohol 'one or two days a week', and 32 per cent said that they drink alcohol 'most days'. Only 12 per cent said they never drink alcohol.

In this case a life course perspective can once again illuminate current behaviour. Jude, for instance, first used alcohol to numb the loneliness of being a closeted young lesbian in a strange city:

> I'd already taken to drink [...] to fill in the hours of getting off the bus and getting back on the bus in the morning... I saw no one, you know? [...] So I'd taken to buying cheap sherry, to try and tell myself that I was normal.

After a brief, unhappy lesbian relationship, she decided:

> If I do what my mother says I'll be a lot happier. I'll be able to keep this under wraps; it's not worked out; etc. etc. And then I found [a husband], who was as boring as hell, and I didn't think he'd be too demanding... and then there was 20 years of marriage. [...] It was terrible. [...] It went on for 20 years, and it was only when the boys were settled at 18 that I decided I couldn't stick this any longer. For a start, I did not want that thing in me again! It made me feel totally degraded, violated, upset... I didn't like the mess, I didn't like any of it. Nothing. [...] I had to get drunk to have any sex with him.

These were difficult years for Jude: one of her sons suffered severe brain damage and became permanently disabled; her father died; her mother developed dementia and became dependent on her:

> Interviewer: And all during these 20 years there was never any relationship with another woman?
>
> Jude: I wouldn't. I thought deeply about my marriage vows, and I thought, I'm not going to. And there was just a succession of repressed emotions really, it was dreadful. And I must say that was when I started drinking quite heavily, you know.
>
> (Jude, born 1944, interviewed 16 October 2012)

Five per cent of older lesbians in the WLT survey reported using recreational drugs, in all cases this being some form of marijuana. Guasp (2011), on the other hand, found that nearly twice this number of older lesbian, gay and bisexual people (9 per cent) had recently taken illegal drugs, and are more likely to take recreational drugs than heterosexual people. Those in social categories C2DE (skilled/unskilled manual workers, unemployed and pensioners) were twice as likely to use drugs as those in social categories ABC1 (professional and managerial, clerical) (p. 15). The apparent discrep-ancy between the two surveys could be accounted for by several factors, including social class, but these results could also suggest that older gay men are more likely to use recreational drugs than older lesbians. These initial findings have salience for substance abuse prevention policies, and the targeting of user communities with relevant public health information and support.

## Physical disability

Despite these patterns, mobility and physical disability were seen as the most serious problems faced by respondents. Health and healthcare came at the top of the list of things that respondents worried about for the future: 29 per cent said that physical disability was currently a problem for them, 35 per cent reported having a life-limiting illness or physical condition, and 14 per cent claimed a state welfare benefit, disability allowance, attendance allowance or 'blue badges' for parking. Mumtaz, for instance, lives alone and worries what may happen if her disability worsens:

> That's the most frightening thing. [...] My mobility's very poor. I walk with a stick, I refuse to use a wheelchair – I don't know if I could, because I don't know if my arms are strong enough to lift the wheelchair into the car if I needed to go anywhere, and I certainly don't have a wheelchair-accessible home.
>
> (Mumtaz, born 1950, interviewed 1 October 2011)

The support of a partner can make a significant difference to quality of life. Aine suffers from arthritis and uses a wheelchair. She and her partner Merle spend a good deal of energy managing Aine's access needs so that they can continue to travel and enjoy their retirement:

> Merle: [T]he largest project [...] was going to Spain, overland. So we do things like that; we try and plan ahead. We have to think

of all different ways to do it, because it's not like everybody else who can just jump onto a bus, we have to plan it quite carefully so that you [speaking to Aine] can get on...

Aine: Yes, Merle's very considerate in trying to work out transport situations... I do my best if I can, I will have a go at doing something, I don't let anything defeat me! So, yeah, we do manage to get around quite well really ... people are more considerate now of people with a disability, so even at the hotels and places it's much easier.

Interviewer: When you go to a hotel together, which thing gives you the most difficulty, your disability or the fact that you're a couple of lesbians?

Merle: I suppose it's the disability.

Aine: The disability, probably. If they haven't got, say, a lift. We always have to ask.

(Merle, born 1945; Aine, born 1941, interviewed 20 November 2010)

Having a visible disability can make other aspects of a disabled person's identity, such as their emotional or sexual needs, invisible. Another interviewee, Anna, worried that her physical disability was preventing her from finding a partner:

I really would love to have a relationship with a woman, but I just have such difficulties ... I look on the websites, and... I don't know... they seem to be very sporty, and I've got my blue disablement badge... [because] I've got a huge number of things wrong with my spine. I can hardly walk. I'm in a lot of pain. [...] But I'd definitely... I'd just like to see somebody, and share things with them, and care for somebody...

(Anna, born 1945, interviewed 10 April 2011)

Jones and Ward have pointed out the need for service providers to 'look beyond organisational categories' and to 'recognise service users as individuals with distinctive life histories, perspectives and values, all of which have implications for the type of services people need' (2010, p. xiii). They argue that people who have non-mainstream gender and sexual identities can benefit significantly from a holistic person-centred approach which considers all the different facets of their identity together. Interviewee Shaz (born 1945) is known to the health service as she suffers from epilepsy, and is disabled by arthritis and uses a mobility scooter. She also has a psychiatric history. Her social workers, on the other hand, know her as a service user who was homeless and has recently been rehoused in sheltered accommodation. Shaz is also a lesbian, an identity that ties together many of the 'facts' of her life-story. It was only when she was referred to a local housing project that she found emotional support and unconditional acceptance of her lesbian identity from the project workers, one of whom was also a lesbian. This recognition of her many-sided self has clearly been a contributory factor in her rehabilitation.

Cruikshank (2008) has reflected on the way in which an individual's multiple identities interconnect at different life-stages, so that one identity may obscure others. Interviewee Elaine, whose partner was severely disabled during the last years of her life, remembers that sometimes it was neither sexual identity nor her disability which caused the most pain:

Elaine: [She] would get abuse in the road, when she was trying to get into her car, from people driving through… But that was to do with her being a black woman. And a very, very large black woman, as well. It wasn't to do with her being a lesbian.

Interviewer: So would you say that you met with more discrimination on those grounds?

Elaine: I would say, definitely yes. Yes.

(Elaine, born 1941, interviewed 1 October 2010)

However, eight out of ten survey respondents had experienced discrimination at some time because of their sexual orientation, and two-thirds believed that lesbians generally suffer discrimination. These experiences and beliefs will have an impact on their expectations of how they will be treated in the future, and on the way they approach health and social care services as users.

## Experience of mental health services

Guasp (2011) found that older lesbian and bisexual women are more likely to have a history of mental illness than either heterosexual women or gay men. Thirty-one per cent of our survey respondents reported that they had been in psychotherapy or counselling, specifically in relation to their lesbianism, and 4 per cent were in psychotherapy or counselling at the time of the survey. These statistics do not, of course, include those with mental health issues who have never sought help. The interview data showed that not all the women who have received psychotherapy or counselling did so voluntarily; several, particularly when they were young, were sent for psychiatric treatment in order to 'cure' their homosexuality:

> [O]ne day one of my boyfriends [...] poked around in my writing case and found a letter to [woman lover]! Whereupon he told everyone, all the people he knew from back in college. [...] And as a result he made me promise to go to a psychiatrist; which I did, just for the sake of it. [... I] met a very nice Freudian psychiatrist who, after about four sessions, said, 'I don't think there's much wrong with you, darling; I think your boyfriend's got a problem.' And that was it. So I ditched the boyfriend, and thought, sod it. I am what I am.
>
> (Philippa, born 1938, interviewed 8 May 2011)

Philippa's experience was more positive than many, and she tells this story now with a defiant humour, but not everyone survived so well. 'JJ' is much younger, but her mother still thought lesbianism was an illness to be cured. Here JJ recounts what happened after her first girlfriend left her:

> JJ: I was devastated ... no one to talk to. [...] I tried to slit my wrists. I didn't make a very good successful game of it. My mother decided then I needed to go into [mental hospital]. [...] So they put me in there for six weeks.
>
> Interviewer: What happened in there?
>
> JJ: I had shock treatment. [...] I had two or three of them, until I collapsed and they discovered I had a faulty heart valve, so they couldn't give me any more. [...] And I came out of there, still totally lost...
>
> (JJ, born 1949, interviewed 16 October 2011)

## Secrecy, stigma and rejection

Our interview data shows that following a stigmatised lifestyle involved considerable mental and emotional stress, particularly for those who came to their lesbian identities early in life. The strains of secrecy, internalised homophobia, social and moral disapproval by others, including close family, all took their toll. However, like Philippa's psychiatrist, Jude's doctor did not regard her lesbianism as an illness; but he recognised the stress she was under because of it:

> Jude: I had a bit of a breakdown ... I was so lonely, you know. There was no one, no one at all. [...] There was no one I could tell anything to, about how I felt.
>
> Interviewer: And you were dealing with all that stuff on your own ... did you still think at that stage that it was wrong, what you felt?
>
> Jude: Yes. I thought it was terrible. Why God picked me to be like that... [...] I did go to the doctor eventually, and he said to me – because I did tell him, and I said, 'Please don't write it down in the notes!' – I told him that I thought I was gay. And he said, 'Look it doesn't matter!' I said, 'It does to me!'[...] So anyway, he sent me off to [the local] hospital for some seeing-to in the brain [laughter].
>
> Interviewer: What did that consist of?
>
> Jude: Oh, counselling and antidepressants.
>
> (Jude, born 1944, interviewed 16 October 2011)

If hiding was stressful, coming out could be even more so: rejection by a parent was an experience faced by several interviewees. JJ remembers what happened when she came out to her mother:

> [S]he was vile. Which was [...] really upsetting, because I'd always been very close to my mother. She'd been my best friend. [...] She called me a dirty slut. And lots of other hard things, really... No, that wasn't a pleasant time. And you did feel totally isolated, that you couldn't talk to anybody.
>
> (JJ, born 1949, interviewed 16 October 2011)

Sandy's experience of telling her mother was particularly traumatic. She was still in her teens when her first woman lover left her, and she took a drug overdose. Afterwards, like Jude, she attempted to conform to social expectations:

> He was [...] ever so gentle, a really nice guy, and I wanted to be like everybody else. So I got engaged to him, even though I couldn't bear him near me sexually.

Shortly before the wedding she realised she couldn't go through with it:

> So I broke it off [...]. My mother was distraught, we had a huge
> row. And on the morning of my birthday, we had this huge row in
> the morning, and I went off to work; and when I came back from
> work she'd had a cerebral haemorrhage, and she'd died without ever
> regaining consciousness. So you can imagine what that did to me.
>
> (Sandy, born 1943, interviewed 2 December 2010)

Attitudes towards lesbians have changed in line with the effect of the
progressive social movements since the 1960s and 1970s, making self-
disclosure easier for some. The WLT survey shows that most participants
are far less closeted now than they were 30 years ago. Seven out of ten said
that 'most' of their family now know about their sexual orientation, and
another 14 per cent that some of their family know. However, nearly 6 per
cent said that, even now, no one in their family knew, or knows, of their
lesbian identity:

> I couldn't ever tell anyone. My sisters – well, years ago, in the 1970s
> I think it was, there was this programme on television about these
> kind of women... you know. And afterwards I heard my one sister
> say to the other, 'They are disgusting, aren't they? They all ought to
> be shot.' So I never dared say anything.

Fear of such condemnation, shame (Munt, 2007), and the internalised
homophobia that went with that fear kept Edith silent through a long
married life. Just once, when the woman she had fallen in love with found
another partner, Edith broke her silence:

> I rang up – oh, what did they call themselves? [...] the Samaritans.
> Yes, I rang the Samaritans once, and told them. I mean, they didn't
> know me and I didn't know them, it didn't matter... And the woman,
> she was sort of laughing. She said, 'Oh, what do you do when you're
> with your husband? Do you just lie back and think of England?' And
> I put the phone down. I thought that was the most... She shouldn't
> have been in that job.
>
> (Edith, born 1919, interviewed 1 December 2009)

One of the highest costs of being closeted can be the lack of support from
others at times of grief and stress. One in six of WLT survey respondents

have experienced the death of a lesbian partner. Brief comments from the anonymous questionnaire responses do hint at unacknowledged relationships and disenfranchised grief:

> She died when I was on holiday and the relatives arranged the funeral to take place before I returned.

> Could not disclose our relationship, as her family were unaware of it, so the grieving was lonely.

> Could not talk to my closest friends about my grief as they did not know I was gay.

> Her family contested the will… tried to pretend we weren't lovers…

> She died just before civil partnerships were recognised. Legally, it was the fact that I was not next of kin; financially, her pensions died with her; emotionally, there were any number of people who thought I'd just lost a friend.

Even in the era of civil partnerships (which became legal in 2005), the habit of secrecy can be hard to break. Kathryn has experienced damaging homophobia in the past and this affects her expectations about revealing herself now:

> My partner and I live as sisters to most of our friends. I would like to be able to live as a lesbian couple for once in my life. However the fear of discrimination and recrimination prevents my partner from ever being able to take this step. If we both could do it, I am sure we could cope together but not individually.
>
> (Kathryn, born 1949, written autobiography)

Angela stays in the closet even though it increases her sense of isolation:

> I feel isolated here. I mean, I always wanted to live in a village, which is fine, but village life can be insular, and very narrow-minded and gossipy, and I would never, never come out here, at all. There have been one or two very nasty incidents about that sort of thing, and I would never ever come out, because village people, they're not very well educated in the ways of the world. So it's difficult on one's own.
>
> (Anna, born 1945, recorded autobiography)

This rural/urban split reflects popular belief considering the supposed backwardness of country attitudes. Queer scholars have debated this paradigm: Richard Phillips, David Shuttleton and Diane Watt (1999) were the first to comprehensively tackle rural sexualities; Halberstam (2005) has critiqued the celebration of metrocentricity, and Mary L Gray (2009) in *Out in the Country* argued that nowadays young queer people do find spaces to be, but not in the way first imagined – and that class background and familial feelings of belonging can be more important to them than sexual orientation.

## Managing mental and emotional health

In answer to the question 'Who would you turn to for help with emotional mental health problems?' nearly half of women respondents named a friend or partner; only 20 per cent said they would turn to a mental health professional and only 14 per cent to a doctor. Given the enforced psychiatric history of many of our participants, these attitudes are perhaps not surprising, but experiences in the present can also be unsatisfactory. Wintrip (2009) found that LGBT people are continuing to experience prejudice and misunderstanding in mental health services, and that some health managers feel helpless to cope with homophobia in staff. Interviewee Maureen reflected on the lasting psychological impact of living a stigmatised life:

> [W]e all must have been wounded to some extent by our early experiences of rejection, or having to keep things secret; and we do carry those wounds; and sometimes we do drink too much, smoke too much, and all those things – probably more, statistically, I've a feeling, greater than the ordinary population, or people of our class and education and so on – precisely because of those pressures and concealments, and hurts, and wounding of the soul... wounding of the integrity of the person, of the personality; and we carry those wounds with us.
>
> (Maureen, born 1945, interviewed 11 October 2010)

Ideas of a wounded homosexual subject are of course historically enduring. It is remarkable, then, that the large majority of WTL participants now describe themselves as happy and in good emotional health; indeed, nine out of ten participants described themselves as 'very happy' or 'quite happy'. Nearly eight out of ten (78 per cent) rate their mental/emotional health as good or excellent. Although Guasp (2011) found that older LGBT people who are single are more than three times as likely as those who are in a relationship to rate their mental health as poor, this was not so with our sample; single women in the WLT study were as likely to describe themselves as in good mental health as those with partners. These figures point to the mental and emotional resilience many older lesbians have developed over the years in spite of the social stigma they have had to contend with.

## Conclusion

There are many thousands of older lesbians in the UK, but many remain invisible to health services. A habit of secrecy preserved from negative past experiences, particularly around psychological health, make older lesbians wary of engaging with health and social care professionals, and of disclosing their sexual identities to them. Many older lesbians have wrought high levels of emotional resilience, but their hard-won independence can be a barrier to accepting help from others when necessary. The development of successfully inclusive services for such women needs to embrace a life-course perspective in order to understand the subjective experiences of those who have lived often-stigmatised lives.

Unlike many of the chapters in this collection, this chapter is primarily an empirical one. Although the study as a whole challenges some previous theorising about LGBT ageing, and troubles the category 'old lesbian' by demonstrating the intersectional nature of its subjects' overlapping identities, we as authors feel that, in the area of queer health, the issues raised by our research lead logically to issues around education and training, rather than re-theorisation. Nevertheless, there are some conceptual challenges raised by the Women Like That project. Namely, simply seeing The Lesbian as a category of Otherness may not always be helpful when thinking about older lesbians' health needs. Issues around radical invisibility may cloud the assessment of healthcare priorities, seeing 'a lesbian' when in fact what needs to be recognised are a person's immediate and distinctive requirements for dignity and support, as an older citizen. Contrarily, recognising that the person's right to be 'in' or 'out' about their sexuality is their own decision, may lead to better alliances between her and health professionals, based, as they should be, on ethics of mutual respect. Educating with skills and awareness training will hopefully unravel neat social typifications such as 'lesbian', which perhaps over-assume attributions such as 'lonely', 'sad' and 'ashamed' (Dorfman et al, 1995), leading to hierarchical dispensations of pity from healthcare professionals. She may be a lesbian, but she might also have a rich and longstanding network of familial relationships that are not immediately apparent in 'blood'; supporting her in maintaining such crucial links is beneficial to her mental and physical health. Conversely, we should also consider that her social needs may not be linked to her sexual orientation, because in later life other parts of her identity take a more important role, or simply because we should not assume that all lesbians want to socialise with other lesbians, because we 'have so much in common'. To make this assumption is to reduce someone to a stereotype, and forget the intersectionality of their experience. Certainly, established binaries such as the public/private, and visibility/invisibility continue to assert their modernist imperative. These boundaries need not so much deconstructing, as an interrogation for the specific social realities and histories behind them. Finally, we would like to stress to our readers the importance of a life-history model that can accommodate the queer flexibility of an individual's sexual orientation. In that sense, we need to think 'beyond' the categorical imperative of lesbian and what it symbolises in popular discourse. Older lesbians have diverse needs; being a lesbian does not 'trump' other social identities but neither should it be evaded in its specificity either. We cannot assume an older person is heterosexual; we cannot assume that their needs collapse into a monochromatic picture if they are not. Not all lesbians are the same.

## References

Age UK (2012) *Knowledge Hub: Statistics*. Age UK. Available from http://www. ageuk.org.uk/professional-resources-home/knowledge-hub-evidence-statistics/ [accessed 5 January 2013].

Bailey, L (2012) Trans ageing: Thoughts on a life course approach in order to better understand trans lives. In R Ward, I Rivers & M Sutherland (Eds) *Lesbian, Gay, Bisexual and Transgender Ageing: Biographical approaches for inclusive care and support* (pp. 51–66). London and Philadelphia: Jessica Kingsley Publishers.

Berger, R (1990) Older gays and lesbians. In R J Kus (Ed) *Keys to Caring: Assisting Your Gay and Lesbian Clients* (pp. 170–181). Boston: Alyson Publications.

Browne, K & Lim, J (2009) *Older People: Summary of findings report* (Count Me In Too Survey). Brighton, UK: University of Brighton and Spectrum.

Bullough, V (1994) *Science in the Bedroom: A history of sex research*. New York: Basic Books.

Cronin, A & King, A (2010) Power, inequality and identification: Exploring diversity and intersectionality among older LGB adults. *Sociology, 44*(5), 876–892.

Cruikshank, M (2008) Aging and identity politics. *Journal of Aging Studies, 22*(2), 147–151.

Dorfman, R, Walters, K, Burke, P, Hardin, L, Karanik, T, Raphael, J & Silverstein, E (1995) 'Old, sad and alone': The myth of the aging homosexual. *Journal of Gerontological Social Work, 24*(1–2), 29–44.

Edwards, J & van Roekel, H (2009) Gender, sexuality and embodiment: Access to and experience of healthcare by same-sex attracted women in Australia. *Current Sociology, 57*(2), 193–210.

Gay and Grey in Dorset (2006) *Lifting the Lid on Sexuality and Ageing*. Bournemouth: Help and Care Development Ltd.

Gray, ML (2009) *Out in the Country: Youth, media, and queer visibility in rural America* (Intersections: Transdisciplinary perspectives on Genders and Sexualities series). New York: New York University Press.

Guasp, A (2011) *Lesbian, Gay and Bisexual People in Later Life*. London: Stonewall.

Halberstam, J (2005) *In a Queer Time and Place: Transgender bodies, subcultural lives*. New York and London: Routledge.

Heaphy, B, Yip, A & Thompson, D (2003) *Lesbian, Gay and Bisexual Lives over 50*. Nottingham: York House Publications.

Hunt, R & Fish, J (2008) *Prescription for Change: Lesbian and bisexual women's health check 2008.* London: Stonewall.

Jones, RL & Ward, R (Eds) (2010) *LGBT Issues: Looking beyond categories* (Policy and Practice in Health and Social Care series). Edinburgh: Dunedin.

Kehoe, M (1988) *Lesbians Over 60 Speak for Themselves.* New York: Haworth Press.

Kenny, T (2012) *Smoking: The facts.* Leeds: Patient.co.uk. Available from http://www.patient.co.uk/health/smoking-the-facts [accessed February 2014].

Munt, SR (2007) *Queer Attachments: The cultural politics of shame.* Hampshire: Ashgate.

Office for National Statistics (2011a) *Integrated Household Survey April 2010 to March 2011: Experimental statistics: Sexual identity.* Available from http://www.ons.gov.uk/ons/rel/integrated-household-survey/integrated-household-survey/april-2010-to-march-2011/stb---integrated-household-survey-april-2010-to-march-2011.html#tab-Sexual-Identityhttp://www.ons.gov.uk/ons/rel/integrated-household-survey/integrated-household-survey/april-2010-to-march-2011/stb---integrated-household-survey-april-2010-to-march-2011.html#tab-Sexual-Identity [accessed 5 January 2013].

Office for National Statistics (2011b) *Civil Partnerships in the UK.* Available from http://www.ons.gov.uk/ons/rel/vsob2/civil-partnership-statistics--united-kingdom/2011/sb-civil-partnerships-in-the-uk--2011.html#tab-Civil-partnerships-by-sex [accessed 5 January 2013].

Phillips, R, Watt, D & Shuttleton, D (2000) *De-Centring Sexualities: Politics and representations beyond the metropolis* (Critical Geographies). London: Routledge.

River, L (2006) *A Feasibility Study of the Needs of Older Lesbians in Camden and Surrounding Boroughs: A report to Age Concern.* London: Polari.

River, L (2011) *Appropriate Treatment: Older lesbian, gay and bisexual people's experience of general practice.* London: Age of Diversity and Polari.

Stonewall (2012) *Working with Older Lesbian, Gay and Bisexual people: A guide for care and support services.* London: Stonewall.

Traies, J (2012) 'Women Like That': Older lesbians in the UK. In R Ward, I Rivers & M Sutherland (Eds) *Lesbian, Gay, Bisexual and Transgender Ageing: Biographical approaches for inclusive care and support.* London and Philadelphia: Jessica Kingsley Publishers.

Ward, R, Rivers, I & Sutherland, M (Eds) (2012) *Lesbian, Gay, Bisexual and Transgender Ageing: Biographical approaches for inclusive care and support.* London and Philadelphia: Jessica Kingsley Publishers.

Wintrip, S (2009) *Not Safe For Us Yet: The experiences and views of older lesbians, gay men and bisexuals using mental health services in London.* London: Polari.

# 3

## queering older gay male lives: academic theory and real-life research

### – lee price –

In this chapter I will discuss my experiences as a gay man researching with gay men who are older than me. As a healthcare researcher I am primarily concerned with the health and social care needs and experiences of this minority group. I will explore how queer theory could aid my research and some of the challenges I consider this poses in deconstructing concepts of identity linked to sexuality.

My particular interest is culture and diversity in healthcare provision for older people, specifically related to human occupation and the expression of self, as part of my more general interest in minority groups within society. Older people in the UK are increasingly vocal about the healthcare they expect and need. There are, however, minority groups within this older population whose opinion often goes unheard (Age Concern, 2002, 2008). As the number of older people in the UK grows, the need to develop insights into the older population's minority sub-groups becomes increasingly important.

Sixteen per cent of the UK population are believed to be aged 64 and over. In 2006, 4.7 million people were aged over 75, and it is predicted that by 2016 this population will be 5.5 million and will rise to 8.2 million by 2031 (Office for National Statistics, 2007; National Institute for Health Research, 2009). The longevity of older people will result in increased demands for health and social care provision. In anticipation, the UK Government has identified challenges for health and social care providers to meet the requirements of a culturally diverse older population who are expected to have complex long-term health and social care needs (Department of Health, 2001, 2006; HM Government, 2007). One of these minority groups is gay men.

For the purpose of this chapter I refer to men over 60 years of age as 'older'. Males over the age of 64 make up 7 per cent (4.1 million) of the UK population (Office for National Statistics, 2007). Gay men are believed to account for 5 to 7 per cent of the general population (Stonewall, 2009). If it is assumed that gay men could make up 6 per cent of the population of males aged over 64, this currently equates to 250,000 people – a sizeable portion of older UK males. Older gay men also represent a hidden, silent, under-studied population for whom multiple discriminations around sexuality, age, ethnicity, disability and gender may intersect (Age Concern, 2002; European Commission, 2007; Heaphy, 2007).

It therefore appears to be currently opportune in the UK to engage in research that explores the needs of a culturally diverse older population, particularly concerning sexuality and older gay men, but the complexity of the task needs deliberation. The heterogeneity of gay men means they cannot be considered a homogenous group, in much the same way as we cannot consider gay men, lesbian, bisexual and trans people as one group under the category LGBT. Each group has different experiences, motives, values and beliefs, as do the individuals within each of the groups. This notion of categorising people and groups as if they have fixed identities is challenged by Butler (2004). She contests the way people think about others as belonging in categories, and how and why we group and categorise ourselves and others (Browne & Nash, 2010). These theorists state that people should not be defined by a category such as sexuality, arguing that such categorisation, although apparently simplifying the complexity of human life, paradoxically confuses and limits our understanding of diversity. This has the potential to become oppressive when identities are regarded as fixed, and may further alienate and marginalise those deemed threatening or undesirable to society's dominant heterosexual norm.

Hall (2006) argued that social constructions of homosexuality or heterosexuality inform and shape the way that we live our lives. Gay men, for example, have historically been marginalised and persecuted within society. In the twentieth and twenty-first century, gay rights movements in western societies have challenged this marginalisation. Gay men began to be vocal about their lives and in doing so made their space and place in society more obvious by challenging the pejorative labels society applied to their lives, values, beliefs and behaviours. Many used labels such as 'queer', 'fag', etc to invert the purpose of the insult and nullify malevolent intent, using them instead to rally a gay cohesive identity underpinned by the assumptions that these men have a universal or 'essentialist identity of "gay"'.

Although the adoption of this identity could be argued to have helped form the bedrock of the gay rights movement, it remains one that is contested. As argued above, the notion of an essentialist identity was rejected by Butler (2004) who asserted that it renders the subjects invisible, categorising individuals and limiting potential. But many of the men I have researched with were activists in the gay rights movement and I feel uncomfortable using theoretical principles that advocate the rejection of the essentialist identity that focused the gay political struggle. When I am studying this population I am studying a group of men, many of whom, because of socio-historical events, define themselves as gay and associate themselves with like-minded peers. To challenge this identity requires delicacy, because the cohesiveness it brings to some men is fundamental to how they perceive themselves and their space in society. This movement has led to growing societal and political acceptance of gay people as an 'out' self-identified group with social capital and power. But this occupation of essential gay identities and acceptance and promotion of difference is at odds with the notions of queer theory, which regards categories of homosexual and heterosexual as binary views, limiting possible options for individuals and leading to categorisation and marginalisation. Queer theory moves us away from constructs of identity categories and helps us to resist labelling and the limitations this evokes.

Yet while the aim of queer theory is to challenge binary views and promote the notions of fluidity and variability in humanity, this, I suggest, may create a dilemma for researching and establishing the healthcare needs of older gay men. The events that these men have lived through, and in many cases been active in over the past 50 years in the struggle for gay liberation, have involved embracing to positive effect society's categories and labels used to marginalise them, to bring about social and political change. Challenging the notion of a unified subject or entity of 'gay' is problematic for research that purports to represent older gay men because this specific group have become more invisible as a result of presenting a unified grouping. The academic language and discussion of the findings of its research may not resonate with, or have meaning for, the population the work claims to represent. This could represent a gap between research as an academic discipline, steeped in theory, and the lived experiences and day-to-day life of the men.

The expression of self through sexual identity for gay men has become more overt in society in recent years. But by being gay these men were positioned as different, outside the 'norm', or 'other' to society and its services. These services, including healthcare, are considered founded on heterosexual norms. These 'norms' tend to become visible when service providers make assumptions of how people live their lives, their relationships and support networks. This has the potential to marginalise individuals, particularly at times of vulnerability, which older age can bring, when they rely on others for help and support. For example, moving into residential healthcare settings forms the basis of a typical anecdote I have come across in my research activity. One account was told to me by a friend of a man who was becoming increasingly frail and isolated in his home and was relying on his 'family of choice' for support. This 'family of choice' are usually friends who form a family community for the individual in the absence of a biological family, which many older men may be ostracised from. The man's friends encouraged him to consider going into a care home so that he could receive the level of support he needed. His friend who spoke with me said that it was 'the worse thing we could have done', as friends asked 'family' not to visit in case they 'outed' him. His friend told me that that the man was still isolated in the home, but now also lonely because he said he had no one around who was gay, and declined visitors for fear of being vulnerable in what he perceived to be an environment negative to his sexuality. There is little research that explores this phenomenon, probably because it is difficult to recruit participants owing to issues such as 'outing'. Nevertheless, there is a growing group of older gay men whose aspirations are different than the generation before them. They are unlikely to accept having to hide their sexuality after 50 years of fighting for gay rights.

Such examples highlight difficulties for service providers and policy makers in appreciating the individual motives and actions of older gay men, or in recognising that their services may exclude such men. This may stem from providers trying to 'fit' people to services, judging everyone against an assumed heterosexual norm. There is little published healthcare research about older gay men to help or guide service providers and policy makers. The literature that is available tends towards description, and does not employ a substantive critical stance in analysis or discussion. In the remainder of this chapter I will explore topics drawn from available literature related to older gay men and explore potential strengths and challenges of queer theory to explicate the motives, experiences and views of older men related to health and their sexuality.

# Outside mainstream society

Non-conformists appear throughout history. They are the individuals and groups who challenge doctrines and threaten authority in society (Hall, 2006). Same-sex relationships can be seen as non-conformity to society's heterosexual norm and often appear associated with chaos and hedonism. Foucault (1984) commented that in the nineteenth century homosexuality emerged as a 'personage' in society – a 'space' for the sexual non-conformist. This label of homosexual allowed non-conformist individuals to be categorised and separated, and so reinforced and sustained divisions between people (Malpas & Wake, 2006).

The label of homosexuality created a binary with heterosexuality, and homosexual people were seen as antagonists to this norm. From this we can appreciate how this constructed divide separated and alienated gay men, leading to derision, violence and intolerance by a dominant heterosexual group within society. In the current population of gay men aged over 60 years many have fought to establish their social space and capital and, as they age, are now reaching a threshold of growing dependence on services provided for and by society. Healthcare is one such service, but one which is predicated on the societal norm of heterosexuality. What is the first generation of gay activists anticipating as they age? Will they promote gay rights as they enter the new arena of healthcare? How will contemporary healthcare services respond to this challenge?

The challenge for queer theorists is to tackle, through research, and debate this heterosexual/homosexual binary in ways that make sense for the people who see themselves occupying both categories. In terms of the gay men occupying the 'gay' category, this appears to have enabled them to articulate their needs, not in terms of a group marginalised from mainstream society but as one fundamental to its fabric. It seems to help them to discuss and promote recognition as equal society members, but from a stance of differentiation to the norm. As a contemporary critical theory, queer theory has the potential to help older gay men engage with those who are responsible for health service provision, thus enabling the decision makers to transcend conceptual divides of human sexuality and recognise a continuum of sexual practices, experiences and desires, which does not define the person but recognises diversity.

To accept the notions of queer theory, and transcend some of the divides the homosexual/ heterosexual binary has created, may be difficult for both gay men and service providers and policy makers. Sedgwick (1993) may provide some clues to resolving these dilemmas, arguing the need to acknowledge the values, beliefs and practices of different groups in society in order not to blend groups but recognise our diversity. Research based on such principles can help in this endeavour, but I suggest there are limitations. In the area of sexualities research there are dominant accounts and 'voices', which tend to be white, articulate members of social groups. Ethnic disabled, lonely, socially and geographically isolated, and ageing sub-groups of gay men are rarely 'heard'. Queer theory has the potential to ensure that research findings acknowledge and represent diversity in minority groups. This could help healthcare policy and practice to be cognisant of the specificity of an older gay man as a member of a minority group (Namaste, 2000), and recognise representations of older gay men which reify socially constructed essential identities – this stereotype fails to take account of the range and diversity of individuals who are categorised as 'gay'.

## Issues of culture

It can be argued that as we approach work retirement age and the years beyond we seem to become increasingly oppressed as older citizens. The diversity of how we have lived our lives is lost in the category and overarching identity of 'old person'. A report from the UK charity Age UK, formally Age Concern (2008), highlighted this issue, claiming that older people's culture and 'lifestyle' were important but are often neglected aspects of ageing. This included ethnicity, gender and sexuality as culturally important factors for self-identity, image and concept. A particular focus in this report is how older people's expression of self is related to sexuality, and specifically to lesbian, gay, bisexual and transgendered/transsexual (LGBT) people (Turnbull, 2001; Age Concern, 2002).

Older people are often conceptualised without sexual identity regardless of their sexuality. This occludes people for whom sexuality and self-expression form self-identity and meaning making in life (King & Cronin, 2010), an important issue in challenging hetero-normativity in societies. Older gay men have often lived lives that were at odds with dominant views, beliefs and values, and which either positioned them to hide their sexuality or defend it against the prejudice of a dominant norm. We can see that this could influence and give meaning to the way everyday life is lived, and the physical, psychosocial, spiritual and environmental aspects that inform, shape and focus our human occupation (Wilcox, 2006). These aspects should not diminish as we age, with use becoming more proficient in them with practice, experience and expertise (Wilcox, 2006). But older gay lives are multifaceted and although the 'gay' category may have been useful and expedient, at times it can also be limiting and inadequate in terms of the individual (Butler, 1993), and may further marginalise within the category of older people an already marginalised group of gay people.

Gay men are generally represented in social media in stereotypical ways, often for the purpose of entertainment. These and similar representations originate from discourses that fail to embrace diversity, and serve to inform the social construction of 'gay', which tends to be young, white, able-bodied and healthy. This stereotype not only neglects and marginalises groups of men in society, but also sustains marginalisation based on ageing which already exists within gay society. Growing older as a gay man may therefore leave individuals exposed to discrimination within and outside the gay scene, which may be multiplied depending on other demographic factors such as disability or ethnicity. There is an opportunity for theorists to take the 'queer turn' (Hall, 2006), to challenge the social identity of 'gay' to expand and explore this category, enabling diversity within a social group to be acknowledged and valued.

Butler (1993) argued that gendered identity can be viewed as 'performative'. Gender is discursively produced and gains shape over time in the process of performativity. Sexuality follows on from gender production, and becomes visible in the cultural and social. This productive process can be seen in gay culture, and has provided unity and strength over the past 50 years of the gay rights movement. But is self-representation as being 'gay' beneficial in contemporary terms? Current issues of older gay men in relation to healthcare needs are rarely mentioned in research literature. This may be attributed to the current older population of gay men being relatively closeted, because that is how they had to be as young men prior the UK Sexual Offences Act of 1967. Younger generations have lived through different times and the expectations of an older generation may not be acceptable. Hence there is a need for more research in healthcare which bridges the gaps in practice, policy and institutional culture related to sexuality. Queer theory may offer a critical stance to challenge stereotypes and help our understanding of sexuality and how it can shape our everyday lives and occupations, and influence our beliefs, values and motivation.

Age Concern (2002, 2008) recognised sexuality as concerning lives and cultural differences and not simply related to sexual activity, highlighting a cultural dimension to human sexuality. Healthcare providers' knowledge and understanding of the cultural dimension of sexuality in older age could be enhanced through collaborative research work with members of relevant cultural groups. Additionally, queer theory as a framework of analysis may be useful to assist our understanding of issues of minority groups who, due to difference, may not be culturally and socially understood. The social construction of 'gay' appears to foster the notion of difference, which although arguably historically useful to the gay rights movement to provide a focus on a minority group, may now be limiting and unrepresentative of an emerging, articulate, confident and expectant generation of ageing gay men, who may view themselves and peers as a diverse group within society, and who appear not to want to be categorised as different. Queer theory seeks to bridge these social constructions, which foster difference, misunderstanding and prejudice. It seeks to recognise diversity within society as a whole and within the minority groups that exist because of perceived difference (Butler, 2004; McNay, 2007). Such an approach to research could provide explanations and insights around how members of society are categorised and often marginalised with regards to their experiences of receiving healthcare (Ward et al, 2010; King & Cronin, 2010).

## Why the need for sexuality research in healthcare?

Research with older gay men is important. This population are reported to age in a heterosexual normative environment where their socio-historical and cultural differences are not acknowledged (Heaphy et al, 2004; Pugh, 2005). A heterosexual normative perspective appears to be assumed in healthcare in the United Kingdom (Sale, 2002; Heaphy et al, 2004; McNair, 2008). In these environments the lives of gay men are not understood and are open to judgments and assumptions informed by the binary classification of heterosexual/homosexual. This binary is hierarchical: the first is the 'norm' against which the second may be judged (Hall, 2006). Here queer theorists would argue to bridge such classifications, challenging the social construction and order of these identities as a way to attempt to address the power imbalance (Browne & Nash, 2010). But caution may be needed, as the laudable motives of queer theorists could be perceived as potentially disempowering gay men. These men have occupied the societal category of homosexual for most of their adult lives, and have worked to change negative connotations to present positive images and advantages of gay lives. To surrender this position may not prove an easy transition, perhaps creating a further binary of academic/lay perspectives of society. Research has indicated that a heteronormative perspective informs discourses of older people in general and this may influence the appropriateness of, or limit, support for older gay men (Hubbard & Rossington, 1995; Brown, 2002; Kitchen, 2003; Heaphy & Yip, 2006).

According to Age Concern (2002) a heteronormative discourse is inadequate, as is, arguably by association, the heterosexual/homosexual binary. This discourse often represents LGBT people in stereotypical ways and as a homogeneous group. It fails to differentiate between lesbian, gay, bisexual or transgendered/transsexual lives. Age Concern's (2002, 2008) specific arguments that the voice of these older members of society is absent in shaping and influencing healthcare provision are congruent with my research findings of older gay men. My work suggests that older gay men see themselves against the backdrop of a heterosexual society and that their voices are unheard. The challenge for healthcare providers in avoiding inequalities in their services and recognising diversity can be achieved, as Ward et al (2010) advocate, by challenging their own assumptions through engagement with these older men to explore and understand the socio-historical and cultural influences which have helped shape their lives, values, beliefs and behaviours. Ward proposed a rationale of learning through narratives and biographies, which could assist healthcare providers and policy makers to gain insight into the lives and experiences of older gay men.

As previously discussed, the current generation of gay men who are aged 60 years or older have lived through – and frequently been active in – the fight for gay rights. Research that explores their lived experiences through bibliographic approaches could provide insight into their lives and culture to assist healthcare policy makers and service providers. Events and legislation in the United Kingdom have changed the arena for gay men. The UK Sexual Offences Act in 1967 decriminalised homosexual acts between consenting adults, and subsequent legislation has led to gay lives being increasingly open and acknowledged (Tester et al, 2003). Nevertheless, research suggests older gay men may hide their sexuality from health and social care providers to avoid discrimination. This concern is a consequence of past life experiences of prejudice (Sale, 2002; Fish, 2007). Many older gay men grew up ostracised by society and often by their families, so that trust in a heteronormative society and heteronormative services at times of vulnerability may lead to the concealment of their sexuality (Sale, 2002).

An understanding of the lives of older gay men therefore appears problematic. Representations are generally absent in popular media and research literature. This results in issues of an older gay life rarely being discussed in relation to healthcare. Coupled with this, older gay men appear to be difficult to identify and engage in research studies (Lee, 2005). Yet there is an urgency to conduct research with this population to explore and record their experiences and views, if recent healthcare policy and social and cultural change are to be enacted and discrimination avoided (Lavin, 2004). Such research could enhance our understanding; gay lives are not a global experience and not all gay men experience societal freedom or oppression. We need to challenge and reflect on some of the assumptions we make about sexuality and identity. There is a need to recognise that the experience of being a gay man may differ across cultures and ethnic groups within a society, and between countries (Hall, 2006). This is particularly important for older gay men who may experience an additional disadvantage to other older peers, because their views, opinions and issues are further hidden within the gay subculture of society (Heaphy, 2007) and further obscured from a mainstream heterosexual society – perhaps, as queer theorists may argue, as a result of social constructions of 'gay men' and 'old age'. Hall (2006) argued further that categories such as homosexual are social constructions and therefore open to challenge and potential change. Queer theory recognises the specificity of the categories and constructs of society, and through critique could bridge such categories, highlighting the assumptions that inform mainstream society and healthcare providers.

## Accessing and understanding cultural groups

In general, accessing cultural groups is not straightforward for outsiders. According to Hall (1989) there are three levels of culture. The first level is described as those aspects of the culture that are explicit and public. The second level involves assumptions and rules known to the group but rarely shared with outsiders. The third level is thought to be harder for people outside a specific culture to appreciate and understand, and is the deepest level known to all in that cultural group and seldom stated. The notion of cultural levels is contested in postmodern literature, which views culture as fluid, unstable and an ambivalent construct, often understood in relation to other concepts such as power, the political and the social. A realist model such as Hall's could be viewed as representing a tension between essentialism and poststructural identity, and that rather than conceiving of the entity of social groups as having a necessary structure and set of attributes, we should not try to understand group culture in those terms; we should, rather, recognise the diversity of entities. Nevertheless, I have found it a convenient heuristic to help grapple with the complexities of culture.

Adopting Hall's (1989) model can allow healthcare research to explore cultural issues of specific groups on the first level. The second level appears to be harder to access and requires some previous knowledge of the culture in order to be able to ask appropriate questions to deepen understanding. Nevertheless, it is possible to strive towards this through research links to Ward et al's (2010) notion of the use of bibliography and bibliographic approaches in research to understand individual needs and experiences of healthcare services. The final level can, I suggest, be accessible to researchers. However, these researchers must be members of the cultural group – researching from both inside and outside the group (Lee, 2005). It therefore seems important to consult and work with members of the population to be studied throughout the research process in order to establish an understanding of the group at the deepest level of culture possible.

## Developing our understanding

I suggest that to enhance our understanding of this minority group, researchers should strive to recruit and engage older gay men in research activity, ensuring that their voices are heard so that health and social care services are sensitive to their needs and life issues. My current research activity, consulting with older gay men about their health and social care needs, has informed and shaped my research questions and interests. It has helped me to outline a research agenda concerning healthcare provision of older gay men. My aim is to research and understand the life constraints and advantages of a non-heterosexual life (Heaphy, 2007). But as an academic I am faced with a conundrum: queer theory informs me of 'troubles' – that is, the notion of fluid identities and multidimensional facets of individual sexuality (Hall, 2006). The conundrum is how to work and research with men who mostly express identities directly linked to their sexuality, to try to gain insight into this group, whilst recognising the compelling notions of queer theory and employing these in my analysis. As a researcher I feel torn between my responsibilities to the research participants and to academia; I had to gain the trust of these men as someone who would represent their experiences and views, and yet through the application of queer theory I felt I was deconstructing the 'gay' identity they fought so hard for.

My initial contact with the group provided what could be argued as level-one and -two cultural insight, which Hall (1989) suggested outsiders of a group would need. I was invited to talk about my research ideas at a group meeting. The group leader told me I would be 'in for a rough ride'.

He explained that members were antagonistic to the notion of research and researchers. This stemmed from past experiences when they had cooperated with researchers but never found out the outcomes of the research; they felt used. My collaborative approach to researching seemed to make this group encounter easier, but it was tough. The group did have strong negative feelings about research. The second thing the leader advised me was to tell the group from the start that I was gay. This echoed the advice of Lee (2005) and I believe, as my contact suggested, that it helped the group members to associate with me as a member of the gay community who was aware of some of the issues faced by gay men. I felt challenged by this both as a gay man, an identity I value, and as a researcher. Sharing my sexuality with the group was a significant step in the development of my relationship with them. My 'coming out' was steeped in the culture of gay men and a very important aspect of our identity and culture: we choose who to 'come out' to. It is a profound, intimate action of openness about a taboo and holds the chance of acceptance from others or risk of rejection. Coming out to the group demonstrated my trust in them and their acceptance and trust of me to represent them through research. As a researcher using queer theory to analyse and critique my research findings, I feel I compromised my allegiance with the men I worked with and I found it hard to step between the academic notion of queer theory and our lived world as gay men socially categorised as different.

Nevertheless, it seemed to me that the lived experience of being categorised as homosexual by society did have an impact on how these men lived their lives. Previous researchers had informed us that compared to other groups in society, older gay men, by virtue of their sexuality, are more likely to: live alone because they are less likely to have had children (Hubbard & Rossington, 1995); to care for an older relative; and to experience or expect to experience discrimination from healthcare providers (Hunt & Minsky, 2005). Although queer theory can shed insight into the disadvantages of seeing identity and sexuality as fixed, I felt there was a wide gap between this theoretical perspective and the actuality of everyday lives. Such everyday lives are important to me, and I am more interested in the practical implications of research than theoretically driven research. King and Cronin (2010) argued for the establishment of approaches such as queer theory to examine and perhaps challenge heteronormative assumptions. As a researcher I embrace this notion, but, as these authors argued, this is difficult to achieve against ideologies which are pervasive in some societies, and I believe this is the current snag in my thinking, beliefs and values. My position is further informed by the findings of the research consultation groups I conducted, which suggest that the identities of the men are linked to their sexuality and some of the sociocultural and historical aspects of being a gay man during the past 40 or 50 years in UK society.

The following are the issues my work identified in relation to the older gay men's experiences and expectancies of the healthcare they may receive in the UK.

### It is too late to 'come out'

This was in relation to a man finding himself in a situation where healthcare providers may know his sexual orientation, but where this has been something the individual has kept secret over decades from his biological family.

### I want to tell my story to younger gay men

The conveyed need of which was that there was some expressed urgency to share the sociocultural and historical events and experiences, so that a younger generation of gay men could understand the 'fight' for rights which had taken place to achieve the freedoms gay men were now able to enjoy in contemporary UK society. It was clear in the discussions in the groups that the older men thought a predominantly heterosexual society could withdraw these rights, and that gay men should keep up the pressure and not become complacent.

### I want to be accepted as me. I want to be accepted as a person and for my life to be respected

This links to the notions of fluid identity and a rejection of specificity as argued in queer theory. Research in this area may hold the link in helping to bridge what is for me an academic dilemma, as described earlier. Here I can see the value of queer theory as an approach that may assist in deconstructing boundaries and challenging assumptions of predominant ideologies.

### I do not want to give up 40 years of fighting for rights

This issue is the foundation of my thinking in this chapter, which has highlighted what I believe to be the current limitations of queer theory for the type of research activity in which I engage. It challenged me to strive towards incorporating this critique in my research whilst still remaining 'true' to older gay men as research participants and co-researchers, recognising the 'fight' they have made and how this struggle has embedded the importance of our identity formed though occupying the category society places us in for our sense of self and minority group. Queer theory challenges the stability of the heterosexual/homosexual boundary (Hartstock, 1990; Richardson et al, 2006). If it destabilises 'gay men' as an identity category it may weaken the concept of 'self' for individuals, which for the older generation may be difficult to accept.

## How will 'they' treat me when I am alone? I have found many straight peers to be homophobic

Here 'they' refers to heterosexual health and social care staff. This may be difficult for some people to read, but the notion exists in the minds of some older gay men that these staff may treat them unfavourably. The research group had anecdotal evidence and sometimes evidence from media reports of instances where older gay men had been mistreated during times of older age and vulnerability. Research in this area is likely to focus on challenging assumptions, values, and in some instances practices in health and social care provision. This point also linked to the experienced intolerance of heterosexual peers – the peers the older men had struggled with to gain rights and who had actively discriminated against them in the past. Once again, being categorised as homosexual with the derogatory names and labels applied to members of society is not something these men wanted to forget; it was important for them to remember how they were treated. Occupying the category was not something they may want to give up for the sake of an academic theory.

## I need to see someone like me in services

This issue slips back into societal category territory. It indicates the need to feel comfortable and at ease around health and social care staff, who, the participants believed, needed to be gay to understand and be accepting of them. This was partly formed from the idea that if one was in receipt of health and social care as one aged, that this left a person vulnerable. A gay face would help to reassure individuals that they would be valued and taken care of respectfully.

## My cultural differences will not be recognised

Here the issue was of people seeing themselves as different from other older men because of sexuality, which is difficult to challenge given historical events. Then again, this notion of a 'gay' culture could be explored to investigate the minority groups within a minority group. Gay men who have disabilities, or who are from a range of ethnic groups or of different ages, may find themselves at odds with a predominantly white, some would argue middle-class, able-bodied, young gay scene. They may find themselves exposed to multiple discrimination-related categories. Queer theory approaches could be useful in challenging boundaries and categories, giving a voice to individuals.

## Will I be isolated and lonely?

Finally, the fear of being isolated and lonely in older age was clear. The concern that friends would die, and the links with the gay community would dry up, were paramount in the men's minds. Paradoxically, it would seem that actively occupying the category of a minority group could prove disadvantageous if the individual's social circle became contracted. Perhaps we can see here a stronger argument for queer theory approaches and ideals. Perhaps the next liberating step for gay men in our move towards equality will come through a challenging of the constructs and categories of society linked to sexuality; it may be the next challenge this population of pioneers for gay rights will take on. If academics can articulate queer theory to lay groups, then negative or constraining concepts and boundaries of sexuality could be clearly recognised and addressed.

## Conclusions

These all appear to be profound issues in the lives and expectations of these older men, who represent a generation of activists who are now entering older age. This new position in society poses new challenges for this generation: to contest the societal assumptions associated with older age and of sexuality, to achieve recognition as older men who are gay, and to secure healthcare which is appropriate to their health needs and which is cognisant and respectful of them as individuals. Queer theory could offer ways to analyse data, disseminate research findings that are empowering to individuals and services, and promote equality and diversity in healthcare.

# References

Age Concern (2002) *Issues Facing Older Lesbians, Gay Men and Bisexuals.* London: Age Concern.

Age Concern (2008) *Information and Advice Needs of Black and Minority Ethnic Older People in England.* London: Age Concern.

Brown, E (2002) *Lesbian and Gay Issues in Residential Care Homes (Blackpool, Fylde, Preston & Wyre)* Blackpool: Age Concern Blackpool and District.

Browne, K & Nash, C (Eds) (2010) *Queer Methods and Methodologies: Intersecting queer theories and social science research.* Farnham: Ashgate.

Butler, J (1993) Critically queer. *GLQ, 1,* 17–32.

Butler, J (2004) *Undoing Gender.* London: Routledge.

Department of Health (2001) *National Service Framework for Older People.* London: Department of Health.

Department of Health (2006) *A New Ambition for Old Age: Next steps in implementing the National Service Framework for Older People – A resource document from Professor Ian Philp, National Director for Older People.* London: Department of Health.

European Commission (2007) *Tackling Multiple Discrimination: Practices, policies and laws.* Luxembourg: Office of Official Publications of the European Communities.

Fish, J (2007) *Older Lesbian, Gay and Bisexual (LGB) People.* London: Department of Health.

Foucault, M (1984) *The History of Sexuality, Volume 1: An introduction* (Trans. Robert Hurley). London: Penguin.

Hall, D (2006) Gender and queer theory. In S Malpas & P Wake (Eds) *The Routledge Companion to Critical Theory* (pp. 102 –114). London: Routledge.

Hall, E (1989) *The Dance of Life.* New York: Anchor Books.

Hartstock, N (1990) Foucault on power: A theory for women? In L Nicholson (Ed) *Feminism/Postmodernism* (pp. 157–175). London: Routledge.

Heaphy, B (2007) Sexualities, gender and ageing: Resources and social change. *Current Sociology, 55,* 193–210.

Heaphy, B & Yip, A (2006) Policy implications of ageing sexualities. *Social Policy and Society, 5,* 443–451.

Heaphy, B, Yip, A & Thompson, D (2004) Ageing in a non-heterosexual context. *Ageing and Society, 24,* 881–902.

HM Government (2007) *Putting People First: A shared vision and commitment to transformation of adult social care.* London: Home Office.

Hubbard, R & Rossington, J (1995) *As We Grow Older: A study of the housing and support needs of older lesbians and gay men.* London: Polari Housing Association.

Hunt, R & Minsky, A (2005) *Reducing Health Inequalities for Lesbian, Gay and Bisexual People: Evidence of health care needs.* London: Stonewall.

King, A & Cronin, A (2010) Queer methods and queer practices: Re-examining the identities of older lesbian, gay, bisexual adults. In K Browne & C Nash (Eds) *Queer Methods and Methodologies: Intersecting queer theories and social science research* (pp. 85–96). Farnham: Ashgate.

Kitchen, G (2003) *Social Care Needs of Older Gay Men and Lesbians on Merseyside.* Southport: Get Heard/Sefton Pensioners' Advocacy Centre.

Lavin, N (2004) Long-time companions. *Community Care (UK),* July 22–28, 34–35.

Lee, A (2005) The influence of life experiences on attitudes towards homosexuality, and their effects on the way gay men negotiate later life. *Generations Review, 15*(4), 13–17.

Malpas, S & Wake, P (Eds) (2006) *The Routledge Companion to Critical Theory.* London: Routledge.

McNair, RP (2008) Lesbian health inequalities: A cultural minority issue for health professionals. *Medical Journal of Australia, 178*(12), 643–645.

McNay, L (2007) *Against Recognition.* Oxford: Polity Press.

Namaste, V (2000) *Invisible Lives: The erasure of transsexual and transgendered people.* Chicago: University of Chicago Press.

*National Institute for Health Research.* Available from http://www.nihr.ac.uk/Pages/default.aspx [accessed 2 August 2013].

Office for National Statistics (2007) *Key Population and Vital Statistics: Local and health investigatory areas.* Basingstoke: Palgrave MacMillan.

Pugh, S (2005) Assessing the cultural needs of older lesbians and gay men: Implications for practice. *Practice (UK), 17,* 207–218.

Richardson, D, McLaughlin, J & Casey, M (Eds) (2006) *Intersections between Feminist and Queer Theory.* New York: Palgrave Macmillan.

Sale, A (2002) Back in the closet. *Community Care, 1424,* 30–31.

Sedgwick, E (1993) *Tendencies.* Durham, NC: Duke University Press.

*Sexual Offences Act* (1967) London: HMSO.

Stonewall (2009) *How Many Lesbian, Gay and Bisexual People Are There?* London: Stonewall. Available from http://www.stonewall.org.uk/at_home/sexual_orientation_faqs/2694.asp [accessed 2 August 2013].

Tester, S, Valentine, J, Archibald, C & Abrams, I (2003) *How Does Ageing Affect Older People with Marginalised Sexual Identity?* Stirling: University of Stirling and Our Story Scotland.

Turnbull, A (2001) *Opening Doors: The needs of older lesbians and gay men: A literature review.* London: Age Concern.

Ward, R, Pugh, S & Price, E (2010) *Don't Look Back? Improving health and social care service delivery for older LGB users.* Manchester: Equality and Human Rights Commission.

Wilcox, A (2006) *An Occupational Perspective of Health* (2nd ed). Thorofare, NJ: Slack Incorporated.

# 4

## it's a gap, not an overlap: queering bi health

### – kath browne, leela bakshi and georgina voss –

### Introduction

This chapter explores the tensions between bi identities and queer thinking. Bi lives, experiences and identities can be overlooked and subsumed within the category 'lesbian, gay, bisexual and trans'. Whilst homophobia and transphobia are increasingly mentioned in the UK and Global North antidiscrimination contexts, biphobia is often forgotten, as if homophobia were the only form of discrimination that bi people experience. The materialities of bi identities illustrate that the gap between the straight/gay binary has consequences for those who understand themselves, or are labelled, as bi. In this chapter we will show how biphobia can operate in relation to different forms of health concerns, namely sexual health and wellbeing issues arising from experiences of exclusion. We discuss the relationship between bi thinking and queer theory.

Queer can be read in at least two ways: as an umbrella term for LGBTQQI (lesbian, gay, bisexual, trans, queer, questioning, intersex) and other letters that are frequently added to denote gender and sexual difference. Queer is also a non-normative mode of thinking and engaging in activisms that contests the boundaries of normal. In the first section of this chapter we address what each of these uses might mean for bi people who are often overlooked in discussions of LGBT or queer as an umbrella term, and are elided in theorisations of queer as a non-normative subject positioning. We then use this framing to discuss the materialities of bi health through the Count Me In Too research, and conclude with the implications for practitioners.

## Queer or bi?

The relationship between queer and bi is often uneasy. Bisexuality has been theorised in queer theory as an absence, a middle group solely dependent on heterosexuality and homosexuality for its existence, and a cultural and political null (Angelides, 2006). Bisexual theorists argue that the deconstructive approach at the core of queer theory 'effectively makes invisible that which is already a decentred and marginalised subject position' (Gammon & Isgro, 2006). With little consideration of its potential possibilities and pitfalls, the category of 'bisexual' can be read as a 'silenced sexuality' in queer thinking (Barker & Langdridge, 2008). It is important to note that this is not just silent, but *silenced* by insistent reliance in queer theorisation on binaries of heterosexual/homosexual normativities in order to deconstruct them (Seidman, 1994). In the rare instances where bisexuality is mentioned in queer studies it is often commented on with a token mention in the introductory passages of the text, only to be forgotten and ignored in the main body of the work. This silencing is peculiar, given that the category 'bisexual' can be considered to be located on the boundaries of both heterosexuality and homosexuality, and often embraces an identity in flux (Callis, 2009; Erickson-Schroth & Mitchell, 2009). These qualities offer much to 'queer theory's project to point out the impoverishment of heteronormative constructions to point out the complexity of human sexuality' (Anderlini-D'Onofrio & Alexander, 2009). Yet even within this work it is unclear how a fixed category of bisexual, rather than as overlaps of homosexual and heterosexual, would be seen as desirable. As Lingel (2009) cautions, bisexuality should not be automatically associated with fluidity, because to do so leaves it 'without specificity, deliberation or intent'.

Whilst queer thinking has historically challenged 'essentialist' identity-led (in the main, gay and lesbian) political movements (Stein & Plummer, 1994, p. 181), bisexual communities do not have a history of identity politics to either draw on or distance themselves from (Barker & Bowes-Catton, 2009). It is also unclear what queer thinking can pragmatically offer to the issues with which bisexual activism is concerned, such as biphobia in the workplace, social care and, for the purpose of this collection, healthcare provision (Jorm et al, 2002). Recent work has explored how bi people must negotiate the complexities of membership in communities defined by their members as queer, where bisexuality may not be a desirable identity (Lingel, 2009). Moreover, the silencing and invisibilising bisexuality moves beyond queer thinking into organisational and policy settings. Spaces that label themselves as lesbian, gay, bisexual and trans (LGBT) or LGBT-friendly can, in practice, 'know nothing about bisexual people and cheerfully provide services only if they are able and willing to pass as gay or lesbian' (Heath, 2005, p. 88). This can mirror the tokenistic mention of bisexuality in queer theory discourse. Providing services only for those users who identify as heterosexual or gay/lesbian does not create an 'overlap' that encompasses bisexual people. Instead these supposed inclusions create a silenced gap.

This silencing is exacerbated by the lack of research on bisexuality itself. Barker et al (2012, p. 10) note that 'the very invisibility and exclusion of bisexuality ... means that much research to date combines data from lesbian and gay people, or excludes bisexual people from studies'. Work that claims to examine facets of LGBT populations often makes little direct reference to bisexuality itself or fails to consider bi needs specifically (e.g. Hunt & Dick, 2008). Rather, such discussions are reduced to the needs of lesbians and gay men under the auspices of the umbrella term 'LGBT'. Whilst there is an emerging body of research around bisexuality, particularly spearheaded by UK scholars Meg Barker and Surya Monro, a considerable amount of the existing literature silences the lives and experience of bi people – much as the body of queer theory literature does.

Within discussions about bringing queer approaches to service delivery, such as those in this book, there are materialities to the dynamics and interactions between bisexuality and queer thinking in relation to the specific role of identities. Bisexual invisibility is arguably the main problem that confronts bi people when accessing services (Barker & Yockney, 2004). Research that informs the remit and understanding of policy makers exacerbates this invisibility, creating material consequences for those living in the gap of 'the silent B' (Heath, 2005). 'Queering' does not necessarily act as a panacea to this problem – queer deconstructions can fail to acknowledge the importance of identity in service provision. Where heterosexist institutions fail to recognise bi and other minority sexual identities, naming can be a powerful and important act. However, this can run counter to queer desires to challenge identities and categorisations as normalising and regulatory. Identification as bi and naming this category can do more than normalise or regulate, it can be a political act in the face of Heath's (2005) 'silent B'.

Much of the existing research discussing LGBT sexualities fails to acknowledge bisexual identity as distinctive and requiring examination on its own terms. Whilst bi identities, desires and practices have, like queer, the potential to disrupt binaries of heterosexuality/homosexuality, the erasure of bi identity in queer thinking does not bode well for considerations of queering bi health provision. Thus, we are using this chapter to contest the invisibilising of bi health as part of a broader queer/LGBT context.

## Count Me In Too: Research details

This chapter draws on data from the Count Me In Too research project that sought to explore differences between and among LGBT people,and to identify areas of need in Brighton, UK. Brighton is renowned as the 'gay capital of the UK' and is seen by many in the city as 'leading the way on LGBT equalities' (see Browne & Bakshi, forthcoming; Voss et al, forthcoming). In Count Me In Too, LGBT people in Brighton shared their views and experiences, and worked with service providers and others to gather and present evidence that would promote positive changes for LGBT people (see www.countmeintoo.co.uk for further details of how the project was undertaken, findings reports and summaries of findings).

The initial research design and data analysis involved local LGBT individuals and voluntary and community groups and services, as well as statutory services. The data was collected between January and October 2006 using a qualitative and quantitative questionnaire, completed by 819 respondents, which consisted of open and closed questions. The sample details are:

- 6% (n. 47) identified as bisexual; gay men made up 53% of the sample (n. 431) and gay women/lesbians 34% (n. 280).

- 60% (n. 492) of the sample were aged between 26 and 45, with 9.5% (n. 78) over 55.

- 5% (n. 43) of the overall sample identified as trans.

- 20% (n. 160) of the total sample earned an income of under £10,000. However, 32% (n. 24) of those over 55 earned less than £10,000 per year.

The questionnaire was routed, and one section specifically addressed those who identified as bisexual. The qualitative and quantitative data that this section elicited is discussed in this chapter.

Recognising the bias towards representation of a gay, white and 'affluent' grouping in LGBT questionnaire research, 20 focus groups were undertaken. These sought to connect with groups that the LGBT

Community Steering Group understood as multiply marginalised, based on an intersectional understanding of social difference; the research subsequently found the cumulative effect of discrimination that is implied in the Equalities Act 2010 term 'dual discrimination' (see Browne et al, 2010; Browne & Davis, 2008; Taylor et al, 2010) and that is often overlooked in questionnaire data. We targeted people whose experiences of certain issues (such as mental health difficulties and hate crime) may have implications for their experiences of LGBT life. There were also specific focus groups for older LGBT people, trans people, bi people, LGBT people who identified as disabled, and black and minority ethnic LGBT people.

The data for this chapter was reanalysed from that presented in the *Count Me In Too Additional Findings Report: Bi people* (see Browne & Lim, 2008). We have chosen to focus on particular areas of need and exclusion for this chapter in order to highlight specific issues that were raised by LGBT people in our research. We turn now to examine the ways in which the 'silent B' (Heath, 2005) is materialised through bi people's experiences from this research. We begin with a discussion of the place and importance of bi identities, before moving to examine some specific health-related considerations, namely sexual health and the use of mainstream services.

## Materialities of bi health and identities

In this chapter, following from the Count Me In Too research, we use 'bi' as a term to describe the set of practices, spaces, identities and movements that revolve around an identity that is not heterosexual or homosexual, but identifies with a category of 'bisexual'. In Count Me In Too we understood the boundaries of the category of bi as fluid, and this was shared by those who lobbied for the use of the term bi, acknowledging that within this category are people who don't self-identify as bi but recognise the term as politically useful. Respondents to the questionnaire were asked which of a number of sexual identity categories they most identified with. 'Bisexual' was one of the tick-box answers given, so those who ticked this box compose the sample of 'bisexual' (or 'bi') respondents for the purposes of this report. As we noted above, 6 per cent (n. 47) of respondents identified as bisexual. Of course, the sample of bisexual respondents who completed the Count Me In Too questionnaire are not necessarily representative of all bisexual people in Brighton and Hove. This is because some bisexual people do not identify with, or participate in, the LGBT community and would therefore have been very unlikely to have completed the Count Me In Too questionnaire.

It should also be noted that, for the purposes of analysis, 'bisexual' is a matter of identification rather than of sexual 'orientation'. Relatedly, there are some individuals who might, under certain circumstances, be understood as 'bisexual' on the basis of who they find sexually attractive but who identify with other terms (such as 'pansexual') rather than the term 'bisexual'. Because the analysis for this chapter is based on respondents' self-identification with given categories, such individuals would not be classified as 'bisexual' in this report. However, there is a gap here when considering the users of services, as the bi category may encompass more than those who identify as bi people in relation to practices rather than identities, a point we return to below.

In contrast to a growing awareness of lesbian and gay needs and identities in the first decade of the twenty-first century, the 'coordinates of bisexual identities' were felt not to be understood (see also McLean, 2007):

> Audience member: There is something about understanding the coordinates of bisexual identity. I think there's a greater understanding as time goes on of what the gay identity might be, the lesbian identity might be and even the trans identity might be, but I don't get that sense around people understanding what, if you had high self-esteem as a bi-sexual person, what that actually means, what it means to say, 'I'm bisexual'. I don't think the understanding is there at all, so even people who want to be out as bisexual people don't necessarily fit on that.
>
> (Consultation event, April 2009)

Failing to grasp the specificities of bi identities and the possibilities of openly claiming this identification can mean that bi people are overlooked and their needs subsumed within the categories of lesbian and gay. The tensions with queer are important here; rather than seeking to move beyond foundational identities or between heterosexual/homosexual, this audience member identified the ways in which bi identity could not simply be understood only through narratives of exclusion and as distinct from straight and gay/lesbian. In the Brighton context, some bi people carved out space for themselves to celebrate and support bi identities. These stood separate to straight and gay/lesbian, as distinct rather than bridging or combining these identities (see also Voss et al, forthcoming).

Whilst bi identities are often overlooked in queer thinking and LGBT provision, there is thus a need to address bi identities in ways that do more than only locate it within the hopelessness and despair of marginalisation.

In this research, alongside the appreciation of bi spaces, participants discussed bi identities in both positive and negative ways. Some placed bi identities in a list alongside 'lonely and messed up' (questionnaire 489). For others, bi spaces, identifications and interactions offered 'freedom', acceptance and learning:

> **Drew:** I found it initially very hard when I came out as bi. If I had an either straight or a simply gay identity I think personally I would have found it harder to find my way to the kind of alternatives to the scene. There's a flipside to not feeling like you fit in on the scene which is that you have to go and find other things, or you have to set things up yourself and you have to go looking for things that are a bit different, and there is this acceptance thing in the bi community. I've made some really good friends through getting involved with bi stuff here and across the country, which is something I'd never have expected and which comes totally from being bi and getting involved in sort of bi activism organising stuff, and just the feeling that I've got of being accepted as bi in whatever way I choose to do it. The sense I always get from people is that there are 100 ways to do it – you just pick your own one – is something that is kind of filtered back into the rest of my life, and I've found it easier to look at other bits of myself that don't fit in in other people's eyes.
>
> I've found that there's a kind of valuing of diversity in the bi scene which has helped me to value diversity and meet other people elsewhere.
>
> **Cristina:** I just really like the freedom and the thing about being bi is it just allows me to relate to the emotional qualities and just the person. I suppose to think well, 'Now I've got to fit in this little box and I can only relate to you out of this box,' and actually it just doesn't work like that, that's a secondary issue, that's more who I'm dealing with as a human being and that's fantastic, I really like that.
>
> (Bisexual focus group)

The spatial constitution of identities is unmistakable in this narrative, as is the importance of 'being bi' and the significance of naming this and finding 'bi community'. Yet, there were '100 ways to do' bi identities. For Cristina, opening up ways of relating that negate and refute 'boxes' was 'fantastic', and in many ways operationalised queer fluidities and critiques of categories. Thus, even when defining and celebrating bi identities these participants refuted the fixity and homogeneity that *a* bi identity might imply.

Thus, there are complex understandings of bi identities, which draw on queer engagements with identities. These coincided with the desire of some bi people to be recognised and named in all their complexities. The diversity between bi people and the fluidities of identities, whilst respected in many bi spaces in gay Brighton, was not perceived to be valued more broadly. Indeed, bi identities were believed not to even be seen in Brighton's gay scenes or straight spaces. Combining this desire to be named and recognised where necessary with an engagement with queer fluidities with the desire, we now turn to sexual practices and the failure of services in this arena to recognise bi identities and practices that transcend heterosexual/homosexual binaries.

## Sexual health

It was apparent from the Count Me In Too research that the needs of bi people were misunderstood by sexual health services in Brighton, a place that 'should' know and do better than other places for its LGBT populations (see Browne & Bakshi, forthcoming). This went beyond naming identities and moved into the realm of sexual practices, where identities may not relate to the enactments of sexual encounters. There is an extensive literature regarding gay men, men who have sex with men and other sexual practices, and this was reflected in the provision of services and health-related services that seek to cater for this group in Brighton. Bi respondents, however, reported how sexual health information that they received reiterated gay/straight divides, with a dearth of information that specifically addressed bi sexuality and encompassed sexual practices beyond this binary:[1]

> Ruth: I think there's [names of clinics] for gay men, but there's nothing aimed at bisexual people and that's a whole different thing on its own. I mean I'm polyamorous anyway, so I'm sleeping with people from both genders and so there isn't any information that's specifically aimed at bisexual people and about the issues around that.

> Holly: I think it is really important with the bi thing as well that there is an acknowledgement that people may be having sexual relations with both/all genders; they might be having sexual relations with none, and all the implications that come out of that and tying in issues like polyamory as well. The queer sexual health, of women going for tests and being asked, you know, 'How many sexual partners have you had?' and the implication being 'and they're all male'.

Isabelle: [In some] medical environments if you go in as a woman, you get one set of advice, which is like the straight woman's pack about pregnancy and what women get from men, or you go in and you get the gay woman's pack which doesn't tell you anything about pregnancy and things you need to know if you're going to be sleeping with men. It's been my experience that you have to persist in order to get all that information, because they're really kind of, 'But why do you need to know all this?' – 'Because I sleep with different people!'

(Bisexual focus group)

Differentiating sexual health information on the basis of gay/straight and assumptions regarding the gender of partners effect the erasure of bi people's identities (as well as gendered implications in catering for men). Here queer contestations of identities dovetail with bi experiences. However, practices that failed to be contained within easy gay/straight binaries are erased, and understandings do not provide practitioners with the necessary resources and coordinates to work with. These erasures had significant effects. For Isabelle, the 'need to know' required practitioners to contest implicit assumptions that sexual identities and practices are fixed within singular genders that are desired.

While it could be argued that sexual health services need to make certain assumptions about sexual practices in order to provide information, these assumptions become exclusionary when they don't fit the practices they encounter. Unhelpful normativities are created when it is assumed that services for bi people can fit within, or mirror, what is available to those who fit within gay/straight categories. Here queer critiques of normativity are useful for providing tools to recognise the complexities of social lives that defy regulation within particular categorisations of gendered attractions. A service built on assumptions rather than discussion of individuals' situations will inevitably exclude.

Where the 'coordinates of bi identities' (audience member above) are unknown, there is a paucity of understanding of the bi identity group. Indeed while Isabelle defined herself as polyamorous, 78 per cent (n. 31) of bisexual respondents said they usually have monogamous relationships with one person. Sexual health information that is relevant across the grouping of 'bi' may not be possible, but to begin this journey it is necessary to at least recognise the need to take a different approach to that of current lesbian or gay sexual health information leaflets and services where assumptions are made about the (same sex) sexual practices of these groups.

These information sources in turn may serve to educate, inform and shape people's expectations of the sex life they 'should' have. This can work against the narrative of celebration of freedom, space for play and self-determination that Drew describes as 'the feeling that I've got of being accepted as bi in whatever way I choose to do it'. It is clear that deploying a binary frame of sexual practices can make sexual health information not only inappropriate but also actively exclusionary in setting up an ideal heterosexual/gay sexual norm. Moreover, there will most likely be further specific issues that aren't catered for even when the binary between gay/straight is disrupted. Thus, practitioners may always need to discover practices and identities otherwise unknown or unacknowledged. This requires specific attention to be paid to the complexity of individuals, without negating the place of collective identities and groupings, such as bi, in the practices of sexual lives.

## Mainstream services

It was not only in sexual health promotion that queer critiques can both be usefully deployed and contested through addressing the 'silent B'. Mainstream (that is, not LGBT-specific) services[2] were more uncomfortable for bi people to use than for others in the Count Me In Too research, illustrating the need for a consideration of the materialities of sexual identities as they interface with key areas of publicly provided support. In Count Me In Too, bisexual people (26 per cent, n. 11) were more likely to feel uncomfortable because of their sexuality/gender identity when using mainstream services than lesbians (22 per cent, n. 59) or gay men (12 per cent n. 49, p<.002). Experiences of LGBT-specific services indicated some of the issues bi people faced:

> Annie: With regard to domestic violence and abuse, I've had two experiences of being in domestically abusive relationships. On both occasions I've sought help and got really poor services. The first time was when I was with a woman; the domestic violence helpline that I phoned didn't understand LGBT issues at all. The second was when I was with a guy who had serious, serious issues around me being bisexual even though he identified as bisexual. I wanted some help and support around that before it descended into any more drunken arguments at three o'clock in the morning and accusations of I've been flirting with this girl or that girl or the other girl. My experience is, and my feeling is, that bi people aren't terribly well served. I mean

when I phoned up they really didn't understand the issues around my bisexuality either time.

The second time they didn't understand that there were specific issues around bisexuality that were provoking the behaviour in the relationship that was becoming really problematic and that what I needed was someone to talk to who was from the LGBT community that could understand why bisexuality seems such a particular threat to people and how the specificities of that kind of controlling relationship can exercise themselves in power mechanics that are about identity.

(Individual interview, Annie)

Annie describes her experiences of accessing services following incidents of domestic violence. She argues that bi identities are not understood by services or those working in them, illustrating the need to engage with relationships beyond straight/gay binaries. This leads to inadequate service provision where particular aspects of Annie's relationships were not accounted for, including relationships between women, and the ways in which bi identities can contribute to power struggles in relationships. Here, assumptions regarding gender and sexuality intersected to negate Annie's experiences and render bi people as not 'well served'.

The erasure of bi identities has been identified as a key factor in use of services by bi people (Barker & Langdridge, 2008; Barker & Yockney, 2004). In spaces that are perceived to be 'dangerous', bi identities can be carefully managed, while other spaces in Brighton are experienced and used in ways that allow for bi identities:

Sashi: I have to have yearly medicals because I'm on incapacity benefit, and it's the only environment where I'm really keen not to mention it [bisexuality], because I'm really not sure it'll be received caringly, or carefully. But it's quite a spiky environment anyway. It can be a very kind of combative thing, to have a medical, because essentially you're kind of being checked out to see if you're faking. So I'm really conscious that I never talk about my sexuality there ever, because I just wouldn't want them to know more about me than they need to know.

Lucy: I've been exactly the opposite actually. I did engage with a lot of the government services in the last months. I've engaged with the mental health community and I had to fill in a form and I was quite clear I was bisexual and transgendered. The bisexual statement actually got an odd response, the transgender one seemed to be okay, but then it's a kind of freezing with the lady that I was speaking to. I applied to go on the council housing list and I wrote a letter about my history and that was kind of interesting because I went into the fast track place and there was a kind of shock. The guy at the counter [it] was quite clear, he [was] gay and he was trying to be helpful, but it was just like there was this shock, a sort of recoil to what I was presenting them. I've been quite straightforward with housing benefit people as well, because I felt it was important. So I think I just get mixed response coming out.

(Bisexual focus group)

In spaces where there was a reliance on others in judging your 'truthfulness' in order to receive particular services, bi identities can be more 'than they need to know'. However, not telling, not disclosing, and hiding information has costs. Sashi identifies a lack of care as key to her not being out in a spiky, combative environment. Conversely, Annie talks about needing to be out in the context of domestic violence services in order to discuss issues she faced, and people talked about specific practices being relevant in sexual health services. Bi identities are then negotiated beyond sex and relationships, where feelings of being out of place and exclusions on the basis of bi identities play a significant role in how vulnerable LGBT people are supported.

## Conclusion

This chapter augments discussions of queering healthcare, which could be reduced to the needs of lesbians and gay men. It also contests queer deconstructions that can fail to acknowledge the importance of bi identities in the provision of services, as well as the importance that this identity has for individuals. Queer is thus not a panacea for addressing sexuality and social justice; we need multiple approaches, conceptualisations and politics.

Bi identities invite responses that move beyond gay and straight, and in this way are aligned to queer theorising. Bisexuality is not contained or containable within the overlap between gay/lesbian and heterosexual. It is not addressed by simply dealing with same-sex and heterosexual practices and identities. This gap in understanding and service provision has material consequences for people, and there is a need to understand the materialities of bi identities, even where there are queer impulses to deconstruct it. This gap is under-researched, yet it can be explored through recognising bi identity separate to lesbian and gay/straight identities, practices and lives. This is not to negate the complexities of bi identities and the heterogeneity of the grouping that identifies within the category 'bisexual'. On the contrary, queer analyses that deconstruct gay/straight binaries and query normativities are valuable and important for engaging with the shortfalls of services that seek to address LGBT while re-creating normativities around specific assumptions regarding lesbians and gay men.

We have shown how the fluidity of how people define their identities exists alongside a named identity which people define themselves in relation to. We argue that this identity can exist without creating an assumption of homogeneity for individuals within the category. We finish with some insights for practitioners from these findings and discussions.

Practitioners and services can devise services and practices that are responsive to individuals and more inclusive through understanding that conceptualisations of identity are reference points, not necessarily descriptions of individual identities. This could draw on queer theorising that is always seeking to question the boundaries of normativities in order to find 'others' that fail to be included or even recognised. For example, whilst the Count Me In Too data discussed here captured experiences and views of a 'slice' of bi grouping, that is, people who connected with LGBT identity, this is limited. There is a need for recognition of fluidity and diversity, responding to potential sequels of relationship issues and discrimination, as well as sexual practices. This should also be augmented with an understanding of intersectionality within this population, for example, recognising people who are bi and trans, those who are bi with mental health issues and those who are bi and experience domestic violence.

A queer approach that does not negate the import of identities may also require a different methodology to developing services. This is one that does not seek to make normative assumptions about the bi 'population', given the diversity within this population, and does not seek to map fixed coordinates of bi identity. Moving away from assumptions grounded in beliefs and majority, or dominant group practices, requires a queering of thinking in public health services. Manifestations of biphobia, and higher incidences of issues that impacted across the LGBT collective – such as higher incidence of mental health issues and experiences of domestic violence (see Browne & Lim, 2008) – illustrate, however, that there is an importance in accounting for the specifics of marginalised groupings within already disenfranchised communities. However, with this recognition, there is a need for an approach that is wary of normativities and does not seek easy assumptions based on specific categorisations. It is clear from these narratives that there is a desire for services that are open and caring, and that recognise the important role that belonging to a community like 'bi' might hold, without neglecting the diversity within such a collective and the fluidity it might imply.

## Endnotes

1. Of bisexual respondents 28 per cent (n. 11) disagreed or strongly disagreed that sexual health information available in Brighton was appropriate to their sexual practices. Bisexual respondents were the most likely group by sexual identity (39 per cent, n. 15) to disagree or strongly disagree with the proposition that 'information on sexual health available in Brighton and Hove is appropriate to my gender identity or sexuality', compared with 3 per cent (n. 11) of gay men (p=.0005). Only lesbians (25 per cent, n. 58) are less likely than bisexual people (36 per cent, n. 14) to agree or strongly agree with the proposition.

2. In the UK there are health and welfare services that are statutorily provided by local and national government. These are variously termed public sector and statutory services. The complexities of these are beyond the scope of this chapter, but suffice to note that when discussing 'mainstream services' we are referring to these.

# References

Anderlini-D'Onofrio, S & Alexander, J (2009) Introduction to the special issue: Bisexuality and queer theory: Intersections, diversions and connections. *Journal of Bisexuality*, *9*(3–4), 197–212.

Angelides, S (2006) Historicizing (bi)sexuality: A rejoinder for gay/lesbian studies, feminism, and queer theory. *Journal of Homosexuality, 52*(1–2), 125–158.

Barker, M & Langdridge, D (2008) Bisexuality: Working with a silenced sexuality. *Feminism & Psychology, 18*(3), 389–394.

Barker, M & Yockney, J (2004) Including the B-word: Reflections on the place of bisexuality within lesbian and gay activism and psychology: Meg Barker in conversation with Jenni Yockney. *Lesbian & Gay Psychology Review, 5* (3), 118–122.

Barker, M, Richards, C & Bowes-Catton, H (2009) 'All the world is queer save thee and me…': Defining queer and bi at a Critical Sexology seminar. *Journal of Bisexuality*, *9*(3&4), 363–379.

Barker, M, Richards, C, Jones, R, Bowes-Catton, H, Plowman, T, Yockney, J & Morgan, M (2012) *The Bisexuality Report: Bisexual inclusion in LGBT equality and diversity.* Milton Keynes: The Open University Centre for Citizenship, Identities and Governance.

Browne, K & Bakshi, L (2013) *Ordinary in Brighton? LGBT, activisms and the city.* Aldershot: Ashgate.

Browne, K & Davis, P (2008) *Housing: Count Me In Too additional analysis report.* Brighton Spectrum and the University of Brighton. Available from http://www.realadmin.co.uk/microdir/3700/File/CMIT_Housing_Report_April_08.pdf [accessed January 2014].

Browne, K & Lim, J (2008) *Bi People: Count Me In Too additional findings report.* Brighton: Spectrum and the University of Brighton. Available from http://www.realadmin.co.uk/microdir/3700/File/CMIT_Bi_Report_Dec08.pdf [accessed January 2014].

Browne, K, Cull, M & Hubbard, P (2010) The diverse vulnerabilities of lesbian, gay, bisexual and trans sex workers in the UK. In K Hardy, S Kingston & T Saunders (Eds) *New Sociologies of Sex Work* (pp. 197–212). London: Ashgate.

Callis, A (2009) Playing with Butler and Foucault: Bisexuality and queer theory. *Journal of Bisexuality, 9*, 213–233.

Erickson-Schroth, L & Mitchell, J (2009) Queering queer theory, or why bisexuality matters. *Journal of Bisexuality*, *9*, 297–315.

Gammon, M & Isgro, K (2006) Troubling the canon: Bisexuality and queer theory. *Journal of Homosexuality, 52*(1/2), 159–184.

Heath, M (2005) Pronouncing the Silent 'B' (In GLBTTIQ). *Gay and Lesbian Issues and Psychology Review, 1*(3), 88–92.

Hunt, R & Dick, S (2008) *Serves You Right: Lesbian and gay people's expectations of discrimination.* London: Stonewall.

Jorm, A, Korten, A, Rodgers, B, Jacomb, P & Christensen, H (2002) Sexual orientation and mental health: Results from a community survey of young and middle-aged adults. *British Journal of Psychiatry, 180,* 423–427.

Lingel, J (2009) Adjusting the borders: Bisexual passing and queer theory. *Journal of Bisexuality, 9*(3–4), 381–405.

McLean, K (2007) Hiding in the closet? *Journal of Sociology,* 43, 151–166.

Seidman, S (1994) Queer-ing sociology, sociologizing queer theory: An introduction. *Sociological Theory, 12*(2), 166–177.

Stein, A & Plummer, K (1994) 'I can't even think straight': 'Queer' theory and the missing sexual revolution in sociology. *Sociological Theory, 12*(2), 178–187.

Taylor, Y, Hines, S & Casey, M (2010) *Theorizing Intersectionality and Sexuality: Genders and sexualities in the social sciences.* Basingstoke: Palgrave.

Voss, G, Browne, K & Gupta, C (forthcoming) Embracing the 'and': Between queer and bi theory at Brighton BiFest. *Journal of Homosexuality.*

# 5

## queer challenges to evidence-based mental healthcare

## – laetitia zeeman, kay aranda and alec grant –

### Introduction

The discourses of evidence discussed in this chapter follow on from a particular understanding of discourse. Drawing on Foucault, a discourse is a system of statements, institutions, structures and practices that systematically form the objects of which they speak (Foucault, 1974). Discourses do not merely describe reality – they form reality in a specific manner, thereby delivering a particular system of meanings. How we regard the world is shaped by the discourses through which we view the world (Rolfe, 2001). Discourses give rise to structures and institutions populated by professional communities that speak a similar language and practise in accordance to shared values and cultural conventions, governed by policy and legislation. Discourse and power relations produce historically specific and variable subject positions (Lloyd, 2007). Discourses also have material effects as they shape the body in specific ways as seen in actions, bodily gestures and behaviour, which in turn inform discourses.

Biomedicine, informed by scientific modernist assumptions, acts as the most prominent discourse in contemporary western healthcare. Central to this discourse is a set of post-positivist foundational assumptions about knowledge that aspires to objectivity, logical coherence and truth (Freshwater & Rolfe, 2004; Rolfe, 2001, 2005, 2007). Biomedical knowledge is constructed in realist terms as 'out there' waiting to be discovered or found, with the aim to uncover essential truths (Rorty, 1999). Biomedicine assumes there is a preferred form of knowledge where all kinds of knowledge should conform to one representation (Riggs, 2011). The evidence-based movement in healthcare has been criticised as exclusive and normative, since scientific knowledge represses other forms of knowledge (Holmes et al, 2006). Queer readings of evidence-based practice will show how biomedicine produces interdisciplinary normative assumptions which marginalise other ways of knowing. This text interrogates the hegemony of evidence-based practice and suggests how it may be reworked and revised to foster understandings of evidence that is not so bound by normative codes. A queer critique of 'evidence' in healthcare contests the 'truth status' of post-positivist scientific knowledge but develops in dialogue with scientific biomedical and constructionist discourses. Both constructionist and queer epistemologies suggest that multiple representations of knowledge are possible.

However, a critique of biomedicine that unequivocally aims to dismiss the usefulness of 'evidence' repeats the epistemic brutality that some would accuse positivism and post-positivism of (Riggs, 2011). Queer readings of evidence-based practice will resist normative demarcations of intelligibility of what counts as knowledge, evidence and mental health, whilst recognising the provisional and tentative nature of all knowledge claims, including our own. The aim is not to denounce the usefulness of biomedicine, but to recognise diverse ways of knowing that emerge from, and in critical relationship to, modern scientific and interpretive constructionist epistemologies. The chapter will trouble knowledge relations in order to recognise knowledge as embodied and performative, as well as socially constructed and culturally mediated.

As diverse epistemological positions are possible, the biomedical discourse will present knowledge as 'found', and in contrast, social constructionist claims can be regarded as knowledge 'made' where people come together to discuss and agree over time what holds value, thereby supporting the generative nature of knowledge (Brandom, 2000; Hesse-Biber & Leavy, 2007; Rorty, 1999). Queer scholarship regards knowledge as ongoing rather than making truth claims (biomedical) or underlining how communities generate knowledge in interchange (constructionist). An account of biomedical, constructionist and queer epistemologies will follow.

## Biomedical epistemology

Biomedicine turned to evidence-based practice (EBP) in the early 1990s. This discursive shift initially occurred during the Thatcher years in the UK, and the Reagan administration in the USA. Evidence-based practice can be regarded as an extension of a neoliberal managerialist agenda, known for governing professional practice and organisations (Davies, 2003). The movement has influenced health policy, practice and service delivery with the aim to improve healthcare outcomes by integrating clinical knowledge with rigorous evidence, often derived from research or practitioners' observations, to inform decisions about treatment and care, whilst aspiring to take account of service user feedback and choice (Sackett et al, 2004).

Central to the evidence-based narrative has been an assumption of the usefulness of evidence. What works in clinical practice is key to the aim of improving service user outcomes in a cost effective and efficient manner (Rycroft-Malone, 2006). With an expanding range of treatment options available, service user and practitioner choice has increased. Treatment options with best outcomes are promoted providing that they fit with economic and budgetary constraints (Rycroft-Malone et al, 2004). The merits of improved outcomes at reduced costs are rarely disputed; however, health practitioners, academic communities and researchers remain critical (Paley, 2006). Evidence-based practice is a useful but insufficient form of healthcare knowledge (Morse, 2006; Porter & O'Halloran, 2009). The narrative of evidence-based practice accounts for desirable health practice through a scientific lens; however, numerous other representations of knowledge exist (Freshwater & Rolfe, 2004). Due to the inherent power of biomedicine, other discourses are silenced. The evidence-based narrative came about over time and relies heavily on the truth status that scientifically produced evidence achieves (Rolfe, 2007). Comparative studies like randomised controlled trials (RCTs) follow a set of rules to produce evidence (Paley, 2006). Here research rigour is measured against scientific criteria to assess the validity and reliability of research findings. When evidence is produced according to these rules and conforms to scientific criteria, results are represented as a form of 'truth'. Only the most rigorous evidence is selected to inform practice.

The meaning of 'evidence' is imbued with assumptions about knowledge. Such assumptions shift according to the values a specific scientific community subscribes to. As queer and constructionist epistemologies indicate, what we see as evidence is never neutral and objective. An exercise of disciplinary power underlies any concept of evidence (Morse, 2006; Rolfe, 2007). In Foucauldian terms discourses are linked by power relations. Biomedicine as a prominent discourse exerts disciplinary power where preferred forms of evidence are defined (Lupton, 2012). Social, cultural and political values underpin our understanding of evidence whether predominantly scientific research findings or evidence drawn from multiple sources of knowledge.

In its defence, evidence based practice has been faced with the challenge to guard technical scientific knowledge and introduce quantitative research findings to practice, define care pathways and develop clinical guidelines (Traynor, 2009). Technicality of knowledge is tied up with a profession's claim to autonomy and status. Where highly skilled technical procedures are conducted in healthcare, practitioners resort to safety gained in scientific certainty and truth (Traynor, 2009). The post-positivist hierarchy of knowledge supports forms of knowledge that are technical and complex in nature, and that aspire to truth (Porter & O'Halloran, 2009). Normative formulations of desirable evidence, such as systematic reviews of RCTs, serve the political purpose of strengthening the authoritative voice of clinical experts, and in doing so attribute less value to non-quantifiable forms of evidence such as patients' experiences, narratives and choice. However, opportunities for discursive resistance exist. Health professions display a form of disinterest about scientific practices and measuring outcomes in clinical trials, experimental studies and audits (Traynor, 2009).

In an appraisal of different forms of knowledge, Bruner (1986, 1990) makes visible the range of knowledge and distinguishes between logico-scientific knowledge (biomedicine) where people look for proof and causal laws, and narrative knowledge, which is about human connection. In sharp contrast to biomedical scientific knowledge, cause and effect is less important in constructionist narrative knowledge, which is interpretive and reflexive in nature, as meaning is generated between those involved. Biomedicine overlooks the crucial role of narratives in providing an account of situated and embodied knowledge, in contrast to social constructionists.

## Constructionist epistemology

Constructionists expose a range of possible approaches to knowledge generation and hold the view that what counts as 'evidence' is related to shared epistemological assumptions. Knowledge is discursively shaped by academic communities resulting in a perception of it as naturally 'made' (Rorty, 1999). Such knowledge is inscribed by norms and governed by informal rules to determine what a community counts as credible and rigorous (Gergen, 2002, 2006). Constructionism assumes that knowledge can never be value neutral. The objective basis and value-neutrality of post-positivist knowledge is questioned. Objectivity, neutrality and causality are regarded as effects of the biomedical discourse of science through which specific knowledge claims are constructed (Burr, 2003). Hierarchies of evidence that favour scientific methods in the form of RCTs, systematic reviews and meta-analyses over interpretive, narrative and reflexive forms of evidence are brought into contention (Rolfe & Gardner, 2006). According to constructionists, blind acceptance of any form of 'truth' is precarious since the post-positivist hierarchy of evidence is no more than a constructed category relative to a particular scientific, cultural and historical context. A social constructionist critique makes the process explicit by which academic communities come to regard some forms of evidence as more valid and reliable than others. Knowledge upheld as most rigorous, such as RCTs, systematic reviews and meta-analyses (Polit & Beck, 2008), implies that other discursive knowledge representations are sidelined by biomedicine. Alternative forms of evidence, such as service user and practitioner narratives (Grant & Zeeman, 2012; Grant et al, 2011) or interpretive or transformational studies, might yield equally relevant information. However, qualitative evidence is regarded as subjective and less robust by those who see RCTs, meta-analyses and systematic reviews as preferable (Dawes et al, 2005). The path leading to truth is saturated by silenced voices (Gergen, 2003). By placing RCTs at the forefront of what counts as evidence, power, in the shape of academic credibility, and opportunities to gain research funding and influence practice, is given to scientific researchers but denied to others (Rolfe, 2001). Constructionists expose biomedical tendencies to attribute less value to non-quantifiable forms of evidence, in favour of those who produce quantitative evidence by conforming to agreed display rules.

Constructionists encourage health professions to step out of the comforts of a post-positivist biomedical epistemology towards a social epistemology. Objective and a-historic knowledge is questioned where the knower and the known is separated in order to recognise the merits of collective knowing (Gergen, 2003). The meaning-making process by which constructionists decide what counts as evidence is embedded in a range of narrative processes where communities discuss what holds value and agree what counts as 'fact' thereby serving as a form of 'truth'. Deciding whether a treatment option holds value in clinical practice is not something that people do individually, but that occurs between people. Knowledge is not 'held' by individual people but is something that people 'do' together, as a form of action. Knowledge becomes visible as a relational practice where mutual understanding is gained in dialogue between researchers, academics, clinicians, practitioners, service users and carers (Gergen, 2009).

According to constructionists, entering into dialogue means the contributions of all types of knowledge are recognised without making normative assumptions about the value of one type of knowledge over another. A different future is possible where the knower and the known work in partnership to select the most suitable treatment options. This type of collaboration allows for multiple realities and values to intersect where researchers, practitioners, service users and carers work not from a position of 'above' or 'against' but 'with' one another to facilitate collaborative decision making in health practice (Gergen, 2009). This constitutes learning to value the embodied and locally held knowledge of a service user about the impact of a treatment or honouring what practitioners have learnt from their lived experience. This discursive position represents knowledge as plural (Gergen, 2003). This plurality assumes that knowledge is designed to serve a particular purpose and fulfil a specific function, whilst underlining the notion of usefulness of knowledge in a particular context (Gergen, 2006). Biomedical scientific knowledge is most useful when comparing and contrasting treatment options, whilst nursing knowledge might consider provision of psychosocial support during a period of mental health recovery. This form of constructionism, as proposed by Gergen, omits a consideration of the effects of power and the way that knowledge is infused by power relations that lend credence to biomedicine over other disciplines. Constructionist knowledge generation assumes the knower (researchers or health professionals) and the known (participants or service users) co-construct meaning and achieve goals valued by all as a form of relational ontology (Gergen, 2009). Co-construction of meaning occurs where practitioners and service users discuss treatment options drawing on both the evidence base and the experiential knowledge of service users where they hold embodied knowledge of the consequences of treatments or side-effects. A relational ontology will aid development of shared goals where practitioners value treatments that are cost effective and efficient whilst ensuring the safety of service users, combined with service user preferences about treatment options with the least side-effects. Some may argue that constructionist relational engagement plays into the hands of a neoliberal agenda, where evidence-based practice is prevalent when valuing cost effectiveness, efficiency and service user opinion. Instead of measuring outcomes, constructionists like Gergen place an emphasis on the process of knowledge generation where relationships serve as a vehicle for knowledge generation and exchange.

# Queer epistemology

Queer theory emerged in synergy with sociological theorising of gender and sexuality in feminist, lesbian and gay studies that refuses any identity-based foundational categories, such as women, gay, lesbian and trans identities. Queer theory shows how the normative reproduction of gender supports and enables the regulation of sexuality. Queer studies are committed to non-normativity and oppose any practices that demarcate identity, whilst refusing to define a field of operation in respect of any fixed content (Hall et al, 2013). Such theorists loosely cohere around sexuality and the intersection of sexuality and other markers of difference, such as race, ethnicity, class, age, disability and, in this chapter, mental illness.

As far as knowledge is concerned, queer scholarship departs from biomedicine and constructionism by exposing different traditions of knowledge generation in the biomedical, constructionist and queer. This opens up the normative foundation of evidence-based practice to illuminate power relations and whom these work in service of. Queer knowledge draws on poststructural and Foucauldian texts that critique universal truths, causal relationships and ontological coherence prevalent in scientific modernist discourses (Browne et al, 2007). Queer theory is infused with politics that promotes critical consideration of oppressive discourses and identity ideologies that contain normative 'truths'. Queer texts add to our understanding of knowledge by showing how marginalisation occurs in healthcare owing to normative formulations of health, resulting in those who differ from the norm becoming 'ill' or 'mentally disordered'. Due to the inability to escape this violent system of signification, the politics of queer is to resist, subvert and exploit normative values and meanings. Queer scholarship moves beyond understanding of how exclusion occurs, to create spaces where resistance and active disruption can take place or be imagined. This political impetus creates room for difference to disrupt the normative 'truths' of biomedicine to bring about radical social and material change.

In order to achieve this, queer theory studies the relationship between knowledge and the known, in respect of the healthcare subject, with a view to gaining an understanding of how the normative comes about and how it impacts on the material or the body. Performativity is proposed as a theoretical resource in arguing for gendered, sexualised, diverse and plural subjects of knowledge.

Biomedicine is aligned with Cartesian philosophy in representing an autonomous healthcare subject with a natural and essential identity, imbued with agency, autonomy and rationality existing independent of language (Aranda et al, 2012). Such individuals are subjected to truth claims and exercise choice whilst aiming to achieve their health potential. Constructionists assume healthcare subjects who are socially constituted as a product of history, are determined by discourse, and who in turn inform discourses. Constructionist assumptions are helpful for understanding contemporary forms of subjectivity; however, their value neutrality omits the systems that render subjects as culturally and socially invisible due to difference (Lloyd, 2005). This process is now addressed in more detail.

## Queer readings of the normative

Queer and poststructural readings of Cartesian philosophy paved the way for a discursively produced subject that becomes intelligible via binary oppositions. Binaries such as health/illness, ordered/disordered (or the rational/emotional), and heterosexual/homosexual dominated during modernism. Binary categorisations privilege one term over the other, for example, health over illness, or heterosexual over homosexual, or as far as knowledge claims are concerned, preference the rational objective (biomedical) over the subjective interpretive (constructionist and queer). The reader is misled to attribute greater value to one of the binary pair over the other (Sedgwick, 1990), whereas one component cannot exist without the other (Burr, 2003).

Poststructuralists such as Derrida (1974, 1978) deconstruct texts by opposing the 'either/or' 'logic' of binary oppositions and instead follow a 'both/and' approach. This strategy is associated with liberal identity politics, but we see it played out in debates over legitimate knowledge. When studying scientific knowledge claims we consider what these knowledge claims are, as well as the unstated absence or what is excluded. Biomedicine affirms truth, rationality and objectivity, but there exists an 'other' in the subjective, embodied and relational which acts as contrast to that which is affirmed. In that which is taken as immediately present or confirmed, there is always already absence, difference and deferral (Hesse-Biber & Leavy, 2007). Meaning can never be fixed as definitive; meaning is repeatedly deferred and open to reinterpretation. These dichotomous concepts do not exist as opposites, but instead, there is an unavoidable defining of one through the other. The nature of concepts becomes visible in relations between binaries instead of in these terms themselves, where biomedical knowledge values the rational and objective in RCTs, but functions in relation to other forms of knowledge, such as the subjective, embodied and relational in service user accounts or narratives. For other forms of knowledge to be recognised or legitimised, difference in the subjective, embodied and relational has to claim sameness with the dominant norm through assimilation in biomedicine, or alternatively remain marginal or excluded to that which is considered as the 'norm'.

In the work of Butler (1992, 1993, 1999), queer theory suggests a radical rethinking of the subject that would involve opposing the practices of a scientific biomedical epistemology. Radical critique is necessary, as traditional formulations of an essentialist, detached and disembodied subject contribute to inequality, as the bodies, lives and experiences of these subjects are rendered invisible due to difference. In a reformulation of the subject, where the Cartesian logic is dismantled, difference is required to delineate subjects that fall within the norm. Subjects become visible because difference exists. For queer theorists (Butler, 1993) and poststructural feminists (Weedon, 2003; Hesse-Biber & Leavy, 2007), dismantling Cartesian logic is a redundant strategy because binaries cannot be overturned or replaced given the tentative and provisional nature of all knowledge claims.

Queer theory highlights the limitations of previous difference strategies, as to acknowledge difference in pairs leaves intact the linguistic binary that hierarchically positions that which is considered as preferred or normal, as superior to an inferior 'other' (Aranda et al, 2012). As a result, there is no opportunity for that which is represented as different or subject to the norm (healthy/ill or mentally ordered/mentally disordered, heterosexual/homosexual or the objective scientific/subjective interpretive) to be incorporated into an inclusive ideal. During this strategy, difference is not overcome or erased; instead difference has been denied (Lloyd, 2007).

Difference cannot be overcome; on the contrary, the *normative* that becomes visible in dichotomous thinking should be destabilised and disrupted by difference as a political act (Butler, 1993). A politics of difference makes visible the power imbalances and structures of discrimination that underpin the normative (Lather, 2009). Butler draws attention to broader historical and cultural contexts in which binaries appear, where the emphasis on difference becomes a transformational political endeavour with the aim to subvert an oppressive order.

In the context of healthcare, this kind of politics uncovers processes where mental health subjects are formed within the health/illness and mentally ordered/disordered binaries (Lupton, 2012). The political aim of queer scholarship is to disrupt this form of dichotomous thinking by difference, for example, through the refusal of mental health service users, consumers or people in prison to be labelled as mentally disordered, and individuals reclaiming the term 'mad' by participating in 'Mad Pride'. This cultural and social event interrupts the confines of labelling that occurs via institutional psychiatry and biomedicine. People cohere around a common purpose and create a shared space, separate to institutional psychiatry and the norms whereby they are defined as disordered. The collective practice reclaims the term mad and serves a political purpose of resistance. This kind of politics sharpens the focus on disrupting the normative where difference as signified in the term 'mad' is reclaimed, to stand illuminated in its own light. During Mad Pride, psychiatric survivors celebrate how far they have come from exclusion in asylums to contemporary survivorship where people cohere as organised groups around art, music, life narratives, films, poetry and community events. The movement presents the history and culture of psychiatric survivorship through the stories of those who lived the experience, through a range of mediums. Mad Pride provides the forum to link with others who reject cultural stereotypes based on gender, sexuality, ethnicity and disability to challenge sexism, heterosexism and racism. The lives and cultural practices of survivors are made visible to promote social inclusion of people with psychiatric histories (Grant et al, 2011). Mad Pride also remembers those who did not survive as a result of adversity they faced within and outside the psychiatric system (Costa & Reaume, 2008).

## Queering knowledge in mental health

Queer knowledge aims to make life possible for those who are excluded, marginalised or presented as unintelligible within a normative discursive regime (Lloyd, 2007). Within the realms of the social and cultural, an 'exclusionary matrix' is involved in the formation of subjects where regulatory practices will determine who is recognised as viable and who exists as 'other' (Butler, 1993). Cultural intelligibility as proposed by Butler (1999) concerns the formation of a normative framework that provides the conditions governing who can be recognised as viable subjects. Mental health service users and survivors only become intelligible where they are culturally or socially recognised; for example, owing to their visibility at Mad Pride, service users become socially recognisable. The human normative is produced in particular racial, cultural and knowledge frameworks (Lloyd, 2007). Evidence-based practice acts as a knowledge framework that renders mental health service users invisible owing to its preferencing of the scientific, rational and objective in forms of knowledge, such as RCTs and systematic reviews, which detach service users from their histories, contexts, larger narrative structures and overarching discourses. Normative violence occurs whereby lives become invisible when service users are silenced, or their narratives and experiences remain unheard. A queer critique of biomedicine reveals this form of normative violence, where service users are discounted as viable beings.

## Queering embodied knowledge

The relationship between materiality and discourse is relevant to mental health. This relationship does not represent a form of life materialised through the body, but the way that the interplay of discourses and materiality is constitutive of life itself (Ruffolo, 2009). A scientific biomedical epistemology attempts to define and impose notions of the normal and the natural through an essentialist human subject. Discourses produce the bodies they govern; for example, discourses of health and biomedicine produce the bodies they regulate. Drawing on a Foucauldian notion of the productive function of language, thus discourses bring into material being the bodies they claim to describe. Mental health subjects are discursively produced as a constitutive effect of the practices of power and knowledge, where the material is measured against a normative ideal. Biomedicine creates health subjects with bodies that are neutral, rational and fragmented. Biomedical knowledge studies the body as an object, detached from its narrative structure and context, functioning like a machine with organs as parts (Fox, 2012). Mental illness is seen as a malfunction that leads to the body of service users (the known) being closely examined and dissected by professionals (the knower) in an attempt to observe symptoms. Confirmation of symptoms leads to diagnoses and treatments in the form of medication and therapy.

Constructionists see the body as a biological entity without reducing physiology to mechanical functions, instead seeing the body as an entity partially determined by social and cultural forces (Twigg, 2006). The body is discursively shaped and becomes a vehicle for culture as a carrier of psychosocial or physical pain (Fox, 2012), which follows on from mental illness or emotional or psychological trauma, as seen in facial expressions, tears and physical states such as lethargy.

Queer critiques the normative by uncovering the regulatory function of biomedicine and the material effects that come about as a result. Within healthcare the normative provides parameters for health, mental order and wellbeing. In delineating health, biomedicine brings difference into sharp focus by categorising subjects who deviate from the health ideal as ill, 'other' or disordered (Lupton, 2012; Seidman, 1997). The body becomes territorialised by biomedicine where symptoms are assessed, diagnoses are made and treatment regimes are prescribed. Biomedical norms determine when bodies are valued for their health or when they require assessment, diagnosis, treatment and intervention. The 'diseased bodies', 'fat bodies', the 'sexually deviant' or 'mentally disordered' become intelligible via medicalised systems, for example through psychiatric classification and diagnosis where signs and symptoms of abnormal behaviour are clustered according to the *DSM-5* (*Diagnostic and Statistical Manual of Mental Disorders: 5th edition*) in the USA and/or *ICD-10* (*International Statistical Classification of Diseases and Related Health Problems: 10th revision*) in the UK and Europe, and given labels such as major depression, bipolar affective disorder, generalised anxiety, bulimia, etc.

Queer theory proposes performativity as a theoretical tool to disrupt this form of normativity. Rather than classifying people or fixing identity in categories, mental health can be perceived as performative via a self-reflexive process of becoming over time. During performativity the subject, as gendered and sexualised, remains unstable and open to re-articulation. Mental health could gain shape through a range of acts, which are reviewed, changed and integrated over time. Just at the 'body becomes its gender' (Butler, 2002, p. 523) where gestures, bodily acts and practices are acted and re-enacted during performativity as a process, where gender is inscribed on the body; the mental health of a service user is shaped by biomedical knowledge systems and its related practices over time. The body becomes a surface for history whereupon cultural norms are written (Butler, 1987). The body therefore becomes a concrete scene of cultural struggle during the process whereby liveable lives are negotiated to determine which 'bodies matter'. Consider surgical scars or marks that service users may carry as a result of self-harm or psychiatric treatments – such as the side-effects of anti-psychotics. A psychiatric survivor gives an account of these side-effects narrated in *Our Encounters with Madness* (Grant et al, 2011) where he states '… I was coerced, as a condition of my discharge, to have injections of Depixol in my buttock every two weeks. These produced horrendous side-effects of extreme restlessness and extreme sedation simultaneously…'

(Voyce, 2011, p. 52). Due to the external visibility to others of the side-effects of sedation or restlessness, the body becomes the surface whereupon cultural struggle is inscribed. The body signifies cultural struggle, which impacts on the way others respond to psychiatric survivors. Can this form of difference be recognised and understood? Recognition of difference will determine whether lives become viable.

## Queer interconnections

Queer scholarship actively critiques the process whereby biomedicine fixes subjects owing to normative categorisations and diagnoses. The biomedical notion of a scientific essentialist subject is questioned by queer theorists who suggest that subjects can never be fixed but that they remain plural, fluid and open to re-articulation. Subjects are in a process of becoming, and remain subjects in process (Kristeva, 1982). Derridean texts suggest the inconceivability of any fixed identity, such as an 'ill', 'mentally disordered' or 'homosexual' person, because any formulation is open to constant deferral and re-signification (Lloyd, 2007, p. 12). The queer subject is coloured by ambiguity and shaped in narrative that gains viability through performativity as a process of actions, activities, iteration and reiteration to become a form of 'materialisation that stabilises over time to produce the effect of boundary, fixity, and surface we call matter' (Butler, 1993, p. 9). The mental health subject is the location of contested and contradicting forms of embodiment in the biomedical, constructionist and queer. The process of performativity holds power due to its persistence and instability. The body is held in tension via the biomedical (diseased body), constructionist (socially determined body) and the queer (body marked by difference) discourses.

If we propose queer reformulations of knowledge, subjectivity and the body as replacements to biomedical evidence (which maintains difference), or constructionist knowledge (which is value neutral), we repeat the epistemic violence some would accuse biomedicine of. A discursively plural understanding of knowledge, subjectivity and the body is required to prevent this form of violence from recurring.

## Discursive plurality

Deleuze and Guattari's (1987) metaphor of rhizomes serves as a non-normative backdrop for biomedical, constructionist and queer discourses to coexist in healthcare practice. Rhizomes are complex botanical structures like grass or ginger that are connected systemically in a broad range of roots, nodes and lines rather than consisting of a singular structural tree-like form. Rolfe and Gardner (2006) applied this metaphor to evidence-based practice as a way to accommodate and accept contradicting positions and dissent. When the metaphor is extended to discursive traditions of knowledge generation, a rhizomatic understanding suggests intersecting linear multiples in the biomedical, constructionist and queer, instead of separate structures each with a viable centre, as trees with trunks. There is no central stable core or a coherent origin in each discourse that pre-exists. The ultimate truth that biomedicine aspires to is replaced by a range of representations of reality that comes about as an effect of knowledge and power relations. Within each discourse, knowledge is part of an endless process that remains always in process. Like the rhizome that permeates boundaries and multiplies, epistemologies interconnect as part of a web of nodes shared between plants. The intricate rhizomatic web contains many plants that, each spring, shoot to form new lines in multiple directions. The rhizome suggests knowledge as a cyclic form of an eternal return that becomes visible in open questions, the unknown and reiteration in thought. Knowledge is plural where constructionist and queer knowledge is made, unlike scientific biomedical knowledge claiming to be of a higher dimension or a form of truth waiting to be discovered.

In the metaphor of the rhizome, multiplicity of knowledge occurs against the backdrop of power relations. A rhizome can be split or broken at a specific place but will regrow from one of its numerous lines. We are unable to do away with knowledge constructions of a particular discourse. A critique of discourses is not an attempt at suppressing or doing away with knowledge but more like a pruning action. Rhizomes always come back once disturbed. During any interference the plant rebounds from a different line, with vigour. Discourses such as the biomedical, constructionist and queer develop in dialogue with one another and require the other as a form of pruning.

Rhizomes form segmentary lines that become lines of flight. Binary oppositions or dualisms in rupture are like drawing a line of flight. Lines of flight refer back to one another just as each of the binaries in a binary pair (health/illness, mentally ordered/mentally disordered, heterosexual/homosexual, the scientific rational/interpretive embodied) needs the other for its meaning. Healthcare organisations categorise health and illness to restore power to scientific biomedicine just as the rhizome confirms its existence via a process of territorialisation. Within healthcare organisations, groups hold micro knowledge waiting to erupt via lines of flight. Change in our views of evidence will occur along lines of flight when queer questions the normative of biomedicine. Developments in queer knowledge and re-affirmation of biomedicine are intricately connected as part of the same rhizomatic web. Three discourses in the biomedical, constructionist and queer are all in a process of becoming; they intermingle and require one another for their evolution. Development of discourses occurs without similarity or replication of the other. Within each discourse knowledge is never complete and always evolving during an incoherent and multifaceted transformational process. The rhizome cannot be defined in terms of an entrance into plurality or multiplicity.

Discursive boundaries between the biomedical, constructionist and queer become obsolete during a letting-go of borders that separate knowledge-making communities. Discourses are linked through linear multiplicities that follow on from and feed into a plane of consistency where knowledge becomes the sum of many parts (Ruffolo, 2009; Heckert, 2010). Movement with only biomedicine refers back to a fixed core (tree) whereas movements with the biomedical, constructionist and queer rescind borders and continuously evolve. The process of valuing scientific evidence over other forms of knowledge is underpinned by narrative processes that communities discuss and agree between people. Knowledge is what people 'do' together, becoming visible as a relational interchange where mutual understanding is gained in dialogue.

In the world of healthcare and staunch biomedical assumptions about what counts as evidence, rhizomatic thinking would lead to healthcare systems and practices that move from hierarchical representations of knowledge where biomedical scientific evidence is preferenced, to a mutual valuing of diverse systems of knowledge generation.

## Conclusion

The rhizomatic metaphor lends meaning to discursive plurality with knowledge as relational where the biomedical, constructionist and queer interconnect. The implications for evidence-based practice are that equal respect could be afforded to different knowledge-making communities. However, owing to the prominence of biomedicine, less dominant forms of knowledge continue to be marginalised. Transformation of the monoculture of the evidence-based movement occurs at intersections or connections, where queer disrupts the normative of biomedicine and subverts, not for its own sake, but to revise knowledge-making processes, relations and values. To queer is to pay attention to the specificity of the biomedical/social constructionist discourse and the way these have to keep reworking understanding of evidence and knowledge. Queer works on these fracture lines and pursues plurality and contests the normative diseased body within health/illness or ordered/disordered binaries of biomedicine, whilst actively engaging with dissent to recognise the provisional nature of all knowledge. The opportunity to transform healthcare practice occurs at the brinks and margins of knowledge generation, with a queer epistemology questioning the normative in binary linguistic systems to resist labels in iteration and reiteration over time. Practitioners work in the tension of naming or not naming their service users (ordered/disordered, healthy/ill) in the binary language of biomedicine and psychiatry. Resisting binaries means entering into non-normative practices where service users as healthcare subjects are not fixed via categorisation, for example depressed, bipolar or borderline, but remain constantly open to re-articulation. As long as queer knowledge maintains a critical engagement with normative fixing of meaning, biomedicine will remain under scrutiny.

To queer is to open up the normative base of evidence-based practice, to trouble and expose the working of power relations, and to make visible those whom these work in service of. The range of epistemologies reveals the partiality of all positions, and how the relatedness of diverse forms of knowledge is shaped in power relations. Biomedicine as dominant discourse has to police its boundaries and find new ways to exclude and make certain its claims. The evidence-based movement is an example of biomedicine redrawing its boundaries and asserting its claims.

Queer maintains a position of critical reflexivity in our politics of resistance, where we acknowledge the usefulness and limitations of all knowledge, including our own. Queer does not ask for assimilation or assume that all knowledge is equal, as this will forgo or erase specificity. Queer celebrates difference by remaining outside to disrupt that which is easily overlooked or represented as the norm. The task of queer knowledge is to do justice to the lives lived and cared for in the name of evidence-based practice. The undertaking demands that we queer the conditions of knowledge production, and consider the power relations where the production of knowledge takes place, whilst identifying new intersections with Deleuze, which allows for a socially just understanding of knowing or evidence to emerge.

At the points where discourses intersect on their boundaries, energising, innovative and disruptive approaches to healthcare knowledge, which combine a broad range of evidence, become viable (Denzin, 2011; Hesse-Biber & Leavy, 2007). The vehicle for transformation of research, theory and practice is mediation and negotiation, rather than imposing, dominating or suppressing disagreements about the nature of knowledge or what counts as evidence (Mishler, 2005; Guba & Lincoln, 2005). This implies that a colouring of epistemologies can occur (Denzin, 2010, 2011). Practice will benefit from developing a critical politics of knowledge where practitioners, service users and the public come together in dialogic spaces to contest commonly held assumptions about knowledge and evidence by valuing lay knowledge that holds the potential to support social networks that are central to collaboration and the participatory processes of healthcare (Gibson et al, 2012). These knowledge spaces take the shape of meetings, conferences and interactive events, such as Mad Pride, as initiated by service user groups. They are an exciting development where patient and public involvement could lead to interchange with health professionals on equal terms. In these spaces experiential and embodied understandings of mental health challenge medicalised views of best evidence utilised to make decisions about care, without involving service users (Gibson et al, 2012). Within these spaces knowledge too takes on different forms from the abstract and objective to the relational, affective and embodied found in the complexity of service user and carer narratives, situated in their larger historical and biographical contexts. Here, practitioners, service users and lay people remain open to mutually enriching dialogue whilst critically questioning biomedicine via everyday acts of resistance, where biomedicine aims to dominate or fix meaning. These subversions are iterated and reiterated in behaviour, bodily gestures, conversations and relations. A more nuanced awareness of the humanity and individuality of each mental health service user becomes available, instead of focusing on broad-based similarities that come about because of the persistent reproduction of common classifications and normative categories of mental illness.

## Acknowledgement

With thanks to *Nursing Inquiry* where this paper was first published as: Zeeman, L, Aranda, K & Grant, A (2013) Queer challenges to evidence-based practice. *Nursing Inquiry*. Accepted for publication May 2013. Available online from http://onlinelibrary.wiley.com/doi/10.1111/nin.12039/abstract [accessed January 2014]. Reproduced with permission.

# References

Aranda, K, Zeeman, L, Scholes, J & Santa-María Morales, A (2012) The resilient subject: Exploring subjectivity, identity and the body in narratives of resilience. *Health: An Interdisciplinary Journal for the Social Study of Health, Illness and Medicine, 16*(5), 548–563.

Brandom, R (Ed) (2000) *Rorty and His Critics.* Oxford: Blackwell.

Browne, K, Lim, J & Brown, G (Eds) (2007) *Geographies of Sexualities: Theory, practice and politics.* Aldershot: Ashgate.

Bruner, J (1986) *Actual Minds, Possible Worlds.* Cambridge, MA: Harvard University Press.

Bruner, J (1990) *Acts of Meaning.* Cambridge, MA: Harvard University Press.

Burr, V (2003) *An Introduction to Social Constructionism* (2nd ed). Hove: Routledge.

Butler, J (1987) *Subjects of Desire: Hegelian Reflections in Twentieth-century France.* New York: Columbia University Press.

Butler, J (1992) Contingent foundations: Feminism and the question of postmodernism. In J Butler, J & JW Scott (Eds) *Feminists Theorize the Political* (pp. 3–21). New York: Routledge.

Butler, J (1993) *Bodies that Matter: On the discursive limits of 'sex'.* London: Routledge.

Butler, J (1999) *Gender Trouble: Feminism and the subversion of identity.* New York: Routledge.

Costa, L & Reaume, G (2008) Mad Pride in our mad culture. *Bulletin: Information for consumer/survivors of the mental health system, those who serve us, and those who care about us, 374*(July 14), 2–4. Available from http://www.csinfo.ca/bulletin/Bulletin_374.pdf [accessed January 2014].

Davies, B (2003) Death to critique and dissent? The policies and practices of new managerialism and of 'evidence-based practice'. *Gender and Education, 15*(1), 91–103.

Dawes, M, Davies, P, Gray, A, Mant, J, Seers, K & Snowball, R (2005) *Evidence-based Practice: A primer for health care professionals.* London: Elsevier.

Deleuze, G & Guattari, F (1987) *A Thousand Plateaus: Capitalism and schizophrenia* (Trans. B Massumi). London: Continuum Books.

Denzin, N (2010) Moments, mixed methods and paradigm dialogs. *Qualitative Inquiry, 16*(6), 419–427.

Denzin, N (2011) The politics of evidence. In N Denzin & Y Lincoln (Eds) *The Sage Handbook of Qualitative Research* (4th ed) (pp. 645–657). Thousand Oaks, CA: Sage.

Derrida, J (1974) *Of Grammatology.* Baltimore, MD: Johns Hopkins University Press.

Derrida, J (1978) *Writing and Difference.* Chicago: University of Chicago Press.

Foucault, M (1974) *The Archaeology of Knowledge.* London: Tavistock.

Fox, N (2012) *The Body.* Cambridge: Polity Press.

Freshwater, D & Rolfe, G (2004) *Deconstructing Evidence-based Practice.* London: Routledge.

Gergen, KJ (2002) Beyond the empiricist/constructionist divide in social psychology. *Personality and Social Psychology Review, 6*(3), 188–191.

Gergen, KJ (2003) Beyond knowing in organizational inquiry. *Organization, 10*(3), 453–455.

Gergen, KJ (2006) Theory in action. *Theory & Psychology, 16*(3), 299–309.

Gergen, KJ (2009) *Relational Being: Beyond self and community.* New York: Oxford University Press.

Gibson, A, Britten, N & Lynch, J (2012) Theoretical directions for an emancipatory concept of patient and public involvement. *Health, 16*(5), 531–547.

Grant, A & Zeeman, L (2012) Whose story is it? An autoethnography concerning narrative identity. *The Qualitative Report, 17*(36), 1–12.

Grant, A, Biley, F & Walker, H (Eds) (2011) *Our Encounters with Madness.* Ross-on-Wye: PCCS Books.

Guba, E & Lincoln, Y (2005) Paradigmatic controversies and emerging confluences. In N Denzin & Y Lincoln (Eds) *Handbook of Qualitative Research* (3rd ed) (pp. 191–216). Thousand Oaks, CA: Sage.

Hall, D, Jagose, A, Bebell, A & Potter, S (2013) *The Routledge Queer Studies Reader.* London: Routledge.

Heckert, J (2010) Intimacy with strangers/intimacy with self: Queer experiences of social research. In K Browne & C Nash (Eds) *Queer Methods and Methodologies* (pp. 41–54). Farnham: Ashgate.

Hesse-Biber, SN & Leavy, PL (2007) *Feminist Research Practice.* London: Sage.

Holmes, D, Murray, S, Perron, A & Rail, G (2006) Deconstructing the evidence-based discourse in health sciences: Truth, power and fascism. *International Journal of Evidence-Based Healthcare, 4*, 180–186.

Kristeva, J (1982) *Powers of Horror: An essay on abjection* (Trans. Leon S Roudiez). New York: Columbia University Press.

Lather, P (2009) Against empathy, voice and authenticity. In A Jackson & L Mazzei (Eds) *Voice in Qualitative Inquiry: Challenging conventional, interpretive, and critical conceptions in qualitative research* (pp. 17–26). London: Routledge.

Lloyd, M (2005) *Beyond Identity Politics: Feminism, power and politics*. London: Sage.

Lloyd, M (2007) *Judith Butler: From norms to politics*. Cambridge: Polity Press.

Lupton, D (2012) *Medicine as Culture: Illness, disease and the body* (3rd ed). London: Sage Publications.

Mishler, E (2005) Patient stories, narratives of resistance and the ethics of humane care: A la recherché du temps perdu. *Health, 9*(4), 431–451.

Morse, J (2006) The politics of evidence. In N Denzin & M Giardina (Eds) *Qualitative Inquiry and the Conservative Challenge*. Walnut Creek, CA: Left Coast Press.

Paley, J (2006) Evidence and expertise. *Nursing Inquiry, 13*(2), 82–93.

Polit, D & Beck, CT (2008) *Nursing Research: Generating and assessing evidence for nursing practice*. Philadelphia: Lippincott Williams & Wilkins.

Porter, S & O'Halloran, P (2009) The postmodernist war on evidence-based practice. *International Journal of Nursing Studies, 46*(5), 740–748.

Riggs, DW (2011) Queering evidence-based practice. *Psychology and Sexuality, 2*(1), 87–98.

Rolfe, G (2001) Postmodernism for healthcare workers in 13 easy steps. *Nurse Education Today, 21*(1), 38–47.

Rolfe, G (2005) The deconstructing angel: Nursing, reflection and evidence-based practice. *Nursing Inquiry, 12*, 78–86.

Rolfe, G (2007) Validity and the fabrication of truths: A response to Porter. *Journal of Advanced Nursing, 60*(1), 108–109.

Rolfe, G & Gardner, L (2006) Towards a geology of evidence-based practice. *International Journal of Nursing Studies, 43*, 903–913.

Rorty, R (1999) *Philosophy and Social Hope*. London: Penguin.

Ruffolo, D (2009) *Post-Queer Politics*. Farnham: Ashgate.

Rycroft-Malone, J (2006) The politics of the evidence-based practice movements. *Journal of Research in Nursing, 11*(2), 95–108.

Rycroft-Malone, J, Seers, K, Titchen, A, Harvey, G, Kitson, A & McCormack, B (2004) What counts as evidence in evidence-based practice? *Journal of Advanced Nursing, 47*(1), 81–90.

Sackett, D, Strauss, S, Richardson, W, Rosenberg, W & Haynes, R (2004) *Evidence-Based Medicine: How to practise and teach EBM* (2nd ed). London: Churchill Livingstone.

Sedgwick, E (1990) *Epistemology of the Closet.* Berkeley, CA: University of California Press.

Seidman, S (1997) *Difference Troubles: Queering social theory and sexual politics.* Cambridge: Cambridge University Press.

Traynor, M (2009) Indeterminacy and technicality revisited: How medicine and nursing have responded to the evidence-based movement. *Sociology of Health & Illness, 31* (4), 494–507.

Twigg, J (2006) *The Body in Health and Social Care.* Basingstoke: Palgrave Macmillan.

Voyce, A (2011) On schizophrenia. In A Grant, F Biley & H Walker (Eds) *Our Encounters with Madness* (pp. 51–52). Ross-on-Wye: PCCS books.

Weedon, C (2003) *Feminist Practice and Poststructuralist Theory* (2nd ed). Oxford: Blackwell Publishing.

# troubling the normative mental health recovery project: the silent resistance of a disappearing doctor

## – alec grant and helen leigh-phippard –

### Introduction

This chapter is composed of two parts – a discussion that sets out its theoretical basis and a subsequent dialogue conducted between the authors which is framed by this discussion. The theoretical basis for the chapter is a pragmatic amalgam of postmodern, queer, autoethnographic and poststructural narrative identity principles. The dialogue – which draws on our witness accounts as mental health survivors – privileges Leigh-Phippard's story. Overall, the chapter utilises queer principles to the extent that it is 'at odds with the ... legitimate, the dominant' (Halperin, 1995, p. 62) in its deliberate disruption and transgression of the normative project of mental health recovery (Plummer, 2005). In keeping with the poststructural basis of queer theory, we regard the markers of such identity as socially constructed, contextually determined, fluid and emerging (Tilsen & Nylund, 2010; Jackson & Mazzei, 2012).

From the above context, we aspire to some of the claimed shared concepts and purposes of autoethnography and queer theory (Holman Jones & Adams, 2010; Adams & Holman Jones, 2011). This includes the deliberate use of dialogue as a progressive qualitative device to resist the kinds of colonialising representational practices we critique in part one of the chapter. Krumer-Nevo and Sidi (2012) argue that dialogue allows for a reflexive exploration of issues and contexts, a resistance to othering, and the creation of the possibilities for change in the utilisation of plural, fluid voices. In summary, building on our developing critique in part one, the use of dialogue as both representational practice and autoethnographic tool aids our attempt to rescue difference from the pathologising tendencies of institutional psychiatry in the context of a broader commitment to social justice and change.

We trouble current mental health nursing-policy literature, which discursively coheres around institutional psychiatry and other related textual constructions of 'recovery'. Developing from a basis in, and extending the dialogue around, our ongoing narrative inquiry work (Grant et al, 2011, 2012), we hopefully model the potential for local stories to contribute to new explorations of what 'recovery' might signify.

Institutional psychiatry has the discursive power to attempt to bully into silence any account that troubles its operating assumptions. It will become apparent as this chapter unfolds that this can happen in several connected ways. In keeping with related policy and professional texts, the big stories of institutional psychiatry have a sanitised veneer concealing a less-than-pristine subtext. In contrast, little – local, individual or small-group – stories simultaneously graphically expose and protest in reaction to those. Big stories shout, 'Behave! Know your place!' Little stories consistently reply that they won't. Big stories hijack the emerging identities central to the little stories, often in value-laden, gendered and infantilising ways. Little stories try to pick up and reassemble the narrative pieces later, frequently in novel and dignity-restoring ways.

## Part one: Theoretical underpinning

### Discursive practice and discourses-in-practice

Little stories need to be understood in the context of the broader discourses that make them possible. We assume that people account for themselves at the interstices of discursive practice and discourses-in-practice (Holstein & Gubrium, 2000). Discursive practice refers to how subjectivity is produced, performed and constructed – for the purposes of this chapter, through the experience of storytelling. In this poststructural context, experience and identity are assumed to be simultaneously co-produced, enacted and performed in narrative, rather than fixed and stable. Discourses-in-practice relate to the broad possibilities for drawing on culturally available meaning at any one time and place to construct individual and shared stories (Bakhtin, 1981; Holquist, 2002).

Discursive practice and discourses-in-practice inscribe subjectivities within provisional, performed and emerging witness accounts of a troubled world (Pillow, 2003). Such stories are always situated, making contextual sense in relation to the experiences of people, at specific points in time and space (Bakhtin, 1981; Holquist, 2002). Their cultural bases include the organisational contexts of institutional psychiatry.

## Implicit organisational narratives and their refusal

The shared interpretive schemes of organisational culture, or its implicit narratives (Smircich, 1983; Richardson, 1997), can inform 'the way things are done around here' in the practice environments of institutional psychiatry. They include tacitly held organisational rules and related practices to which mental health workers are socialised. Resulting enacted realities may be far removed from what is portrayed in the sanitised accounts of psychiatric care and treatment appearing in policy texts (discussed below). However, they can impact on service users to the extent that their mental health problems, or sometimes unrelated but stigmatised aspects of their behaviour, become that by which mental health workers and others define them in a comprehensive and discriminatory way (Thornicroft, 2006).

In this context, however, the settings where institutional psychiatry is either practised or contested, materially, interpersonally and textually, are potential discursive spaces for the production of variable meanings and experiences by staff and service users and survivors (St Pierre, 2009; Spry, 2011). What is produced may run counter to, or in parallel with, policy-based stories about what constitutes 'treatment' or 'intervention' in conferring negative local identities on service users. Conversely, users and survivors may reject such locally imposed biographies by re-storying alternative personal realities (Grant et al, 2011).

The master narratives of institutional psychiatry, mediated by local implicit organisational narratives, often trump enacted stories of individual service users and survivors. However, the last two decades have witnessed the development of a corpus of oppositional stories, produced and circulated along with corresponding new possibilities for action and radical change (eg. Church, 1995; Grant et al, 2011; Costa et al, 2012). The implications for citizenship emerging from this include the growing acceptance of non-medicalised differences between people. Although possibly a utopian aspiration, it is to be hoped that such re-storying of life narratives, personally and collectively, may result in the categories of 'mental health user' or 'survivor' becoming increasingly less culturally meaningful over time (Cresswell & Spandler, 2013).

## Narrative re-storying

'Re-storying' one's narrative has been described as a transformational act in the development of individual and collective identity and difference (Cresswell & Spandler, 2013; Grant & Zeeman, 2012; Richardson, 1997). Drawing on a clothing store metaphor, people can 'try on' new stories for size once they are in the public domain (Adams, 2008; Alcoff, 2009). Speaking or writing subjectivities into existence also generates possibilities for transgressive and resistant discursive positions, disrupting privileged or colonial voice (Burr, 2003; Chaudhry, 2009).

Category- and identity-refusing narratives have the potential to allow for storied, contested meanings to be re-inscribed and reinstituted within emerging narrative communities in the development of a postmodern critical social consciousness (Alcoff, 2009; Soja, 1989). The stories written in *Our Encounters with Madness* (*OEWM*) (Grant et al, 2011) challenge, contest, trouble, expose as contradictory, critically interrogate, disrupt and problematise the normative project of mental health recovery. This includes the ways in which individuals come together in re-storying their positions in ways that both exceed and are relatively distinct from such constructions.

'Recovery' in *OEWM*, as in other texts, frequently signifies liberation from invalidating societal and institutional practices, including that of institutional psychiatry (Thornicroft, 2006; Pilgrim, 2009). In this context, 'treatment', including 'nursing care', becomes a recovery issue when experienced as a narrative assault on the identities of users of mental health services. Moreover, users' reactions to such 'treatment' and 'care' often compounds such assault experiences when these trigger further discriminating and denigratory responses by mental health workers.

## The recovering patient in mental health nursing-policy literature

All of this represents individuals and groups within the provisional and heuristically useful categories of 'user-survivor' and 'mental health worker' antagonistically relating to each other on the basis of their inevitably different takes on reality (Holquist, 2002). The 'official' construction of recovery proceeds from the tacitly accepted authority of institutional psychiatry. This is reflected in the *Chief Nursing Officer's Review of Mental Health Nursing*, which constructs the gender neutral, compliant, homogenised and relatively silent recovering patient in keeping with discursively available positions proceeding from its own circular logic: that specialist nursing staff in specialist work settings know best what recovery means in the context of their professional and environmental specialisms (DH, 2006).

In this policy document, recovery is argued as an inclusive construct. However, a tension appears between its apparent support for the practices and assumptions of institutional psychiatry and its latent stigmatising stance towards users and survivors (Goffman, 1963; Thornicroft, 2006). Its language endorses and assumes the relevance of the cultural hegemony of biomedical interpretations of the recovery concept and related institutional practices. Although 'recovery' is argued as fundamental to 'valuing the principles of equality', a contradiction is introduced between the possibility of full membership of society for mental health service users and the 'limitations caused by illness' (p. 17).

A further contradiction is anticipated in the sentence, 'To work effectively in partnership with service users and carers, it is essential that … [mental health nurses] are able to … offer meaningful choice…' (p. 18). Although the question begged – 'Meaningful on whose terms?' – is not answered, it is argued later in the document that choice should be governed by the environmental circumstances in which mental health nursing practice is carried out, in the context of 'strengthening relationships with service users and carers' (p. 26). The nature of such choice is described as necessarily variable, depending on the environmental context in which nursing care is provided.

Such a privileging of the term 'choice', although apparently cohering with contemporary neoliberal individualising tendencies in British healthcare, actually betrays a rhetoric of collaboration offered more or less exclusively on the organisational environmental terms of institutional psychiatry. In this regard, the statement '… choice will be facilitated by providing good information about different interventions and outcomes and by asserting service users' views…' (p. 26) glosses over the fact that mental health nurses' and users' views do not always happily cohere. Indeed, the shared assumptions of mental health staff around what constitutes appropriate interventions are often privileged over users' views in persuasion or compliance narratives, tacitly underscored at local and national policy levels (Grant et al, 2011).

A frequently illustrated implication emerging from the above is that users can be pulled into dominant narratives of local mental health services in the name of 'recovery' (Grant et al, 2011), in ways that exceed its constructions. Such narrative assaults on identity are often written as compounding and worsening existing distress, and this will be the subject of part two.

# Part two: Narrative assaults on identity

**Alec:** In our research following *OEWM*, I was interested in the ways in which some stories silenced other stories. It seemed to me that the narratives in the book spoke to the ways in which master narratives ghettoised and tidied away societally unwanted experiences. Unfortunately, this functions as a kind of closure on the possibility for some people, officially in 'recovery', of having a viable life. Stories of acute ward business as usual, for example, silenced the need for interpersonal connection, respect and dignity. None of this is recognisable in the sanitised policy accounts of course.

I was struck by the commonalities people expressed with regard to identity hijacking: how they felt abused or stripped of dignity as human beings, which you well illustrated in your chapter and our subsequent research interview ...

**Helen:** I certainly see my passage through mental health services as the story of how I became 'other', of the person that I once was stripped away by a range of behavioural and linguistic practices, and of how the biggest challenge to my mental health became finding ways of living with being 'other' while still trying to be me. Looking back, I am often astonished at how little explanation of my symptoms was offered to me in the first years of illness. My contacts with mental health professionals focused on getting me to accept that my life had changed irrevocably: I had to understand that I was no longer the person I had been before I became ill, and accept that what I thought and wanted had to be subjected to the demands of medical treatment for my depressive and psychotic symptoms. I lost count of the number of times I was told, 'Your life is different now,' and 'You have to accept that your life has changed for good.' Any challenge to this edict was met with the response, 'This is what depression does, it distorts your thinking', 'You're not in the best position to know what you need' and even, more than once, 'You're not in your right mind.' In a short space of time I had gone from being a trusted and respected professional to a patient whose opinion and wishes could be dismissed and ignored. The consequences of this for my sense of who I was were enormous. For a long time I simply didn't know who I was any more.

Inevitably, this change in my status, from working professional to 'severe depressive', defined primarily in terms of mental health problems, had a profound effect on my partner and on our relationship. He found himself redefined as carer and breadwinner, while my relationship with him was redefined by others from partner to burden. Following my discharge from psychiatric hospital my husband came with me to my initial monthly outpatient appointments with a psychiatrist, during which the psychiatrist would have conversations with him about me as if I wasn't there. He would ask, 'How has she been?', 'What's her mood been like?' I felt infantilised, patronised and humiliated.

I was treated as a child, as though I had no capacity to be responsible for my own life. My instinct was to resist this, but resistance was met with accusations of non-compliance, and with the suggestion that I was making things harder for myself by not accepting that I didn't know what was best for me any more. I eventually asked my husband not to come with me to appointments: I didn't want him to speak for me; I wanted to speak for myself. Ironically, I soon learned that if I attended unaccompanied it would be better for me to say as little as possible, as it seemed that whatever I said was misinterpreted as evidence of my disordered mind. So I learned to answer questions in monosyllables or not at all.

**Alec:** One of the things that interested me in *OEWM* was how being caught up in big, stigma- and in your case gender-related narratives left people feeling. Stories suggested that staff assumed this to be acceptable practice. This was something that you and several others in the book wrote about, and something I experienced myself when I was an inpatient.

**Helen:** When I was first admitted to an inpatient ward I was very naïve. I thought it would be no different to going into any other hospital for treatment, but very quickly learned that psychiatric inpatient care wasn't like that. I was admitted as a voluntary patient and had asked for reassurance that I could leave if and when I wanted before agreeing to admission. But once I was on the ward I was told I couldn't leave and could be sectioned if I tried to. When I queried a very large increase in the dosage of my medication (which even at a low dose was causing problematic side-effects), I was told, 'You're in hospital now, you have to do what we say.' When I reported very distressing side-effects of medications I was told first by a nurse, and later by a junior doctor, that the side-effects were all in my mind. And I wasn't allowed to leave until a meeting had been held to determine whether or not I should be sectioned or could be conditionally discharged.

Even as an outpatient there was an implicit threat underlying my treatment during that first year of illness – that if I didn't do as I was told I could be held under section. For example, when I consistently refused a psychiatrist's recommendation to have electroconvulsive therapy he would say, 'If you won't agree to it I could decide that you have to have it, and then it could be administered without your consent.' So the language used to ensure my compliance was backed up by the threat of compulsion.

**Alec:** And I think from your narratives of 'the way things are done around here' that the staff in the institutional psychiatry practice sites you found yourself in were quite defensive. You and others wrote about how you were vilified whenever any of you protested or challenged their business-as-usual.

**Helen:** Yes. It took a long time for me to be 'socialised' into mental health services, but I eventually learned that if I questioned my diagnosis or any prescription then I would be labelled 'non-compliant'. I had to learn to accept that my life had changed, that I would now be either patronised or infantilised by services that appeared to want to control or at least manage me rather than support or help me. Initially I resisted, argued and contested every decision, comment or response I didn't agree with, but over time I learned to give the impression of being compliant. I learned in particular to be silent, to say as little as possible, becoming that stereotype of mental health services – the silent service user, because anything I said could be written down out of context, misinterpreted, reinterpreted and used against me.

Over a period of months I went from being vocal and non-compliant to silent and invisible. I now think that this reflected an internal process in which my sense of self was disappearing. Every time that old professional assertive me had resisted, challenged or questioned, I had been ignored, dismissed and even threatened. I no longer knew if I could trust my own instincts, but I also knew that the medications I was being given weren't working and were making life harder, not easier. I didn't trust the treatments being offered to me so I became invisible. I visited the psychiatrist once a month, listened to what he said, took the prescriptions he gave me, but, after obediently taking them for many months and suffering side-effects that no one cared about, with no obvious improvement to my mental health, I stopped using them. Not taking them made no difference and for a long time no one else knew that I wasn't taking them. I resisted silently because I was afraid of the potential consequences of vocal, visible resistance.

It does seem to me that in those first years, before I was moved to a community mental health team (which was a huge improvement on inpatient and outpatient psychiatric treatment), I received very little 'care' of any kind. The focus was very much on getting me to accept the recommended treatment, even when it didn't help and often seemed to me to make things worse. The sense of powerlessness that this evoked in me was almost certainly more detrimental to my mental health than the hallucinations I was living with.

For five years I tried to preserve what I could of myself, of the old self, by giving the appearance of a passive, if still often non-compliant, patient. That silent resistance was very important to me – I had lost so much of the old me but I didn't know what to replace it with. Resisting silently was a way of keeping what was left, from a fear that I could easily lose that too.

**Alec:** Yes, we all shared in our stories a critique of what passes for 'care' and 'treatment' in institutional practices, practices that seem equally taken for granted by staff. Along with other writers in the book, you mentioned being storied in nursing and medical records in selective, value-laden and derogatory ways, which indicated that moral judgements were being made rather than illness or care ones?

**Helen:** In my case I felt that I really didn't know who I was any more. The person I thought I was simply didn't match up with who I was being told I was: when I challenged anything I was treated like a belligerent toddler rather than an adult. And that had such a huge impact on my self-esteem and my self-confidence, to the extent that it was sometimes easier to accept the dominant psychiatric story rather than fight it, and to be complicit in the stripping away of important parts of my identity. A good example of this is the way in which I accepted the gradual disappearance of my professional title (Dr) from my medical notes and from my life.

I was awarded a PhD in 1991 and was working as a university lecturer when I first became unwell: I was (and still am) registered as Dr at my GP surgery, so all referral letters, prescriptions and other documents sent from there refer to me as such. When I first entered mental health services this title aroused some curiosity: What was I a doctor of? What did the title mean? Was I a medical doctor? However, after a year or two of mental health problems this title gradually disappeared from use by mental health services – it was still in all correspondence from my GP surgery but was no longer used in my psychiatric notes and referrals, prescriptions that originated from mental health services, or in correspondence to my GP or me.

For a long time I accepted this – I didn't feel like a doctor of anything any more. That title belonged to the other me, the professional me who had existed but was no longer. But I also didn't question its disappearance because I didn't want to make waves; I didn't want to challenge its non-use. But I wonder now why it disappeared, particularly since my GP still uses the title and so when I use other NHS services I am still referred to as Dr. Was its disappearance a simple accident, a process of a few key individuals not bothering to enter it as a title in online records so it simply wasn't there anymore? Or was it deliberate – a judgement on the part of someone in mental health services that its use wasn't appropriate, that it somehow undermined a power balance between professional and patient?

More generally, I have often been treated very judgementally by a range of NHS services, not just mental health ones. I've been described in my hospital notes as 'intense', 'difficult' and 'always demanding attention', and was perturbed when I accessed my confidential hospital records by the extent to which my mental health history seemed always to take primacy over the symptoms of any medical problem I was being treated for.

The most obvious example is in relation to the range of neurological symptoms not long after I first started hallucinating. For the first year or so that I was suffering these symptoms my psychiatrist insisted that they were side-effects of the psychiatric drugs he was prescribing. But the symptoms persisted long after I had stopped taking any medication, and when I eventually told my psychiatrist that I had not been taking my medication for some months, so the symptoms couldn't be medication side-effects, I was referred to a neurologist.

I saw him regularly for a number of years concurrently with psychiatric appointments. Each time, he would ask about my symptoms and then tell me in a roundabout way that they were imaginary. He insisted that the problem with patients like me was that they would look up their symptoms on the internet and then decide that they had a terrible disease and demand that the NHS diagnose and treat it. The solution, he told me, was to return to work: not working was giving me too much time to dwell on psychological symptoms. Having finally accepted medical retirement after some years of resisting it, to be told that the problem now was that I didn't have a job, and the only cure was to get a job, left me feeling absolutely hopeless.

I was caught in a web of health professionals who contradicted each other and did absolutely nothing to help me. When I followed their advice it made the situation worse, not better. And even after all these years I still struggle to engage with any health services for fear of being judged on account of my mental health problems.

I was eventually diagnosed with a brain tumour, discovered during a CT scan ordered by an ear, nose and throat consultant because I was having problems both with my hearing and with balance. I had been seeing a psychiatrist for almost five years and a neurologist for around three years at that point, and I often wonder if that tumour would ever have been found had I not had a scan for a hearing problem. I had a craniotomy to remove the tumour but my symptoms persisted, and I found myself being bounced between psychiatric and neurological services once again. However, I had been moved from outpatient psychiatric care to a community mental health team following my craniotomy and found that I now had an excellent community psychiatric nurse (CPN) and so I decided to disengage from medical services as much as possible and focus instead on managing my symptoms with the help of this CPN.

Eight years on, I still have no idea which of my symptoms are neurological/physical and which psychiatric: those kinds of distinctions make no sense to me anymore. I experience symptoms, whatever their cause, and I need to manage them. A recent diagnosis of fibromyalgia has made my situation both more complicated and simpler: it has added to the complexity of diagnoses but, since the focus in fibromyalgia treatment is on symptom management, this fits very well with my own approach to my symptoms. It does, however, leave me wondering if those early 'imaginary' symptoms were in fact the first signs of fibromyalgia some 13 years ago.

**Alec:** Perhaps a final thing that we might talk about, that you and others wrote about in *OEWM* and subsequently talked about with me in research interviews, is the potential and actual power of writing one's story. This includes the power of narrative to expose abusive practices carried out in the name of institutional psychiatry, and how writing can help in the development of acceptance and compassion for self and others and in teaching mental health nurses. You say similar things in your chapter, in talking about being a facilitator of therapeutic story-telling in teaching nurses, and in your role as policy and service configuration influencer. Along with others, you highlight the pride you've experienced in becoming an active member of the mental health recovery movement and the positive shift from stigma-based shame about having mental health problems to becoming a fighting, tenacious self/woman/mother/exposer/survivor of poor and abusive institutional psychiatry.

**Helen:** I've been storying my experiences of mental health services for about eight years now, but mostly orally in the classroom with nursing students rather than in writing. So writing is the latest stage in a long process of developing my own narrative of my experiences. But I resisted writing my story for a long time. For many years, the only way I could find of managing the very difficult emotions around the loss of my career was to put them in a box and to regard that self as someone I had once been but was no more. I was no longer an academic. I was a former academic.

Returning to a university environment to talk to student nurses about my experience was initially challenging although my situation in the university now was very different from my former position as an academic. Nevertheless, I found myself rediscovering old teaching skills and a familiar love of being in the classroom. I was a lecturer again, but not quite. I was, and am, a service user lecturer, but it is the 'service user' that defines that role, not the lecturer.

The invitation to contribute to *OEWM* came at around the same time that a counsellor suggested to me that I might find it therapeutic to write my story down, so I accepted it. And once I began writing I found it difficult to keep the former academic under control. I tried to write as a service user, set out my raw experience as it was, but the academic in me insisted on building an argument and drawing conclusions. I think that writing experience was perhaps more difficult for me than for some of the other contributors because I had written for publication before as an academic: I was afraid to open the box and allow parts of the former me, the person I once was, to become again. Yet looking back now I can see that this was the beginning of an empowering and therapeutic process of locating the old me and letting her coexist with the new one.

In the months that followed the publication of *OEWM* we began to collaborate on a number of different writing projects and, almost unnoticed at first, other parts of the former me began to emerge; perhaps most noticeably, after some years of ignoring world news because it reminded me too much of that lecturer in international relations I had once been, I began to watch news on television, listen to it on the radio, read the papers and engage politically in debate, especially via Twitter. This re-emergence of that former researcher/lecturer/analyst is important, because one consequence of it is that I have begun to think about and analyse more deeply my experience of my mental health problems and of the mental health system.

I have begun to understand how the response of others to me and to my mental ill-health shaped the person I became. That's been very empowering as I've spent so much of the past 13 or so years being angry at myself, for thinking and feeling the way I do, becoming who I am, and for not resisting more, especially when I first became unwell. Writing has helped me to understand that it wasn't 'all my fault', that I was part of a system that had effectively removed most of my power to resist, and that I didn't know then what I know now – I didn't have the knowledge then that might have helped me resist more effectively and preserve more of the important parts of my self-identity.

And at a very basic level, writing my story has allowed me to record my own authentic version of events in contrast to the 'official' version that exists in my hospital notes. That official story is so powerful: those notes follow me everywhere and I have no power to change them – even accessing them is a lengthy process. So being able to create an alternative story and have it published is certainly an empowering process – my story becomes meaningful not only because it has helped me to come to terms with my life but also because it challenges the accepted story enshrined in my hospital records.

## Coda

Working environments privilege the meanings of people who are employed there over 'customers' or 'users' of the services provided in those environments. Hierarchies of descending privilege are apparent in both mental health practice and policy texts, and are played out in NHS research which has an ironic mandate of service user involvement. As a service user, Helen has been involved in the development of such research for a number of years. Yet she sits, time and again, in research meetings (in which she's usually the lone service user representative), listening to academics and clinicians insisting that they can't involve users in research because they don't have the necessary skills. She is a committee member because of her research experience as well as her service user experience, but in this environment continues to remain very much the other, the disappearing doctor.

# References

Adams, TE (2008) A review of narrative ethics. *Qualitative Inquiry, 14*(2), 175–194.

Adams, TE & Holman Jones, S (2011) Telling stories: Reflexivity, queer theory, and autoethnography. *Cultural Studies <=> Critical Methodologies, 11*(2), 108–116.

Alcoff, LM (2009) The problem of speaking for others. In AY Jackson & LA Mazzei (Eds) *Voice in Qualitative Inquiry: Challenging conventional, interpretive, and critical conceptions in qualitative research* (pp. 117–135). London and New York: Routledge.

Bakhtin, MM (1981) *The Dialogic Imagination: Four Essays by M M Bakhtin* (Ed. M Holquist, Trans. C Emerson & M Holquist). Austin, TX: University of Texas Press.

Burr, V (2003) *Social Constructionism* (2nd ed). London and New York: Routledge.

Chaudhry, LN (2009) Forays into the mist: Violences, voices, vignettes. In AY Jackson & LA Mazzei (Eds) *Voice in Qualitative Inquiry: Challenging conventional, interpretive, and critical conceptions in qualitative research* (pp. 137–163). London and New York: Routledge.

Church, K (1995) *Forbidden Narratives: Critical autobiography as social science* London and New York: Routledge.

Costa, L, Voronka, J, Landry, D, Reid, J, McFarlane, B, Reville, D & Church, K (2012) Recovering our stories: A small act of resistance. *Studies in Social Justice, 6*(1), 85–101.

Cresswell, M & Spandler, H (2013) The engaged academic: Academic intellectuals and the psychiatric survivor movement. *Social Movement Studies: Journal of social, cultural and political protest, 12*(2), 138–154.

Department of Health (DH) (2006) *From Values to Action: The Chief Nursing Officer's review of mental health nursing.* London: Department of Health.

Goffman, E (1963) *Stigma: Notes on the management of spoiled identity.* Englewood Cliffs, NJ: Prentice Hall.

Grant, A & Zeeman, L (2012) Whose story is it? An autoethnography concerning narrative identity. *The Qualitative Report, 17*(72), 1–12.

Grant, A, Biley, FC, Leigh-Phippard, H & Walker, H (2012) The book, the stories, the people: An ongoing dialogic narrative inquiry study combining a practice development project. Part 1: The research context. *Journal of Psychiatric and Mental Health Nursing, 19*, 844–851.

Grant, A, Biley, F & Walker H (Eds) (2011) *Our Encounters with Madness.* Ross-on-Wye: PCCS Books.

Halperin, D (1995) *Saint Foucault: Towards a gay hagiography.* New York: Oxford University Press.

Holman Jones, S & Adams, TE (2010) Autoethnography is a queer method. In K Browne & CJ Nash (Eds) *Queer Methods and Methodologies: Intersecting queer theories and social science research* (pp. 195–214). Farnham: Ashgate.

Holquist, M (2002) *Dialogism: Bakhtin and his world* (2nd ed). London and New York: Routledge.

Holstein, JA & Gubrium, JF (2000) *The Self We Live By: Narrative identity in a postmodern world.* New York: Oxford University Press.

Jackson, AY & Mazzei, LA (2012) *Thinking with Theory in Qualitative Research: Viewing data across multiple perspectives.* London and New York: Routledge.

Krumer-Nevo, M & Sidi, M (2012) Writing against othering. *Qualitative Inquiry, 18*(4), 299–309.

Pilgrim, D (2009) *Key Concepts in Mental Health* (2nd ed). London: Sage Publications.

Pillow, W (2003) Confession, catharsis, or cure? Rethinking the uses of reflexivity as methodological power in qualitative research. *International Journal of Qualitative Studies in Education, 16*(2), 175–196.

Plummer, K (2005) Critical humanism and queer theory: Living with the tensions. In NK Denzin & YS Lincoln (Eds) *The SAGE Handbook of Qualitative Research* (3rd ed) (pp. 357–373). Thousand Oaks, CA: Sage Publications.

Richardson, L (1997) *Fields of Play: Constructing an academic life.* New Brunswick, NJ: Rutgers University Press.

Smircich, L (1983) Concepts of culture and organizational analysis. *Administrative Science Quarterly, 28,* 339–358.

Soja, E (1989) *Postmodern Geographies: The reassertion of space in critical social theory.* London: Verso.

Spry, T (2011) *Body, Paper, Stage: Writing and performing autoethnography.* Walnut Creek, CA: Left Coast Press.

St Pierre, EA (2009) Afterword: Decentering voice in qualitative inquiry. In AY Jackson & LA Mazzei (Eds) *Voice in Qualitative Inquiry: Challenging conventional, interpretive, and critical conceptions in qualitative research* (pp. 221–236). London and New York: Routledge.

Thornicroft, G (2006) *Shunned: Discrimination against people with mental illness.* New York: Oxford University Press.

Tilsen, J & Nylund, D (2010) Heteronormativity and queer youth resistance: Reversing the discourse. In L Moon (Ed) *Counselling Ideologies: Queer challenges to heteronormativity* (pp. 93–104). Farnham: Ashgate.

## 7

# breaking the grip: a critical insider account of representational practices in cognitive behavioural psychotherapy and mental health nursing

## – alec grant –

### Introduction

The story I tell is based on accumulated experiences in over 30 years of practice, teaching, supervision, research and writing in the disciplines of cognitive behavioural psychotherapy (CBP) and mental health nursing. I claim to write this narrative as a critically reflexive insider (Mills, 1959/2000; Pillow, 2003), in a representational style governed by integrated meta-autoethnographic, poststructural representational, and critical principles. Drawing selectively from my own published work and other relevant texts, my story extends and consolidates an autoethnographic ethic of testimony (Grant, 2010a) with regards to a critical exposure of abusive representational practices in cognitive behavioural psychotherapy and mental health nursing.

Although my writing aspires to the poststructural in ways that I will describe below, I make no attempt to decentre myself or my voice (Jackson & Mazzei, 2009). This is because I choose to use the rhetorical device of biography in the construction of a credible witness account of a topic area (St Pierre, 2009). This contrasts markedly with a conventional biographical appeal to truth from a coherent liberal-humanist subject: 'truth' told in an absolute sense, by a reliable author moving through a backdrop of reliably apprehended time and space. My story is just one of many that could be told, but it is told from the position of three decades of the shifting historical constitution of my emerging selves (Jackson & Mazzei, 2012). That said, I hope that this account of representational positioning within the discursive fields of cognitive behavioural psychotherapy and mental health nursing proves useful in challenging the normative hegemonic practices of each.

## Methodological and theoretical background

Similar to queer theory, poststructural autoethnographic work challenges the legitimate, dominant and hegemonic, in an explicit commitment to social justice and change (Holman Jones & Adams, 2010; Adams & Holman Jones, 2011). Poststructural and related readings of critical theory assume subjectivities inscribed by and within discourse (Calhoun & Karaganis, 2001; Kincheloe & McLaren, 2005). The challenge for reflexive writers working within this area is therefore to acknowledge their own discursive inscription, while simultaneously interrogating the patterns of meaning making and action they were caught up in. Doing so allows for narrative re-storying, or telling tales in ways critical of dominant meaning production, which in turn contributes to the development of counter-hegemonic pockets of resistance (Grant & Zeeman, 2012; Grant, Short & Turner, in press).

Such resistance is needed in worlds and times where subjectivity is, through repetition, increasingly connected to discursive, hegemonic structures of power. These structures are discursive in that, after Foucault, they form the objects of which they speak. This means that they privilege, sanction and legitimise certain statements and ways of socially constructing, describing, interpreting and acting in relation to the world at particular times, places and institutional locations, while de-privileging and marginalising others (Fairclough, 1992). These structures are hegemonic in that they remain relatively dominant and largely unchallenged in society.

From a critical theoretical perspective, dominant discourses discipline and routinise life and behaviour to the extent that the margin of human unpredictability, or margin of freedom, increasingly narrows. Calhoun & Karaganis (2001, p. 194) argue from a postmodern and poststructural critical standpoint that 'criticism and theory are best used to increase the size of this margin, breaking the grip – if in only occasional ways – of predictable action and habit'. This chapter attempts to do just that: as a critical insider in cognitive behavioural psychotherapy and mental health nursing, I want to continue to develop my sustained, small contribution to breaking the grip of their insidious, often harmful, discursively grounded representational practices, which often escape critical academic, professional and public gaze.

In troubling such practices, I don't want to suggest neat solutions to them, although some possibilities may be more or less implicitly apparent to readers in what follows and at the end of the chapter. In keeping with poststructural challenges to coherent and stable identities and accounts, I will leave myself, my narrative, and possible futures unfinalised (Holquist, 2002; Jackson & Mazzei, 2012).

The description of my socialisation into a mental health practice biography that follows marked the beginning of my feeling compromised by the need to maintain commitments to irreconcilable positions, and my attempts to resolve this.

## Straddling two paradigms

From a background in mental health nursing (1974–1983), I trained in cognitive behavioural psychotherapy (CBP), and practised in this discipline from 1983 to 2009. During this time I gained a BA (Hons) in psychology and social science and an MA in psychotherapy, attempting to reconcile cognitive therapy with existential philosophy in my master's dissertation. After spending 14 years as a CBP practitioner in the NHS, nearing the end of my PhD fieldwork period (my thesis eventually emerging as a critical ethnography of the organisational mediation of clinical supervision among mental health nurses), I began a career in higher education. From that point I led nationally validated courses in CBP at diploma, then degree, then master's levels, for over a decade.

Although initially seduced by the scientific basis of CBP and the moral high ground that this conferred, I increasingly experienced myself as less and less of a cognitive behavioural mainstream practitioner over the years. Indeed, from my early days in the modality I was often taken to task, both by my original teachers of the approach, and, later, by my clinical supervisors, for over-focusing on my relationships with clients and issues in their lives that were argued as peripheral to their central problems.

My awareness of my clients' difficulties consistently always either exceeded, problematised, or both, their difficulties according to how those were represented in either psychodiagnostic terms by the *DSM-IV* (APA, 2000) or, through the 1990s, the British National Institute for Health and Clinical Excellence guidelines. This was reflected in my formulations of clients' problems, which always, for me, deviated markedly from their one-dimensional treatment protocol equivalents. This tension would eventually be reflected in the text I co-wrote and was lead editor for: *Assessment and Case Formulation in Cognitive Behavioural Therapy* (Grant et al, 2008a).

In this book, although I tried to honour the relevance of both protocol-driven (general or nomothetic) and individual (specific or idiographic) formulations in CBP, my heart was in the latter. I illustrated narrative accounts of the development of clients' problems as much as I could from their own perspectives, using highly detailed diagrammatic formulations and their own narrative accounts of the experience of therapy and their relationships with therapists. With few exceptions (Chase Grey & Grant, 2005; Short, 2005), including clients' voices in this way remains a very unusual representational practice in CBP.

My undergraduate social science education sensitised me to problems with realist evidence-based claims, my broad postgraduate studies to non-positivist and existential explanations of the distress that constitutes the human condition, and my doctoral studies to the insidious power of organisations, from micro to macro, in constructing the realities of those within them. From the late 1990s on I brought this awareness into the CBP writing projects I led with my ex-students and colleagues from other higher education institutions, in a developing critique that became increasingly focused on the representational practices of the approach.


## CBP, organisations and representational practices

Influenced by postmodern and poststructural organisational theory, I led the call for an increased awareness of the link between organisations (from micro, or local work setting, through to macro, policy determining) and practice in relation to CBP (Grant et al, 2004a; Grant et al, 2008b). I did this in an attempt to help make practitioners aware of the argument that socially constructed, implicit organisational narratives, or shared interpretive schemes, influence representational practices and thus impact on relationships (Smircich, 1983a,b; Richardson, 1997). I argued that this both happens in ways that usually escape the awareness of organisational members (Morgan, 1997), and undermines attempts to improve the quality of psychological care (Grant & Mills, 2000; Poole & Grant, 2005).

A related rallying call, the first of its kind I believe in a British CBP text, was a critique of representational assumptions deriving from so-called, evidence-based practice in mental health (Grant et al, 2004b). I argued that many CBP practitioners and researchers suffered from 'paradigm entrapment', which resulted in them constructing and thus relating to their clients and their clients' experiences in particular ways at the expense of others. To redress such a restricted methodological vision, I called for a revised and broadened evidence-based agenda. In this regard, I built on the work of the North American postmodern CBP revisionists (Lyddon & Weill, 1997; Russell Ramsay, 1998) to argue that this would:

> ... speed the paradigm advancement of CB psychotherapy towards an evolving position where the personal meaning-making and narratives of clients and practitioners are accorded much greater respect than is presently the case.
>
> (Grant et al, 2004b, p. 232)

I later developed this idea in a call for the evidence-based agenda underpinning CBP to embrace paradigmatic pluralism (Grant, 2009), arguing for a distinction between narrow and broad appraisals of the evidence-base, including in relation to representational practices. My experiences in CBP teaching in higher education locally and further afield in the UK, as external examiner and workshop leader, suggested that narrow appraisals were frequent and often the norm.

Based on what I perceived to be a need to accord much greater and appropriate respect to the therapeutic relationship, I argued that a narrow view marginalised its significance and importance. From a narrow perspective, client identities were viewed in reductionist and one-dimensional, rather than complex, ways. The client and her or his problems were often conflated – seen as one and the same thing. In terms of dialogic and representational politics, the issue of control over what could be talked about was often weighted towards the therapist. Because of the low status accorded to the patient over the organisation and content of CBP practice, problems in the relationship emerging in the dialogue between the client and therapist were often ignored, glossed over, resisted or treated defensively, rather than accorded respect and explored sensitively.

## The politics of representation in the CBP dialogue

In mental health, as in other areas of life, how one describes another is never neutral. Language and representational practices constitute reality, and on that basis reductionist representations of people are often likely to facilitate reductionist mental health interventions. If the narrow representation of a person, in terms of her or his problems, is allowed to substitute for the person in broad, contextual, and flesh and blood terms, then they may well be treated as if all they are is their problems.

A fairly common example from my past CBP teaching and supervision experience will serve to illustrate this point. The thread of the dialogue between a therapist and client in a CBP session is often policed by the therapist to keep the client 'on track'. The dominant construction of reality is shaped by the norms and assumptions of the approach, and precedes and discursively positions therapist and client, thus giving the lie to 'collaborative working'. Consequently, if the client wants to talk about issues that are outside of the session agenda, the therapist may well discount their importance and relevance to therapy.

This may happen, for example, in relation to a therapist's slavish adherence to an agoraphobic treatment protocol (Grant et al, 2008a) because this seems to fit the client's problems. Unfortunately, when this occurs a large amount of contextually relevant and important information and dialogue can be sidelined, for example, in the case of women whose 'agoraphobic' problems only make sense in the broader context of their unhappy relationships.

## Philosophy of science influences on representational practices

In a further attempt to challenge the hegemony of positivist evidence-based practice in CBP (Grant, 2010a), I critiqued this on the basis of how its underpinning philosophy influences representational practices. CBP readers and practitioners are rarely introduced to discussions at this level, and I hoped to show readers how the fundamental differences between modernist and postmodern and poststructuralist worldviews led to irreconcilable sets of assumptions around those practices. I acknowledged that the language and logic of postmodern writers were unlikely to be recognised or accorded credence by their modernist, quantitative-experimental counterparts, and invited the CBP community to consider the potential for new forms of writing. In arguing that this would provide correspondingly new windows into the lives of their clients and themselves, I specifically advocated autoethnography that:

> Allows for narrative writing which has hitherto been eclipsed by, and is critically subversive of, dominant medical, psychological and psychotherapeutic accounts ... allowing autoethnographers to break away from the constraints of realist writing ... (and which aims) to describe the experience, and journey, of human suffering and recovery in ways which are deeply moving and free of the wholesale mediation of psychodiagnostic assumptions and language.
>
> (Grant, 2010a, p. 280)

## Re-focusing towards representational practices in mental health nursing and mental health

However, towards the end of the first decade of our new century, I became more and more aware that I may have been guilty of gross naïvety in trying to make the changes described above in a culture which, according to an ally within CBP writing, is characterised by 'paradigmatic antipathy' (Bennett-Levy, 2008). While I continued to believe that the arguments I made in my writing were valid and important, I felt increasingly disillusioned with a psychotherapeutic community whose concerns deviated markedly from my own.

I consequently withdrew from master's course leadership, supervision, practice and writing at the University of Brighton in 2009. I had always kept an interest in mental health nursing, my original discipline, and was on the editorial board of the *Journal of Psychiatric and Mental Health Nursing*, contributing some of my own articles to this journal and peer reviewing others. I thus transferred my critical focus on representational practices to mental health nursing and institutional mental health more generally.

This was timely, as my own mental health and addiction problems through the first decade of the new century had led to my increased involvement in using autoethnography as a form of therapeutic applied social and human science. On the basis of my experiences, I took to task what I felt were double standards in mental health nursing:

> I spend 4 days on an acute ward in a British state hospital. Apart from an intake interview and regular checks to make sure I am still alive, none of the nurses speak with me. They just stick their heads round, smile (or not) and disappear again. It is like a mad and boring Punch and Judy show – now you see them, now you do not. Although I do not come out of my room for the whole 4 days, I occasionally do covert checks on them. They are all usually gathered around the nurses' station … talking with each other – laughing and joking. Although I feel very scared, I also feel angry with them.
>
> (Grant, 2010b, p. 114)

Why should I have been angry? Colleagues had recently added support to the voluminous literature on qualified mental health nurses on acute wards privileging administrative-managerial tasks over interpersonal-therapeutic ones (Clarke & Flanagan, 2003). My anger was more about the gap between the ideological rhetorical imperative to represent nurse–patient relationships in a sanitised and idealised way, and the organisational behaviour of mental health nurses which gave the lie to this. Since the mid-1970s, when I trained to be a mental health nurse, positive changes and improvements in this area have been talked up, often with little or no compelling evidence to support such claims.

For several years I had engaged in an extended oppositional debate with key cultural leaders in mental health nursing about their version of mental health recovery: *The Tidal Model* (Barker & Buchanan-Barker, 2005; Buchanan-Barker 2009). My PhD research and subsequent experiences of teaching, supervising and consultancy work with mental health nurses convinced me that institutional and organisational factors determined in large part how nurses were socialised into the custom and practice of acute wards. Because of this, anti-therapeutic behaviour, constituting business as usual, often far outweighed modernist, context-neutral claims that nurses could live up to the Tidal Model's commitments to, among other things, valuing the client's voice and language. I argued that the work of Barker and Buchanan-Barker represented a broader tendency in mental health nursing in promoting a bourgeois fantasy model which implicitly claimed to transcend organisational and practice constraints. Consistent reports of organisational subjugation of service users and clients down the years, and my own experiences, give the lie to this.

## The survivor movement and representational practices

In recent years, my experiences of breakdown treatment and recovery (Grant, 2006; Short et al, 2007; Grant, 2010a,b) have led me to increasingly define myself as a mental health survivor, where 'survival' is defined as battling with and working through invalidating social practices, including the representational practices routinely employed in the day-to-day work of institutional psychiatry (Pilgrim, 2009). These practices, often disparaging and hurtful, include what is said and written about clients or patients, in day-to-day exchanges and in nursing and medical records.

In my current survivor research, I promote the use of narrative for individuals who wish to write their own biographies, and re-story themselves into the future on their own terms, often in ways that are independent, critical, or rejecting of patienthood. This enables those who have experienced toxic, institutional psychiatric representational practices to positively re-story their lives (Grant et al, 2011) rather than remaining victims of imposed biographies. In our narrative research and practice development work, my associates and I use the rationale of 'writing for recovery' to facilitate this (Grant et al, 2011, 2012a,b). In the process of re-storying themselves, individuals often describe in stark detail the stigmatising abusive ways they have been represented in the name of mental healthcare and treatment, for example:

> Big Ben is chiming 11a.m. across the river. It's wet and miserable. I think it's Thursday … My unwashed matted hair stinks … Sticky discoloured saliva is leaking slowly from the corner of my mouth … I am shivering. I can smell the sweet sickly smell of a rotting banana … on the pillar-box-red quarry-tiled window sill … Somebody I do not immediately recognise suddenly bursts into the room. He hasn't knocked … 'Are you getting up?' he shouts. 'You have been in bed all day.' 'I'm tired', I whisper. I feel afraid … He has power. 'Don't you want to get better? … Get up you *cunt*.'
>
> (Short, 2011, p. 131)

## Emerging theoretical and related issues

Thus far, I have argued that representational practices in CBP tend to privilege clients' problems over relationships, when relationships are often central to those problems. I asserted that this is frequently reflected in one-dimensional, decontextualised problem formulations. At broader cultural levels, I discussed my attempts to help CBP practitioners and other mental health practitioners become more aware of how they are often caught up in micro- to macro-organisational narratives which shape representational practices. In terms of the theoretical assumptions that shape CBP practice, this can include what I described as 'paradigm entrapment', which privileges particular ways of representing clients and their difficulties over others. I then went on to discuss the circumstances that led to my refocusing my representational concerns to institutional psychiatry and mental health nursing theory and practice, and my current identity and research focus in the mental health survivor movement. As critical insider narrative material, all of this speaks to a broader set of theoretical issues and related concerns. I will conclude this chapter with a selective discussion of some of those.

From the perspective of critical applied and clinical psychology, psychological therapy and mental health, Marecek and Hare-Mustin (2009) assert that mental health systems always reflect the values of the era they correspond to. The knowledge and language associated with mental health systems are always shaped by their social context, often in conflicting ways. The language used in contemporary 'evidence-based' CBP may jar with some of the crude street language used by some mental health nurses in inpatient settings. However, both reflect and are drawn from dominant discursive themes, ideologies and preoccupations of our times, and serve in the continual reproduction of asymmetrical power relationships between mental health worker and client (Pillow, 2003).

In a circular way, hegemonic discourses shape representational practices in CBP and mental health nursing, in terms of what is seen and what can be said by its practitioners, thus reifying macro- and micro-organisational realities. Available discursive terms highlight certain features of people, relationships and situations at the expense of other features, and thus inform, construct, and allow for discursive positions that people can occupy, live within and experience from those positions.

For example, most cognitive behavioural therapy books, including the ones I have co-edited and written, implicitly celebrate humane, altruistic values, ethical practice and a dispassionate scientific outlook. However, in relation to representational practices, I hope I have argued sufficiently well that these claims don't always stand up to scrutiny. The language used in evidence-based mental health interventions traps people in stories. These stories may misrepresent them, socially disadvantage them, disempower them, and discriminate against and stigmatise them (Thornicroft, 2006; Grant et al, 2012a).

From a narrative ethical perspective, great care should be taken over how people are represented. However, some communities may claim the exclusive right to define and portray individuals in particular ways, with unfortunate consequences. These include cognitive behavioural and mental health representations of people which are reductionist and which do immense disservice to emotional and contextual lives.

This highlights the issue of language as a site of the struggle over representation and meaning. People create myriad meanings about themselves and others through engaging with each other in everyday life practices. The ways in which we can be abusively or humanely represented, or can represent ourselves in texts, can never be exhausted, as language and meaning is an infinite and ever-shifting dialogic and cultural resource (Holquist, 2002). This facilitates the constant emergence of different communities of textual meaning making (Frank, 1995; Richardson, 1997), implicating the relevance of both narrative ethics for representational practices (Adams 2008) and re-storying to reflexively resist hegemonic constructions of identity (see Grant & Leigh-Phippard, this volume).

In contrast to such representational plurality and differentiation, it is notable that a reductionist trend in the representation of human suffering in the cognitive behavioural literature has continued to go largely unchallenged in its roughly 40-year history. With a handful of exceptions, including my own work (Chase Grey & Grant, 2005; Grant et al, 2008a), readers would be hard put to spot a real, fleshed-out, life-contextualised person in much of the mainstream British CBP and policy-informed treatment literature. Instead, individuals with problems are usually described as sanitised bundles of symptoms, emotions, cognitions, behaviours or treatment outcomes.

The representation of such passive selves – at worst waiting to be plugged into so-called evidence-based protocols – corresponds to a representation of their 'treatment'. This is always contained within a simple linear trajectory of start (problem), middle (treatment), end (no problem), follow-up (still no problem, hopefully). To paraphrase Jeannette Winterson, a convenient assumption of life as a motorway is suggested, with clear exit points, rather than a confusing maze. Such an algorithm of CBP practice falls short in responding to the complex, the contextual and the unpredictable in human lives. This leaves the question begged as to why so many British CBP practitioners and other mental health workers appear to insufficiently question stripped-down and simplistic representations of people and lives.

One reason for this may be found in CBP's discursive historical basis and its related socialisation of practitioners. Reductionist, fragmenting and decontextualising representations of human suffering derive from the positivist philosophy of science tradition. This subsumes an objectivist theory of knowledge (Crotty, 2003), which holds that things in the material world, including people and mental health 'disorders', have an intrinsic meaning in reality.

The positivist tradition governing quantitative-experimental science influences forms of representation in the cognitive behavioural and related literature. This usually displays a wholesale dismissal of the relevance of the fact that people have lives and often rich contextual referents. In terms of the status of the evidence underpinning evidence-based practice, it is assumed that the most objectively valid and useful knowledge of people's mental health and psychological difficulties is gained via quantitative-experimental research along the lines of the natural sciences.

This reifies the construction of quasi-medical, categorical, a-theoretical, a-personal, de-contextual forms of representations of 'psychopathology', informing and represented by mental health diagnostic and classification systems, and clinical practice guidelines in the United Kingdom. *DSM-IV* (APA, 2000) criteria frequently inform selection for randomised control trials, the outcomes of which influence the development of treatment protocols for CBP. This amounts to a form of circular neopositivist logic where walking bundles of psychopathology, rather than people, become the focus of evidence-based psychotherapeutic help.

It is to these discursively derived representational practices that members of the CBP and evidence-based mental health communities are socialised. Given the hegemonic authority of evidence-based practice, many British cognitive behavioural psychotherapists find what they take for granted in the approach, including its representational forms, so self-evidently rational that meaningful objection to it is difficult (Bohart & House, 2008). Why should this be the case? Anticipating the later emerging poststructural general position of discourses informing subjectivity, Berger & Luckmann (1966) argued the ways in which people can become socialised into *plausibility structures*. From the outset, individuals training in CBP are exposed to pre-existing structures of belief and related practices. Because positivism informs both the legitimacy of quantitative-experimental research and ways of conceptualising human suffering, a kind of moral order constantly underpins and polices CBP representational and related therapy practices.

As a result of this, many practitioners may come to develop a *natural attitude* towards such practices – a sense of an obvious, taken-for-granted reality that couldn't be any other way. The fact that reductionist representations of individuals and their problems have largely gone unchallenged in most of the CBP literature, since its burgeoning as a therapy modality from the 1970s, speaks to the durability of dominant discourses of positivism informing evidence-based mental health practice.

## Ideology – some concluding remarks

Finally, representational practices are of course ideologically shaped in the service of dominant discourses. Key intertwined ideological strands informing mental health practice include the evidence-based movement and liberal and neoliberal humanism. How these strands construct 'reality' camouflages their status as ideology, in the promise of benevolence and helpfulness. In this way they arguably simplify the world, producing a 'dangerous illusion', wherein oppressive and colonising normative identity practices are reified in a totalising one worldview (Lincoln et al, 2011).

The success of ideological work masks contradictions in lived experiences. For example, representations of neoliberalism proceed from liberal humanist assumptions of the coherent person, having a fixed and complete identity that is ontologically prior to her or his positioning in the social world (Jackson & Mazzei, 2012). Such an individual is therefore exempt from discursive inscription and can thus exercise autonomy, freedom, and rational choice and engagement in and with their lives (Brown & Baker, 2012). Neoliberal ideological work constructs those choices as natural, timeless, power-neutral, context-neutral and in people's best interests, rather than contingent, replete with power at a contextual, including organisationally contextual, level, with the potential to be disadvantageous, subjugating and harmful.

It is on this basis that 'evidence-based CBP' is constructed and represented, as the careful accumulation of rigorous scientific evidence to support specific interventions for specific disorders, to which no rational person could disagree. In related terms, the recovery-focused Tidal Model of mental health nursing interventions holds as a fundamental premise, 'The idea that the person remains entirely in charge of himself [sic]' ... (Buchanan-Barker, 2009, p. 685).

In socialising new clients to the CBP model, therapists are probably more likely to highlight the fact that according to the evidence base underpinning psychotherapy, CBP emerges as the frontrunner in the rational choice and engagement stakes. They are less likely to talk about the often vociferous debate and disagreement over the fundamentals of this discourse, including what constitutes 'evidence' and related assumptions, informing often polarised views on both sides of the Atlantic (eg Norcross et al, 2006).

In working according to Tidal commitments, the mental health nurse must apparently regard the service user as someone with a valued story – the individual 'voice of experience'. Curiosity is then exercised by nurses as they adopt the apprentice role to learn from service users and help the latter group reveal their personal wisdom, while giving them the gift of their time (Buchanan-Barker, 2009). Drawing on the metaphorical underpinning of the model, Tidal nurses will presumably therefore have to believe that they really are coherent individuals working unproblematically in dialogue with other coherent individuals.

They must assume that they can take the time to float safely and at leisure with their clients in a kind of smooth and balmy therapeutic sea. They needn't worry about troubled waters affecting the integrity of their Tidal raft, or about being shanghaied by unwelcome others navigating and dominating well-established routes in much bigger vessels. This illusion is not likely to sustain consistently on dry land. The organisations in which people engaged with the Tidal Model exceed imagined therapeutic dyads. These organisations are frequently more discursive shapers of damaging identity and representational practices than they are neutral backdrops to helpful and therapeutic nursing interventions made in the name of recovery.

The grip continually needs to be broken. By definition, this is a never-ending aspiration. However, it would include a narrative inquiry agenda that facilitates the production of new stories about what it is like and what it means to reclaim positive identities separate from the worst excesses of policy and professional constructions: stories that demand contextual representation on their own terms; stories that unrelentingly contest institutional psychiatric and related representations; stories that recognise and engage with the politics of difference.

# References

Adams, TE (2008) A review of narrative ethics. *Qualitative Inquiry, 14*(2), 175–194.

Adams, TE & Holman Jones, S (2011) Telling stories: Reflexivity, queer theory, and autoethnography. *Cultural Studies <=> Critical Methodologies, 11*(2), 108–116.

American Psychiatric Association (APA) (2000) *Diagnostic and Statistical Manual of Mental Disorders* (4th ed), Text Revision. (*DSM-IV-TR*). Washington, DC: American Psychiatric Association.

Barker, P & Buchanan-Barker, P (Eds) (2005) *The Tidal Model: A guide for mental health practitioners.* New York: Brunner Routledge.

Bennett-Levy, J (2008) Personal communication.

Berger, P & Luckmann, T (1966) *The Social Construction of Reality.* New York: Doubleday.

Bohart, AC & House, R (2008) Empirically supported/validated treatments as modernist ideology, 1: Dodo, manualization and the paradigm question. In R House & D Loewenthal (Eds) *Against and for CBT: Towards a constructive dialogue?* (pp. 188–201). Ross-on-Wye: PCCS Books.

Brown, BJ & Baker, S (2012) *Responsible Citizens: Individuals, health and policy under neoliberalism.* London and New York: Anthem Press.

Buchanan-Barker, P (2009) Reclamation: Beyond recovery. In P Barker (Ed) *Psychiatric and Mental Health Nursing: The craft of caring* (pp. 681–689). London: Hodder Arnold.

Calhoun, C & Karaganis, J (2001) Critical theory. In G Ritzer & B Smart (Eds) *Handbook of Social Theory* (pp. 179–200). London: Sage Publications.

Chase Grey, J & Grant, A (2005) Cognitive behavioural therapy: Helping the client find her voice. *Mental Health Practice, 8*(8), 34–37.

Clarke, L & Flanagan, T (2003) *Institutional Breakdown: Exploring mental health nursing practice in acute inpatient settings.* Salisbury: APS Publishing.

Crotty, M (2003) *The Foundations of Social Research: Meaning and perspective in the research process.* London: Sage Publications.

Fairclough, N (1992) *Discourse and Social Change.* Cambridge: Polity Press.

Frank, AW (1995) *The Wounded Storyteller: Body, illness and ethics.* Chicago and London: The University of Chicago Press.

Grant, A (2006) Testimony: God and aeroplanes: My experience of breakdown and recovery. *Journal of Psychiatric and Mental Health Nursing, 13,* 456–457.

Grant, A (2009) Evidence-based practice and the need for paradigmatic pluralism in cognitive behavioural psychotherapy. *Journal of Psychiatric and Mental Health Nursing, 16,* 368–375.

Grant, A (2010a) The evidence base and philosophical debates in CBT. In A Grant, M Townend, R Mulhern & N Short (Eds) *Cognitive Behavioural Therapy in Mental Health Care* (2nd ed) (pp. 273–285). London: Sage Publications.

Grant, A (2010b) Autoethnographic ethics and rewriting the fragmented self. *Journal of Psychiatric and Mental Health Nursing, 17,* 111–116.

Grant, A & Mills, J (2000) The great going nowhere show: Structural power and mental health nurses. *Mental Health Practice, 4*(3), 14–16.

Grant, A & Zeeman, L (2012) Whose story is it? An autoethnography concerning narrative identity. *The Qualitative Report, 17*(72), 1–12.

Grant, A, Biley, F & Walker H (Eds) (2011) *Our Encounters with Madness.* Ross-on-Wye: PCCS Books.

Grant, A, Biley, FC, Leigh-Phippard, H & Walker, H (2012a) The book, the stories, the people: An ongoing dialogic narrative inquiry study combining a practice development project. Part 1: The research context. *Journal of Psychiatric and Mental Health Nursing, 19,* 844–851.

Grant, A, Biley, FC, Leigh-Phippard & H, Walker, H (2012b) The book, the stories, the people: An ongoing dialogic narrative inquiry study combining a practice development project. Part 2: The practice development context. *Journal of Psychiatric and Mental Health Nursing, 19,* 950–957.

Grant, A, Mills, J, Mulhern, R & Short, N (2004a) Organisational factors impacting cognitive behavioural practice. In A Grant, J Mills, R Mulhern & N Short (Eds) *Cognitive Behavioural Therapy in Mental Health Care.* London: Sage Publications.

Grant, A, Mills, J, Mulhern, R & Short N (2004b) A critique of evidence-based mental health and its relationship to cognitive behavioural psychotherapy. In A Grant, J Mills, R Mulhern & N Short (Eds) *Cognitive Behavioural Therapy in Mental Health Care.* London: Sage Publications.

Grant, A, Short, N & Turner, L (in press) Introduction: Storying life and lives. In N Short, L Turner & A Grant (Eds) *Contemporary British Autoethnography.* Rotterdam: Sense Publishers.

Grant, A, Townend, M, Mills, J & Cockx, A (2008a) *Assessment and Case Formulation in Cognitive Behavioural Therapy.* London: Sage Publications.

Grant, A, Townend, M & Sloan, G (2008b) The transfer of CBT education from classroom to work setting: Getting it right or wasting the opportunities? *The Cognitive Behaviour Therapist, 1,* 27–44.

Holman Jones, S & Adams, TE (2010) Autoethnography is a queer method. In K Browne & CJ Nash (Eds) *Queer Methods and Methodologies: Intersecting queer theories and social science research* (pp. 195–214). Farnham: Ashgate Publishing.

Holquist, M (2002) *Dialogism: Bakhtin and his world* (2nd ed). London and New York: Routledge.

Jackson, AY & Mazzei, LA (2009) *Voice in Qualitative Inquiry: Challenging conventional, interpretive, and critical conceptions in qualitative research.* London and New York: Routledge.

Jackson, AY & Mazzei LA (2012) *Thinking with Theory in Qualitative Research: Viewing data across multiple perspectives.* London and New York: Routledge.

Kincheloe, JL & McLaren, P (2005) Rethinking critical theory and qualitative research. In NK Denzin & YS Lincoln (Eds) *The SAGE Handbook of Qualitative Research* (3rd ed) (pp. 303–342). Thousand Oaks, CA: Sage Publications.

Lincoln, YS, Lynham, SA & Guba, EG (2011) Paradigmatic controversies, contradictions, and emerging confluences, revisited. In NK Denzin & YS Lincoln (Eds) *The SAGE Handbook of Qualitative Research* (4th ed) (pp. 400–432). Thousand Oaks, CA: Sage Publications.

Lyddon, WJ & Weill, R (1997) Cognitive psychotherapy and postmodernism: Emerging themes and challenges. *Journal of Cognitive Psychotherapy, 11*(2), 75–90.

Marecek, J & Hare-Mustin, RT (2009) Clinical psychology: The politics of madness. In D Fox, I Prilleltensky & S Austin (Eds) *Critical Psychology: An introduction* (2nd ed) (pp. 75–92). London: Sage Publications.

Mills, CW (2000) *The Sociological Imagination: Fortieth anniversary edition.* New York: Oxford University Press. (Original work published 1959)

Morgan, G (1997) *Images of Organization* (2nd ed). Thousand Oaks, CA: Sage Publications.

Norcross, JC, Beutler, LE & Levant, RF (2006) *Evidence-Based Practices in Mental Health: Debate and dialog on the fundamental questions.* Washington, DC: American Psychological Association.

Pilgrim, D (2009) 'Recovery' and current mental health policy. *Chronic Illness, 4,* 295–304.

Pillow, WS (2003) Confession, catharsis, or cure? Rethinking the uses of reflexivity as methodological power in qualitative research. *Qualitative Studies in Education, 16*(2), 175–196.

Poole, J & Grant, A (2005) Stepping out of the box: Broadening the dialogue around the organisational integration of cognitive behavioural psychotherapy. *Journal of Psychiatric and Mental Health Nursing, 12,* 456–463.

Richardson, L (1997) *Fields of Play: Constructing an academic life.* New Brunswick, NJ: Rutgers University Press.

Russell Ramsay, J (1998) Postmodern cognitive therapy: Cognitions, narratives, and personal meaning-making. *Journal of Cognitive Psychotherapy: An international quarterly, 12*(1), 39–55.

Short, NP (2005) Vocal heroes: The views of two people who experienced a cognitive behavioural approach for their difficulties: Their narratives are accompanied by a commentary from the therapist. *Journal of Psychiatric and Mental Health Nursing, 12*(5), 574–581.

Short, N (2011) Freeze-frame: Reflections on being in hospital. In A Grant, F Biley & H Walker (Eds) *Our Encounters with Madness* (pp. 131–138). Ross-on-Wye: PCCS Books.

Short, N, Grant, A & Clarke, L (2007) Living in the borderlands; writing in the margins: an autoethnographic tale. *Journal of Psychiatric and Mental Health Nursing, 14,* 771–782.

Smircich, L (1983a) Concepts of culture and organizational analysis. *Administrative Science Quarterly, 28,* 339–358.

Smircich, L (1983b) Studying organizations as cultures. In G Morgan (Ed) *Beyond Method: Strategies for social research* (pp. 160–172). Beverly Hills, CA: Sage Publications.

St Pierre, EA (2009) Decentering voice in qualitative inquiry. In AY Jackson & LA Mazzei (Eds) *Voice in Qualitative Inquiry: Challenging conventional, interpretive, and critical conceptions in qualitative research* (pp. 221–236). London and New York: Routledge.

Thornicroft, G (2006) *Shunned: Discrimination against people with mental illness.* Oxford: Oxford University Press.

# 8

## narratives of the resilient subject in health and social care

### – kay aranda and laetitia zeeman –

### Introduction

In this chapter, we aim to explore different stories of resilience through critical and queer theory, specifically feminist theories and engagements with poststructuralism, and especially the concepts of recognition and performativity as discussed by Judith Butler. The chapter is based on a previously published paper and reproduced here with permission.

### Background

International research and policy interest in resilience has increased enormously in the last decade (Bartley, 2006), with much public health policy in the United Kingdom now frequently citing resilience as a valuable resource with which to promote health and wellbeing (Darzi, 2008; Marmot, 2010). Moreover, resilience has become central to discussions on health inequalities in the UK, forming part of a broader trend towards asset- or strength-based as opposed to deficit-based models of health. As such, individuals' and communities' capabilities and resourcefulness to respond to problems or ability to generate active solutions have become central to many planned public health interventions (Bartley, 2006; Wilkinson & Pickett, 2009).

We take this growing interest in resilience and health as our starting point in order to explore the resilient subject. Resilience literature and scholarship is a rich and expanding field, with valuable empirical research findings informing practice, even though its conceptual limits and its normative base are increasingly recognised and discussed (Ungar, 2004; Bottrell, 2009). There is, however, relatively less explicit discussion of the relationship between resilience and notions of the subject and their identity, subjectivity or body. Drawing on feminist poststructuralism, and Judith Butler's work in particular, we explore the potential of these understandings of the subject and the body for resilience research, theory and practice.

We recognise that categorising such an enormous and expanding field into just three narratives inevitably simplifies what is in reality vastly overlapping and complex. Yet these narratives provide a useful heuristic framework with which to outline various disciplinary homes and theoretical assumptions involved in the many conceptualisations of resilience, and they serve to highlight the consequences and implications of such positions for practice and research. Our understanding of narratives draws upon the review of narrative research, which demonstrates how stories commonly relate to one of three themes: personal experiences, events, or broader sociocultural discourses (Squire, 2008). It is mainly the latter understanding we utilise to outline three broad discourses or narratives of resilience.

This chapter is divided into three sections. First we briefly review definitions of resilience and the two dominant epistemological positions previously noted within resilience research. These are commonly referred to as ecological and constructionist (Ungar, 2004, 2010); we name these positions as resilience 'found' and 'made'. Second, and from within each narrative, we interrogate the conceptualisations of the subject, the key features of such, and the potential strengths and limits of each. Finally, we then move on to suggest the potential of a third narrative of resilience as 'unfinished' in order to explore the potential of a feminist poststructural subject for resilience research.

## Definitions

Resilience is now a term that has arguably become part of everyday popular cultural discourse. It is a word associated with inner strength or resourcefulness and the ability to bounce back following adversity or trauma (Hart & Blincow, 2007). The concept originally emerged in engineering, with its earliest use in health in medicine to describe patients' recovery from trauma, followed by its entry into psychology and especially child development and psychiatry (Boyden & Mann, 2005). Resilience also resonates well with other asset- or strength-based approaches and concepts found in public health or sociology, such as salutogenesis (a sense of coherence and social capital) and as such, it is now increasingly popular in health policy discourse (Bourdieu, 1990; Almedom, 2005; Lundman et al, 2010).

Despite there being ongoing debates over conceptual clarity or theoretical usefulness (Luthar & Brown, 2007), core to any definition of resilience is the ability to react and adjust positively when things go wrong; that is, resilience occurs in the presence of adversity (Ungar, 2005, 2008). This has been further categorised as good outcomes despite high-risk status, or sustained competence under threat, or even recovery from trauma (Boyden & Mann, 2005). Given its original disciplinary base in clinical psychology, child development and psychiatry, children and young people are the subject of much resilience research, especially those with complex needs or deemed to be at risk of developing psychosocial symptoms. This tends to include those with behavioural, psychological or neurobiological problems, or those having experienced traumatic events in childhood or adolescence (Masten, 2001; Luthar & Brown, 2007; Rutter, 2007). The narratives of Story One and Two broadly share these understandings of what resilience is and who the subjects of resilience are, but where resilience resides, and how it is achieved and why, differ.

## Story one: Resilience found

As Masten (2001) has argued, after two decades of research into children growing up in disadvantage – where, initially, resilience researchers identified what were thought to be special, resilient, innate attributes belonging to the remarkable few – the great surprise has been to discover the ordinariness of the phenomenon of resilience. Resilience is then the capacity to negotiate ordinary developmental tasks in the face of mounting adversity, and is associated with a combination of risks and protective factors and processes, in either the child or environment (Masten, 2001; Rutter, 1993, 2007). Initially, what were taken to be internally generated traits have additionally become externally derived or located assets or protective processes. These processes and assets include attachment and access to supportive relationships with caring, competent adults, either in the family or community, and individual attributes such as positive self-esteem and motivation. This recognition of the role the environment or ecology plays draws attention to the quality of social relationships, processes, networks and communities, and the mutuality and circularity of such (Luthar & Brown, 2007). These understandings of resilience seek to build on and conserve children's and young people's own assets and resources for promoting change (Goldstein & Brooks, 2006, p. 6) and have led to more practically focused interventions like resilient therapy (Hart & Blincow, 2007).

Together, this research represents Story One, or what has been called the classic epistemological position of resilience, drawing as it does on systems theory and/or biomedical or psychological models of child development (Ungar, 2004; Bottrell, 2009). Most often methodologically driven by positivism and quantitative methods, its focus is on predictive and casual relationships and transactional processes that cause or promote resilience. This is a story of resilience found mainly within individuals, even when viewed as socially caused or derived, as it is seen as a variable psychological attribute, operating at an individual level, though arising from repeated interactions between a person and their environment.

This story draws upon a familiar discourse, originating as it does in the modern biomedicine or 'psy' science disciplines with its commitment to the project of human emancipation and liberation and improvement in the human condition. These social reforming tendencies found with 'psy' disciplines are known to construct or invent and privilege a particular conception of the individual, even when recognising the influence of the social (Burman, 2008; Rose, 1998). This is the well-known Cartesian subject in possession of a coherent or stable sense of self and identity, desirous of self-knowledge and imbued with reason, agency and independence. This subject becomes the psychological norm. Again, a recognised corollary of this norm is to position others; so those deemed devoid or deficient or lacking in one or more of these normal or natural attributes, like the ability to cope or be resilient, become problematic. Therefore, those failing to be resilient may, like all other welfare subjects, become positioned as 'invariably dependent, unpredictable, and unable to act in their own interests' (Frost & Hoggett, 2008, p. 439). This justifies professional interventions in the form of support or therapy, which contains an implicit and at times explicit moral imperative for the subject to be resilient. This assumption of personal responsibility and desire for the normal or healthy subject to want to be resilient further reinforces a focus on the individual and their personal capacities and responsibilities to adapt, cope or succeed (Bottrell, 2009).

When resilience is assumed to be 'natural', arising within or from the individual, it easily becomes seen as devoid of or detached from interests or values, and thus any normative foundations are overlooked (Ungar, 2005, 2010). One consequence of this is to ignore or deflect attention from the powerful role of societal norms and the authority of experts to control and regulate what constitutes normal, healthy or good outcomes, which in turn reinforces and perpetuates unexamined notions of the supposed 'normal' family or childhood. As Ungar (2005, 2008) suggests, resilience is therefore not naturally or normally occurring but culturally and socially produced, this challenge to what constitutes resilience and who is deemed to be a resilient subject is the focus of Story Two.

## Story two: Resilience made

Resilience made is the constructionist story of resilience, whereby resilience is not something we have, but something we do (Ungar, 2004, 2005, 2008, 2010). Drawing on a Foucauldian analysis, resilience becomes more than a description of reality: it becomes a social practice, a form of action reproducing or potentially challenging the dominant social order (Ungar, 2005). Drawing on a constructionist lens, the International Resilience Project explores these different and diverse understandings of resilience across cultures and contexts (Ungar, 2005, 2008; Ungar et al, 2007). The project demonstrates both the heterogeneous and homogeneous features of resilience as diverse, chaotic, complex, fluid, relative and material, located in particular contexts and generated, nurtured and sustained through actions and relations (Ungar, 2008, 2010). In one setting, the youths' resilience was found to be complex, but reflective of different tensions and degrees of access to seven mental health-enhancing experiences, which they negotiated simultaneously (Ungar et al, 2007). These experiences included material resources, supportive relationships, a sense of belonging and control and justice, and the importance of a sense of one's self and purpose. Resilience, therefore, is argued to result from the ongoing iterative and interactive navigations and negotiations between selves, communities and environments (Ungar et al, 2007).

An important consequence of understanding resilience as 'made' is to question social relations and the power to define what becomes a risk, a protective factor, or a resilient outcome, as previously discussed. This draws attention to the social construction of difference and diverse forms of resilience. Therefore, what constitutes resilience is called into question (Munford & Sanders, 2008; Bottrell, 2009; Theron & Malindi, 2010). In a study of young people from an inner-city public housing estate, labelled with challenging behaviour, Bottrell (2009) found young women used these labels to actively resist normatively or socially ascribed identities, and that such activities were central to their sense of resilience. Similarly, Munford and Sanders (2008) demonstrate how marginalised young women use socially disruptive or challenging behaviour to create spaces that allowed them to share their experiences and increase their supportive relationships, and to develop their own sense of gendered subjectivity and, in so doing, resist normative understandings.

The subject at the centre of Story Two is sometimes premised upon modern and postmodern understandings of the socially constituted subject. As Burr (2003) suggests, while both understandings draw upon social constructionism, the former focuses on the role of the subject in the construction of social reality, whereas the latter challenges this fundamental notion of the sovereign subject; instead, it focuses on the social construction of all reality and turns our attention to how the subject is constituted or produced and disciplined or regulated. This latter postmodern subject is one which begins to overlap with Story Three, and is where the subject is produced or constituted by discourse but is, at the same time, constrained by, for example, discourses of resilience, health and wellbeing (Ungar, 2004, 2008, 2010). This postmodern understanding of the subject radically questions the notion of the modern subject and the individualism of Story One. As Ungar (2005) shows, the assumed sovereignty of the modern subject which underpins these previous accounts of resilience is illusory; as he states, 'to say I am resilient is to be mistaken – the "I" of which we speak is a cultural artefact, a product of history and as such is socially, politically, and relationally constructed' (2005, p. xxiv). However, aside from Ungar's (2005) explicit endorsement, and though present in Story Two, the subject is seldom referred to directly. Moreover, the consequences of a postmodern subject for questions of identity and resilience are not discussed more fully, though they are alluded to in recent research where questions of fluidity or identity and resilience are beginning to be considered as significant (Ungar et al, 2007; Munford & Sanders, 2008; Bottrell, 2009; Ungar, 2010).

Indeed, valuable though this social constructionist story of resilience is, the particular mechanisms or processes that generate the subject as unstable and open to rearticulation still need to be understood more fully (Lloyd, 2005). For while identities are now commonly conceived of as mobile, complex, entangled and relational, the mundane or everyday detailed ways that identities are worked at, produced and understood by subjects, and connected to broader social forces, practices, movements or action, still require further empirical demonstration and theoretical explanation (Wetherell, 2009a, 2009b).

Additionally, even though constructionist accounts repoliticise narratives of resilience and recognise the socially constituted subject, there can still remain a tendency to externalise these differences and leave untroubled foundational categories of an incompatible essentialist subject. Thus, much empirical research retains the binaries of the individual and society, and of culture and nature (Gergen, 2009). This leaves the focus of theory and research on an inner and a social outer world, offering a causal template for human action which shapes resilience and the resultant resilient subject. Thus, when resilience is described as relational it can imply relations between bounded, separate, unconnected individuals, rather than being theoretically articulated as a relational ontology as Gergen (2009) suggests.

Moreover, a strategy validating plural manifestations of resilience may also be limiting. Recognising and validating difference in resilience does much to challenge or disrupt the dominant or normative discourses and criteria, and gives voice to marginalised stories. However, philosophically, difference often represents the 'Other', or that which is excluded, treated as an inferior, transient or variant of a dominant norm or unity (Butler, 2004a). Epistemologically, to claim inclusion on the basis of sameness or to validate or valourise difference is known to be limited; it leaves intact that which is considered the same, normal or natural and superior to a then-always inferior-positioned notion of difference. For queer theorists and poststructural feminists (Weedon, 1996; Seidman, 1997) these binaries must instead be constantly destabilised or disrupted by difference. Finally, constructionism's preoccupation with the meaning given to behaviour means a corresponding lack of attention to the unthought, unspoken, unthinkable and unspeakable (McNay, 2008). Therefore, while Story One and Two provide useful perspectives for theorising the subject in resilience research, a further potential contribution may be found in feminist poststructural understandings of the subject. This story provides a lens through which to consider the resilient subject, enabling different questions to be asked and additional understandings to be generated regarding what resilience is, where it resides and how it develops. Moreover, this story explicitly draws our attention to resilience in distinctive ways by questioning its relationship to identity, subjectivity and the body. This is the subject who is the focus of Story Three.

## Story three: Resilience unfinished

To view resilience as unfinished is to place the subject under critical scrutiny. While Story Two and Three agree resilience is socially constructed, Story Three privileges a dialogic, reflexive self, generated relationally and whose subjectivity is negotiated through embodied, affective and historically and culturally situated biographies (Butler, 1990, 2004a, 2004b; Lloyd, 2005; McNay, 1999, 2008). Making sense of our experiences from pre-existing systems of language and meaning found in discourses means that who we are, our sense of self, and our identities are at once privately experienced, but also relationally and collectively lived, being produced through complex psychic, personal and collective identifications and dis-identifications (Lawler, 2008). We are therefore subjects who are always the site of competing and conflicting forms of embodied subjectivity (Burr, 2003), imbued with agency, but equally constrained through being subjected to broader discourses or forces (Weedon, 1996).

## The performative subject

Judith Butler's notion of performativity (1990, 2004a) provides resilience theory and research with an understanding of the subject that is not an external expression of an internal essence, but is instead a self 'manufactured through a sustained set of acts' (Butler, 1990, p. xv). This is a gendered subject who is the product of a complex interplay of discourses, norms, power relations, institutions and practices. Butler suggests that performativity is understood as an embodied, citational practice. This is a practice composed of daily bodily behaviours, gestures or acts requiring repetition over time, which introduces a temporal dimension to considerations of subjectivity or identity. The reiterative power of discourse in our daily re-engagement with or re-experience of gender norms, already socially established, produces the phenomenon of gendered identity.

Thus, gender identity is not a stable identity; it is 'an identity tenuously constituted, instituted in an exterior space through stylised repetition of acts' (Butler, 1990, p. 140). Subjectivity, or our sense of self, is never a description of experience but an expression of a normative, regulatory ideal. Butler's example of 'girling the girl' usefully shows the multitude of practices, customs and norms from birth, through which gender identity is performed (Butler, 1990, p. 111). The subject's agency to resist or subvert norms is located in the compulsion to repeat and in the variations of those repetitions or citations. As Lloyd (2007) suggests, the performativity that produces a gendered subject is also the site where a critical agency becomes possible. It is this instability of performativity that opens up possibilities for destabilising or subverting the dominant regulatory order. In attempting to understand the paradoxical nature of power and its relationship and role in the subject's formation, Butler's theory of agency draws upon Freud and Lacan, but specifically Foucault's concept of *assujettissement*. A subject is produced and results from a subjection to disciplinary power but equally, at the same time, this produces or constitutes a becoming. The gendered subject is an effect of power, but in order for power to persist, it must be reiterated, with the subject, the site of this reiteration (Butler, 1997). It is this process of activation that produces a subject who can act to either resist, or submit, or even become passionately attached to subjection (Butler, 1997).

If the resilient subject is reimagined as performative rather than as stable or socially constituted, then this subject and their resilience becomes unfinished, always in a process of remaking or becoming. This is achieved through embodied, individually and collectively lived biographies, identities, and emotional and unconscious processes. The resilient subject becomes someone who at any given time, across their biography or lifespan identifies, or misidentifies in complex ways with demands to be resilient, as children or teenagers, as mothers or as workers, or as gay, disabled or old. This is a resilient subject who in turn can comply or collude, subvert or resist discourses of resilience governing and disciplining arenas like health and social care.

The performative resilient subject requires us to explore critically how the broader discursive fields present in health and welfare constitute this subject; for example, discourses of positive psychology or public health and the policy focus on health and wellbeing. Additionally, the concept of performativity offers theoretical tools for exploring the micro or mundane; the everyday ways in which resilience is generated; the detailed talk, feelings and behaviours, activities and relationships experienced through particular bodies. It leads to an exploration of how subjectivity or individually experienced identities relate to other socially or publicly available identities like those of welfare client, patient, or as an individual or 'family at risk', or how these interact with other citational practices, like those of ethnicity, age or class.

When the resilient subject is viewed as 'unfinished' or constantly in a process of becoming or remaking, a critical space opens up for exploring resilience's temporal dimensions. This offers radically different theoretical grounds than, say, those of psychology, which views resilience and ageing developmentally and chronologically. Hence the potential scope of resilience research extends to include manifestations beyond childhood or adolescence to the forms resilience might take in mid-life, for example, during women's experiences of the menopause (Lindenmeyer et al, 2008; Hyde et al, 2010), or at differing times of distress and depression (Dowrick et al, 2008). This understanding of the subject and subjectivity provides further grounds for exploring not only how, but also why, subjects express resilience differently and indeed why this might be especially necessary. In queering resilience, Brown and Colbourne (2005, p. 264) relate the lived experience and life stories of young lesbian, gay and bisexual (LGB) people. They show how young people realise their resilience by actively locating personal and community resources to maximise their life opportunities in a society predicated on homophobia and heterosexism (Brown & Colbourne, 2005, p. 272). Queering resilience, they argue, results in a focus on the non-normative, on challenging the expectations and assumptions of heteronormativity. It also demands we pay attention to the fluidity or, as we would argue, the performativity of resilient identities and practices.

A performative subject who comes to understand their self only through and in relation to others is in turn always linked to recognition. As Butler (2004a) suggests, while we are produced through norms of recognition, we are never completely determined by such. She reminds us how easily subjects are 'undone' or where certain subjects go unrecognised or where lives are lost, for example, to disadvantage and poverty. This undoing is brought about by a lack of recognition. Only when we experience recognition are we constituted as socially viable beings, as being acceptable or included. In other words, recognition becomes a site of power where some are recognised, while others are not. While Story Two pays attention to the normative consequences of resilience, a performative subject highlights the importance of recognition. This further aids our understanding of why some subjects are recognised as resilient and others not. More importantly, as stated, a preoccupation with meaning given to behaviour in most resilience research means a corresponding lack of attention to the unthought, unspoken, unthinkable and unspeakable. This attention to subjectivity and the psychic or unconscious extends conventional accounts of resilience to be inclusive of a gendered subjectivity and the other.

Jessica Benjamin's (1995, 1998) psychoanalytical account of gendered subjectivity examines the constant tension between recognising the other and asserting the self. From a psychoanalytical viewpoint exclusion is always already an illusion (Benjamin, 1998, p. 102) for to exclude means to relocate, and what psychically gets relocated is always a repudiated or unacceptable part of the self in order to shore up an individual's identity. Thus the relation between the self and the other is not to be overcome but understood as always intersubjectively related. To do so practically would mean acknowledging moments in all our biographies when we first recognised others and our self as different, or our self as the other. This would be particularly useful for practitioners working to promote resilience in developing a critical reflexivity to their practice; helping them to explore their sense of difference and otherness, or what are less acceptable or less easily expressed feelings of anger, disgust or fear (Rudge & Holmes, 2009; Aranda & Jones, 2010).

Moreover, Butler (2004b) proposes a form of recognition based on a shared corporeal vulnerability, whereas much resilience research ignores or denies the body, or assumes it to be natural, fixed and stable. Yet considerable work now exists which theorises and empirically demonstrates the significance of the body in relation to moral or ethical concerns over what makes for a good life, and specifically in relation to health, illness and care (Foucault, 1980; Butler, 1993, 2004a, 2004b; Grosz, 1994; Davis, 1997; Shildrick, 2002; Shilling, 2003; Williams, 2003; Turner, 2008). Concepts of embodiment draw attention to the relationship between the physical body and subjectivity and the irreducible fusion of mind and body. Indeed, the centrality of the body to our sense of self, our experiences and relationships and practices are now understood to be continuously shaped by our ongoing bodily engagement with the world. To view the resilient subject as embodied, as poststructural accounts do, draws attention to the ways in which identity, subjectivity and bodies are intimately connected but never neutral. They are always already inscribed or marked with particular meanings of difference, such as class, race, gender, ability and age (Shildrick, 2002; Adkins & Skeggs, 2004; Einstein & Shildrick, 2009). Evidence also shows how the body is monitored and controlled to serve social control functions in and outside of medicine, health or education settings (Williams, 2003; Rose, 2007).

In Julia Twigg's (2006) comprehensive review of the body in health and social care the significance of the cultural turn towards the body is clearly evident. She shows how concepts of the body, embodiment, bodywork and body care are central to the enterprise of health and social care. By exploring various states of health, illness, disability and age, or in particular places or spaces and encounters with medicine, nursing or social care, she documents the centrality of the body. One key example cited is in relation to age and disability. Here Twigg (2006) shows how an analysis of the body in age reveals how particular meanings are inscribed on aging and disabled bodies and how this, along with a politics of appearance, become key to understanding processes of inclusion and exclusion or stigma and shame (2006, p. 171).

Those unacceptable bodies, or bodies that fail to achieve contemporary corporeal norms, are not dissimilar to those bodies that are unthinkable. As Rudge and Holmes (2009) suggest, practitioners rarely openly express disgust and repulsion felt when caring for certain bodies: this, they suggest, not only represents the unsayable or unthinkable but also the presence of the abject other. As Shildrick (2002) reminds us, the monstrous body is easily dismissed when extreme, but most often feared when there is some resemblance or recognition with our self. This indeterminate status, as she says – neither wholly self nor wholly other – is that which we find most deeply disturbing. Given that much resilience research and policy focuses on those most excluded, disadvantaged or deemed socially challenging or unacceptable, exploration of the psychic defence of abjection and the role of the body could prove significant for developing resilience research.

To expand theoretical understandings of resilience in this way challenges dominant theories of the subject found in Story One and Two, although the limits of Story Three are important to note. The radical epistemology of poststructuralism and the cultural, linguistic turn is argued to be more problematic in policy arenas in health and social care (Twigg, 2006). The abstract or discursive nature of these theories and apparent neglect of a material world of disadvantage are key concerns (Bottrell, 2009). But equally, these theories suggest the impossibility of direct knowledge of the world and so undermine the rationale of empirical evidence. This is incompatible with the policy world, which continues to be constituted by Enlightenment values of truth, progress, rationality and a knowable reality. Any research informed by such perspectives is therefore potentially marginalised in key debates and interventions in public policy (Twigg, 2006). Furthermore, these perspectives represent mostly western or European theories and concepts, and obviously there is a need to question the often-assumed universal relevance of such.

## Discussion and conclusion

Deconstructing narratives of resilience and exploring the resilient subject further reveals the centrality but contested nature of identity and the normative expectations of such. It helps us understand how people construct their identities in relation to resilience and how far these are prescribed, or how fluid or fixed a sense of self is. In so doing, questions of identity challenge the notion that resilience is intrinsically or inherently good, or that its promotion is a benign or beneficent activity. As Ungar (2008, 2010) notes, to reveal the normativity of much resilience research means continually asking – resilience for whom and for what purpose? Much resilience literature fails to recognise or engage with these normative aspects, nor is there much acknowledgement of the inherently conservative nature of resilience, requiring as it does an adaptation to systems or forms of power which go unquestioned or remain unchallenged (Leach, 2008; Bottrell, 2009). Given this, contemporary interest in resilience is possibly a further manifestation or extension of a clinical gaze, or neoliberal welfare's disciplinary logic. This dominant discourse governs the healthcare subject by promoting personal responsibility for resilience, arguably similar to current discourses of self-management or self-care (Taylor & Bury, 2007). As Bottrell (2009) suggests, resilience within a neoliberal framework of individualism may mean the emphasis shifts from 'positive adaptation despite adversity to positive adaptation *to* adversity' (2009, p. 334). Reframing resilience to engage directly with normative concerns is therefore vital but these considerations must be connected to critical discussions of power and justice. This is especially so if contemporary interest in discourses of resilience is indeed a response to broader sociocultural narratives of fear, anxiety and powerlessness (Leach, 2008, p. 14).

Our argument for a third story of resilience unfinished – drawing on a feminist poststructural subject – is timely, as it complements several critical and oppositional trends present in social theory, psychology and resilience research. Feminist poststructural accounts of the subject resonate with recent articulations of a 'psychosocial subject' (Frosh, 2003; Frost & Hoggett, 2008; Stenner & Taylor, 2008). Theoretically, this involves more than combining separate accounts of the social with the individual (Frosh, 2003). It is said to represent a paradigm shift that combines the social and individual subject as one seamless, embodied entity, and is conceived of as intimately connected (Frosh, 2003; Stenner & Taylor, 2008). Together, such theorising offers rich resources for asking different questions of and about the resilient subject in health and social care. As a lead advocate of a postmodern approach to resilience, Ungar (2010) has recently argued for the use of epistemological innovations in sociology, ecology and cross-cultural psychology. He explores contemporary family forms and argues that these theories allow us to understand resilience and families as fluid and in flux, not tied to places or spaces. Likewise, the critical or discursive turn in psychology and libertarian or community psychology are indicative of similar trends. Taking their starting point in opposition to biomedical or positivistic psychology, this theoretical work is explicitly political and addresses questions of power and justice. There is a commitment to work in inclusive and egalitarian ways to privilege contextually situated understandings of local or indigenous communities in order to generate health and wellbeing (Watkins & Shulman, 2008). Finally, telling a third but different story of resilience can be deemed a political act and, as such, resistance, rejection and challenge to this story might be expected. As Mishler (2005) suggests, we need to actively engage with dissent and mediate and negotiate rather than impose or dominate, or suppress our disagreements, conflict or tensions. This means maintaining a critical engagement with the normative fixing of meaning so that stories of resilience remain under critical scrutiny and in dialogue with each other.

## Acknowledgement

With thanks to *Health,* where this paper was first published as:

Aranda, K, Zeeman, L & Scholes, J (2012) The resilient subject: Exploring subjectivity, identity and the body in narratives of resilience. *Health: An interdisciplinary journal for the study of health, illness and medicine, 16*(5), 548–563.

# References

Adkins, L & Skeggs, B (Eds) (2004) *Feminism after Bourdieu.* Oxford: Blackwell.

Almedom, A (2005) Social capital and mental health: An interdisciplinary review of primary evidence. *Social Science and Medicine, 61*, 943–964.

Aranda, K & Jones, A (2010) Dignity in health-care: A critical exploration using feminism and theories of recognition. *Nursing Inquiry, 17*(3), 248–256.

Bartley, M (Ed) (2006) *Capability and Resilience: Beating the odds.* London: University College London.

Benjamin, J (1995) *Like Subjects, Love Objects: Essays on recognition and sexual difference.* New Haven, CT and London: Yale University Press.

Benjamin, J (1998) *Shadow of the Other: Intersubjectivity and gender in psychoanalysis.* London: Routledge.

Bottrell, D (2009) Understanding 'marginal' perspectives: Towards a social theory of resilience. *Qualitative Social Work, 8*(3), 321–339.

Bourdieu, P (1990) *The Logic of Practice.* Oxford: Blackwell.

Boyden, J & Mann, G (2005) Children's risk, resilience, and coping in extreme situations. In M Ungar (Ed) *Handbook for Working with Children and Youth: Pathways to resilience across cultures and contexts* (pp. 3–25). London: Sage Publications.

Brown, M & Colbourne, M (2005) Bent but not broken: Exploring queer youth resilience. In M Ungar (Ed) *Handbook for Working with Children and Youth: Pathways to resilience across cultures and contexts* (pp. 263–278). London: Sage Publications.

Burman, E (2008) *Deconstructing Developmental Psychology* (2nd ed). London: Routledge.

Burr, V (2003) *Social Constructionism* (2nd ed). London: Routledge.

Butler, J (1990) *Gender Trouble: Feminism and the subversion of identity* (2nd ed). London: Routledge.

Butler, J (1993) *Bodies that Matter: On the discursive limits of sex.* London: Routledge.

Butler, J (1997) *The Psychic Life of Power: Theories in subjection.* Stanford, CA: Stanford University Press.

Butler, J (2004a) *Undoing Gender.* London: Routledge.

Butler, J (2004b) *Precarious Life: The powers of mourning and violence.* London: Verso.

Darzi, A (2008) *High Quality Care for All: NHS Next Stage Review final report.* London: Department of Health.

Davis, K (1997) *Embodied Practices: Feminist perspectives on the body.* London: Sage Publications.

Dowrick, C, Kokanovic, R, Hegarty, K, Griffiths, F & Gunn, J (2008) Resilience and depression: Perspectives from primary care. *Health, 12*(4), 439–452.

Einstein, G & Shildrick, M (2009) The postconventional body: Retheorising women's health. *Social Science and Medicine, 69*, 293–300.

Foucault, M (1980) Power/knowledge: Selected interviews and other writings 1972–1977, by Michel Foucault. (Ed. C Gordon). Hertfordshire: Harvester Press.

Frosh, S (2003) Psychosocial studies and psychology: Is a critical approach emerging? *Human Relations, 56*(12), 1545–1567.

Frost, L & Hoggett, P (2008) Human agency and social suffering. *Critical Social Policy, 28*(4), 438–460.

Gergen, K (2009) *Relational Being: Beyond self and community.* Oxford: Oxford University Press.

Goldstein, S & Brooks, RB (2006) Why study resilience? In S Goldstein & RB Brooks (Eds) *Handbook of Resilience in Children* (pp. 3–16). New York: Springer.

Grosz, E (1994) *Volatile Bodies: Toward a corporeal feminism.* Bloomington: Indiana University Press.

Hart, A & Blincow, D with Thomas, H (2007) *Resilient Therapy: Working with children and families.* London: Routledge.

Hyde, A, Nee, J, Howlett, E, Drennan, J & Butler, M (2010) Menopause narratives: the interplay of women's embodied experiences with biomedical discourse. *Qualitative Health Research, 20*(6), 805–815.

Lawler, S (2008) *Identity: Sociological perspectives.* Cambridge: Polity Press.

Leach, M (Ed) (2008) *Re-framing Resilience: A symposium report – STEPS Working Paper 13.* Brighton: STEPS Centre.

Lindenmeyer, A, Griffiths, F, Green, E, Thompson, D & Tsouroufli, M (2008) Family health narratives: Midlife women's concepts of vulnerability to illness. *Health, 12*(3), 275–293.

Lloyd, M (2005) *Beyond Identity Politics: Feminism, power and politics.* London: Sage Publications.

Lloyd, M (2007) *Judith Butler: From norms to politics.* Cambridge: Polity Press.

Lundman, B, Aléx, L, Jonsén, E, Norberg, A, Nygren, B, Santamaki-Fischer, R

& Strandberg, G (2010) Inner strength: A theoretical analysis of salutogenic concepts. *International Journal of Nursing Studies, 47*, 251–260.

Luthar, SS & Brown, PJ (2007) Maximising resilience through diverse levels of inquiry: Prevailing paradigms, possibilities and priorities for the future. *Developmental Psychology, 19*(3), 931–955.

Marmot, M (2010) *Fair Society, Healthy Lives: The Marmot Review. Strategic review of health inequalities in England post-2010.* Available from http://www.ucl.ac.uk/whitehallII/pdf/FairSocietyHealthyLives.pdf [accessed 17 June 2010].

Masten, AS (2001) Ordinary magic: Resilience processes in development. *American Psychologist, 56*(3), 227–238.

McNay, L (1999) *Foucault and Feminism: Power, gender and the self.* Cambridge: Polity Press.

McNay, L (2008) *Against Recognition.* Cambridge: Polity Press.

Mishler, EG (2005) Patient stories, narratives of resistance and the ethics of humane care: A la recherché du temps perdu. *Health, 9*(4), 431–451.

Munford, R & Sanders, J (2008) Drawing out strengths and building capacity in social work with troubled young women. *Child and Family Social Work, 13*(1), 2–11.

Rose, N (1998) *Inventing Our Selves: Psychology, power and personhood.* Cambridge: Cambridge University Press.

Rose, N (2007) *The Politics of Life Itself: Biomedicine, power and subjectivity in the twenty-first century.* Oxford: Princeton University Press.

Rudge, T & Holmes, D (2009) Accounting for the unaccountable: Theorising the unthinkable (Editorial). *Nursing Inquiry, 16*(3), 181.

Rutter, M (1993) Resilience: Some conceptual considerations. *Journal of Adolescent Health, 14*, 626–631.

Rutter, M (2007) Resilience, competence and coping. *Child Abuse and Neglect, 31*(3), 205–209.

Seidman, S (1997) *Difference Troubles: Queering social theory and sexual politics.* Cambridge: Cambridge University Press.

Shildrick, M (2002) *Embodying the Monster: Encounters with the vulnerable self.* London: Sage Publications.

Shilling, C (2003) *The Body and Social Theory.* London: Sage Publications.

Squire, C (2008) *Approaches to Narrative Research: ESRC National Centre for Research Methods review paper.* London: NCRM.

Stenner, P & Taylor, D (2008) Psychosocial welfare: Reflections on an emerging field. *Critical Social Policy, 28*(4), 415–437.

Taylor, D & Bury, M (2007) Chronic illness, expert patients and care transitions. *Sociology of Health and Illness*, *29*(1), 27–45.

Theron, LC & Malindi, MJ (2010) Resilient street youth: A qualitative South African study. *Journal of Youth Studies*, *13*(6), 717–736.

Turner, BS (2008) *The Body and Society: Explorations in social theory* (3rd ed). Oxford: Blackwell.

Twigg, J (2006) *The Body in Health and Social Care*. Basingstoke: Palgrave Macmillan.

Ungar, M (2004) A constructionist discourse on resilience: Multiple contexts, multiple realities among at risk children and youth. *Youth and Society*, *35*(3), 341–365.

Ungar, M (2005) Introduction: Resilience across cultures and contexts. In M Ungar (Ed) *Handbook for Working with Children and Youth: Pathways to resilience across cultures and contexts* (pp. xv–xxxix). London: Sage Publications.

Ungar, M (2008) Resilience across cultures. *British Journal of Social Work*, *38*, 218–235.

Ungar, M (2010) What is resilience across cultures and contexts? Advances to the theory of positive development among individuals and families under stress. *Journal of Family Psychotherapy*, *21*(1), 1–16.

Ungar, M, Brown, M, Liebenberg, L, Othman, R, Kwong, WM, Armstrong, M & Gilgun, J (2007) Unique pathways to resilience across cultures. *Adolescence*, *42*(166), 287–310.

Watkins, M & Shulman, H (2008) *Toward Psychologies of Liberation*. Basingstoke: Palgrave Macmillan.

Weedon, C (1996) *Feminist Practice and Poststructural Theory.* Oxford: Blackwell.

Wetherell, M (Ed) (2009a) *Identity in the 21st Century: New trends in changing times.* Basingstoke: Palgrave Macmillan.

Wetherell, M (Ed) (2009b) *Theorizing Identities and Social Action.* Basingstoke: Palgrave Macmillan.

Wilkinson, R & Pickett, K (2009) *The Spirit Level: Why equality is better for everyone.* London: Allen Lane.

Williams, S (2003) *Medicine and the Body*. London: Sage Publications.

# the body queered in health and healthcare

## – kay aranda –

### Introduction

The body is undeniably central to questions of healthcare, with its embodied dilemmas of health and illness, sickness and disease, pain and disability, and life and death. Moreover, contemporary imperatives to improve, modify or fix our bodies in the pursuit of health mean that the body has also become a predominant form of identity or self-expression in western culture, which in turn has generated great academic interest (Williams & Bendelow, 1998; Bendelow et al, 2002; Petersen, 2007; Riley et al, 2008). In this chapter, I explore this growing interest and centrality of the body in health and healthcare through feminism's controversial but ongoing relationship with queer theory (Jagose, 2009). Feminism and queer theory's respective contributions to scholarship on gender, sexuality, health and the body are extensive, and in exploring both perspectives, I will assess each for their creative potential to trouble or undo our understandings of bodies generally, but of the fat body in particular. This is the body at the centre of public health discourses regarding the contemporary global obesity epidemic. In troubling the fat body, I will consider whether these perspectives can collaborate to deepen our understandings or whether their controversial relationship prevents productive engagements.

### Feminism and queer encounters

Past encounters between feminism and queer theory are known to have been strained, tense and fraught with unreceptive dialogues (Jagose,

2009; Showden, 2012). With supposedly deep incommensurability and incompatible epistemologies, both have been repeatedly pitted against each other through a series of oppositions: between their respective focus on the real and material versus the celebratory, imagined and playful, and between the political or structural versus the turn to culture or discourse (Hemmings, 2011; McLaughlin et al, 2012). Queer theorists are therefore censured for concentrating on deconstruction and identifying fluid identities and subjectivities, whilst feminism is reproached for ignoring difference, conflating gender with sexuality, and for focusing on the material instead of the cultural. And while queer activists are criticised for advocating local action through transgression, resistance and disruption, feminists are critiqued for their universalising and collectivist political campaigns and for co-option through their engagement with the state to address material inequalities (McLaughlin et al, 2012).

As a modern social movement, second-wave feminism's claims of shared common identities and experiences initially reinforced these divisions. Tending to reflect the interests and concerns of white middle-class women located in the global north, feminism was increasingly criticised by those excluded or marginalised in its theories or analyses. Encounters with postmodern and poststructural theories further suggested inherent flaws and revealed feminism's own partiality and its failure to recognise its own embedded assumptions and historical and cultural locations. These encounters further reinforced the loss of certainty in the political project of feminism, questioning its naïve commitment to grand narratives of progress and emancipation and, most significantly of all, troubling the possibility of a universal, unified political subject upon which to base political action (Nicholson, 1990; Lloyd, 2005; Hemmings, 2011). In further dialogue with queer theorists, this loss of innocence continued. This was especially seen in questions concerning core concepts such as those of sex and gender: sex could no longer be easily equated to biology or be seen as fixed and innate; nor could gender be easily read off from biology or seen as simply socially prescribed and learnt (Flax, 1990; Butler, 1990).

One response to these critiques was to revisit and revise debates and the respective liberal and radical strategies concerning sameness and difference (Weedon, 1999). These revisions tended to treat difference in two ways. The first was devoted to understanding the impact of class, race or gender on women's identity, experiences and struggles. Thus, when accused of ethnocentrism and imperialism, white middle-class feminism took an additive approach to questions of difference, with gender or sexuality added together with demands for recognition of class, race or ethnicity, disability and age (Davis, 2007; Richardson et al, 2012). However, such moves, whilst appearing inclusive, were criticised as it can mean the specificity of differences become invisible. The second response was to problematise difference for its assumption of shared experience. Though this strategy made the unique nature of differences visible, it still contained tendencies towards homogenising what remained heterogeneous experiences and identities. To draw on this strategy meant retaining a criticality towards all labels or categories seeking to demarcate boundaries based on an assumed commonality of experience (Weedon, 1999), and this marked a move towards anti-normative and anti-essentialist understandings of difference. This move overlaps and was and is suggestive of an emerging shared dialogue between queer and feminist theory. However, queer theory's normative project was politics of a different kind.

## Undoing queer theory

With its intentional indefinability, its openness to possibilities of use and re-signification, its refusal to specify its political project, and its unknowable usefulness and futures, queer theory is not any one thing (Jagose, 2009). Queer theory emerged in response to increasing frustrations with sociology and the social sciences generally. Despite both accepting and challenging foundational categories of sexuality, the sociology of homosexuality or lesbian and gay studies remained narrowly defined as questions of deviance or preference. Lesbians' and gay men's concerns, let alone those of bisexual or transgendered people (LGBT), were seen as too particularistic and hence remained relatively marginal or absent to mainstream sociological critique (Stein & Plummer, 1994). The then relatively new intellectual movement of queer theory was thought to hold potential for rethinking sexual and gender identities and nonconformity in ways that would not reproduce this marginalisation.

Even with queer theory's insistent refusal to be fixed or finally decided, it is nevertheless commonly understood as a hetereogeneous practice for interrogating the natural and taken for granted, the invisible and the normalised. In critiquing a 'minoritising' epistemology of sexuality (Browne, 2010), and though often associated or equated with LGBT people's concerns, queer theory demands the interrogation of all conventional categorisations and analyses. It insists on the interrogation of areas not normally considered sexual, and demands that scholars conduct 'queer readings' of hetero and non-sexualised concerns, issues or texts. This suggests new terrains for rethinking the dominant and marginal, or difference and sameness, and the local and particular in identity construction and power relation (McLaughlin et al, 2012). For these reasons, queer theory offers potential resources with which to interrogate normative understandings of the body.

Nonetheless, a number of charges are levelled at queer theory. As a theory and practice, it is accused of conceptual vacuity and diminishing critical and political value, having failed to deliver on its potential, and worse, of possibly reproducing the exclusionary normalising effects it intended to counter (Seidman, 1995; Jagose, 2009). Queer theory's focus on ambiguity, transgression and contingency is argued to promote individualism, offering little explanation as to how cultural norms are constituted, nor why they persist. Moreover, it is argued to have failed to recognise its own partiality and has tended to neglect the western sociopolitical or economic context in which many of these cultural practices operate (Showden, 2012). Such criticisms are especially significant for an analysis of the body in health and healthcare. Lived experiences of embodiment and material inequalities cannot always be best understood by transgression, contingency or ambivalence. For example, while celebrating a fat body may be an empowering move, the global nature of increasing weight gain, or the emotional experience of inhabiting a socially denigrated large body in western societies, for women and men, remains neglected or marginal (Carryer, 2001; Lupton, 2013). Finally, queer theory's disappointing and frustrating inability to engage with the 'real' world, its failure to account for continuing global inequalities, and its lack of feasible strategies for social transformation or change: all are said to have had disastrous effects for those politically marginalised or excluded (Richardson et al, 2012; Showden, 2012).

## Dialogue and alliances

Though these limitations are clearly significant, there may be more at stake in these arguments and disputes. Hostile debates between feminism and queer theory often amount to battles over an intellectual legacy of who did or said what first. There is also a tendency to overgeneralise and exaggerate differences between both whilst ignoring shared concerns, priorities, overlaps and similarities. Moreover, much criticism tends to concern just one version of feminism – usually radical feminism – and its account of sex and patriarchy (Showden, 2012). This discrepancy is especially evident when comparing queer theory with poststructural feminism. In their engagements with postmodernism and poststructuralism, feminist theorists were developing similar anti-normative and anti-essentialist critiques (Jagose, 2009). Judith Butler's work on troubling and undoing gender and sex (Butler, 1990, 2004) is an excellent example of the creative and highly influential links that emerged between both. These mutual interests tend to be overlooked in these debates when there is in fact a shared, heterogeneous project of social critique in which both have a stake. Furthermore, the increasingly recognised intersections between feminism and queer theory are argued to hold considerable potential and promise (Jagose, 2009; Showden, 2012; Richardson et al, 2012).

The potential for shared dialogue and convergence stems from the recognition of the partiality of all theorising and the growing acceptance from both that agency is constituted by, and constituting of, gender and sexual power relations (Jagose, 2009). Additionally, there is growing recognition of the role of 'discursive and linguistic processes within material relations' (McLaughlin et al, 2012, p. 13), and both concede that each shares a concern with the body through their respective explorations of gender and/or sexuality. Reciprocal interests are evident in their respective anti-normative and anti-essentialist critiques and anti-foundational interrogations of their core concepts of gender and sexuality. The concepts of intersectionality and homonormativity are good examples of further common ground (Richardson & Monro, 2012).

## Intersectionality and homonormativity

Feminism's desire to move beyond the aforementioned additive or list-like approach to difference represents an important move away from prioritising specific identities, for example, gender, age, sexuality or class, over others. This has produced an increasing focus on the significance of *intersectionality* of multiple identities. Derived from Crenshaw (1989, cited by Davis, 2008), this concept originally aimed to highlight how women of colour and their experiences were inadequately accounted for in feminist, anti-racist theories or queer theory. Intersectionality now commonly refers to 'the interactions between gender, race, and other categories of difference in individual lives, social practices, institutional arrangements, and cultural ideologies and the outcomes of these interactions in terms of power' (Davis, 2008, p. 68). To be defined by gender or sexuality alone is now seen as both reductive and theoretically inadequate, even though it may be politically expedient (Fish, 2008). Moreover, intersection theory is suggested to offer possibilities for understanding multiple inequalities without abandoning the politics of social movements (Davis, 2008).

Queer theory's recent ability to move beyond the local and intimate and to comment on social relations is to be found in explorations of citizenship, welfare and equality (Richardson & Monro, 2012). Significant social and cultural transformations in the realm of sexuality point to a number of paradoxes in the production of new citizen subjects: where rights and responsibilities are emphasised and where sexuality is both relevant and irrelevant; where sexuality is both collective and individual,;and where homosexuality is indicative of both a consolidation and subversion of heterosexuality. These trends are captured in the concept of a new *homonormativity*. This is a form of homonormativity that does not challenge but accepts, works with, and sustains and maintains dominant heteronormative assumptions and institutions (Richardson et al, 2012). This is witnessed in claims for inclusion and equality through, for example, the legalisation of gay marriage or a desire for permanency and domesticity in demands for marriage, parenthood, or legal rights to pensions, life insurance or welfare benefits (Richardson et al, 2012).

It could be argued that developments such as these possibly indicate increasing tolerance, acceptance, even normalisation of LGBT people's rights to equality – though possibly more so for those in monogamous relationships, who work and pay taxes, rather than those who identify as gender-fluid or diverse (Richardson & Monro, 2012). However, the changes could also constitute an expansion of neoliberal governance into LGBT lives, producing an individualised, de-politicised and privatised gay culture focused on consumption and domesticity. This may then represent a privatisation of intolerance and prejudice and indicate capitalism's ability to colonise, commodify and exploit LGBT identities and lives (Roseneil, 2000; Richardson & Monro, 2012). Alternatively, such social and cultural transformations in the organisation of sexual relations may be indicative of a destabilisation of homo/heterosexual relations (Roseneil, 2000). Given the postmodern emphases on fluid, ambiguous, non-unified identities, Roseneil, for example, suggests that a number of 'queer tendencies' are working to destabilise and multiply sexual identities, bodies and relations. If so, she suggests, the normal or naturalness of both heterosexuality and homosexuality becomes more readily questioned (Roseneil, 2000).

These new terms of intersectionality and homonormativity suggest continuing and shared interests between feminism and queer theory concerning difference and the politics and inequality of health and welfare more broadly (Yeatman, 1994; Yeatman et al, 2009). For an analysis of the body, these developments can be creatively and productively woven together to allow for a richer analysis of the body in health and illness (Einstein & Shildrick, 2009). The extent to which both feminism and queer theory potentially aid or hinder an analysis of the body, and fat bodies in particular, is discussed next.

## The body

From its initial absence and invisibility in social theory, the body now constitutes an area of immense academic interest (Petersen, 2007). With the cultural turn in the social sciences and humanities, the body as the subject and object of analysis became prominent in many academic areas, but rather less so in health and healthcare until recently (Twigg, 2006). At the simplest level, the body is central to healthcare but, paradoxically, this centrality meant that it was, and sometimes continues to be, overlooked. Moreover, it is a particular body that endures and dominates. This is the bio-scientific medical view of the body: the body as an object, fragmented, functional, viewed from a distance or reduced to systems, organs and cells, and seen as a site of physical processes requiring healthcare interventions (Twigg, 2006). In health and illness this understanding of the body is separated from and devoid of lived experience, emotional content or subjective meaning.

Other theories of the body offer rival accounts, placing greater emphasis on the social, on subjectivity and embodiment. These theories range from interrogating the naturalness of the biological body to demonstrating how the social constitutes and is constituted through the body. This work has shown how the material and social are integral to our understandings, interventions and changing embodied experiences and sense of self (Williams & Bendelow, 1998; Shilling, 2003; Williams, 2003; Turner, 2008; Bendelow, 2009). The significant role of experience and emotion is recognised in understandings of the phenomenological body as the lived body. This is the thinking, feeling, pulsing, moving body which does not replace the biological body but places it into a broader context (Williams, 2006). In states of health the body is often felt as invisibly present, but when interrupted by pain, impairment or illness, people often turn inwards, feeling alienated from the self and isolated from others (Williams & Bendelow, 1998). In this area of scholarship, narratives of suffering, pain or disability, and chronic illness become visible and take precedence, and reveal important relationships between the self and identity through changing biological states (Bury, 1982; Frank, 1995; Williams & Bendelow, 1998; Thomas, 2007; Bendelow, 2009).

## Embodiment

Central to current thinking about the body is the concept of embodiment. In replacing the binary Cartesian mind/body split, embodiment aims to capture the irreducible fusion of mind and body and the dynamic interplay of the person with the world (Einstein & Shildrick, 2009). Embodiment is a process rather than a state – a doing rather than being – and as a set of social practices it brings together questions of structure and agency, or mind and body, to explore how bodies materialise or are realised in a social context – that is, how bodies shape, and are shaped by, social processes, relations and structures. The body is therefore core to our sense of self, our experiences, relationships and practices and the ways these are continuously shaped by an ongoing bodily engagement with the world (Twigg, 2006).

## Feminist theorising on the body

Women's bodies have always been central to feminist theory and politics (Davis, 2007). Feminists were among the first to recognise the significance of the body in debates related to fertility, the control of reproduction and patriarchal power (Bordo, 1993; Davis, 1997; Twigg, 2006; Annandale, 2009). Many early campaigns centred on rights in areas of reproduction, contraception, abortion, or control in childbirth and struggles against violence. This empirical work focused on how women experience their bodies, and how these bodies are implicated in social and cultural practices and are represented symbolically. Therefore, the body was hardly new to feminist scholars, and this embodying of theory is an achievement male scholars on the body are somewhat reluctant to draw on, although they often acknowledge the influence of feminism as a political movement that brought the body to the fore as a topic (Davis, 1997).

Within mainstream sociology, even with its critique of modern science and its initial anti-body stance, female bodies and associated female attributes were actively positioned as inferior and 'other', as mysterious, dangerous, uncontrollable and messy, whilst men were considered to be unencumbered by the material limits of their bodies and so were legitimate, authoritative sources of knowledge (Shilling, 2003). Feminism's major contribution here was to reveal the gendered nature and particularity of all social theory. In 'bringing the body back in', feminism destabilised binaries to allow fears of femininity and questions of power to be addressed and, with this, the historical and cultural constructions of sexuality and gender to be explored (Davis, 1997).

Remarkably, even with the interest in the body and the level of political activism in relation to women and health, feminist theorists were initially reluctant and somewhat ambivalent over theorising issues of embodiment and the body. Second-wave feminism had tended to favour gender over sex as the explanatory analytic, as they sought to move beyond biological determinism and essentialist explanations in favour of a focus on gender and the social processes and power relations implicated in women's oppression. Nevertheless, subsequent debates have proved significant, producing rich analyses of women's health and their embodied practices in health and social care (Davis, 1997; Twigg, 2006; Riley et al, 2008; Taylor, 2010).

Much of this work initially sought to correct the invisibility of women's bodies and health concerns to mainstream sociological research, and challenged the dominant construction of the body in medicine. It sought to counter the dominant biomedical paradigm and its capacity to diagnose, alleviate and cure, and questioned the privileging of this perspective. Feminists interrogated the gendered, normative and essentialist assumptions surrounding the nature of women's bodies and explored the sociocultural and emotional meanings involved in experiences of birth, reproduction, chronic illness, disability and aging (Twigg, 2006; Annandale, 2009; Lupton 2013).

Starting with assumptions that gender is pervasive and essential to understanding contemporary society, feminists sought to deconstruct or destabilise binary thinking to show the mutually dependent and interrelated nature of what felt private with the public sphere, and the gendered division of labour in each. The way gender works directly on the body has shown the ways femininity and masculinity are inscribed physically on bodies, limiting or reducing the space women occupy or move in while reinforcing the extension of men's physical presence and connectedness to the world. Using Kristeva's concept of abjection (Oliver, 1993, 1997), feminists have sought to understand why women's bodies are regarded with unease or distaste: as polluting, threatening, repulsive or grotesque, especially in relation to bodily fluids like menstruation or lactation, for example, where boundaries are breached or are indeterminate (Twigg, 2006; Shildrick, 1997).

With the cultural turn and feminism's engagement with Foucault, there was and continues to be a radical questioning of the underlying acceptance of a reality or distinctions between nature and culture and agency or structure. The focus then turned on denaturalising the female body, deconstructing women's position as autonomous or as other, and rejecting or interrogating the use of experience as an authentic source of knowledge (McNay, 1992; Lupton, 1995; Sawicki, 1996; Burr, 2003; Williams, 2006; Davis, 2007). Using Foucauldian analyses, feminists have sought to understand how women's bodies are both subject to discipline and power but also how they can subvert or transgress bodily norms, for example, in challenging contemporary discourses of femininity or sexuality or motherhood (McNay, 1992; Annandale, 2009).

These cultural and discursive analyses challenge simplistic accounts of universal or shared experiences. For example, work exploring the lives of those living with disability has shown the diversity of experience and the pain or suffering involved in living with impairment. These analyses expose the nature of exclusions as being more than those of a disabling society or questions of access, but of exclusions perpetuated by living with pain, or the emotional or psychosocial impact of living with disability. In undoing or troubling discourses of ableism, this work aims to challenge dominant sociocultural meanings and assumptions of able-bodiedness, which reinforces bodies as separate, autonomous, independent, controlled and bounded. Instead, our shared corporeal vulnerabilities are reinstated, recognised and explored (Shildrick, 1997; Twigg 2006). Drawing on these understandings, feminist poststructural theorising reveals how the body in healthcare is both abject and wanted; is desirable but excessive; is cared for and worked on; but is equally managed and controlled (McNay, 1992; Butler, 1993; Shildrick, 2002; McNay, 2004; Twigg, 2006). These are bodies inscribed or marked with particular meanings and socially dominant norms (Shildrick, 2002), resulting in some bodies being deemed acceptable and others, like fat bodies, as unacceptable. These unacceptable bodies fail to achieve contemporary corporeal norms and/or become abject, or unthinkable.

For queer theorists, these abject bodies often became the starting point or focus of their scholarship for troubling sexuality, undoing gender and compulsory heterosexuality and able-bodiedness. This work has shown the complex, cross-identifications involved in understanding embodiment, seen in the intersections between sexual, gendered and disabled or transgendered embodiment, in the diversity of sexual preferences and the nature of normatively defined but differently positioned bodies (Butler, 1993; Halberstam, 2013; McRuer, 2013). Maintaining anti-essentialist and anti-normative understandings, queer theory insisted and asserts that sexuality is concerned not only with intimate desire or conduct, or to be conceived as drives to be repressed, but is social. Sexuality is therefore embedded in socially organised systems, relations and practices, mediated over time and place, intersected by heterosexuality and gender, ethnicity, class or disability. Sexuality, like gender, is central to questions of individual and collective identity and other social formations (Casey et al, 2010). This queering of sexuality has involved interrogating taken-for-granted assumptions. This is evident in critiques of essentialist assumptions inherent to biographical over-simplifications seen in categorisations like lesbian or gay or older LGBT, or assumptions of sexuality or sexual identity categories as fixed, stable or homogeneous (Cronin & King, 2010). Such work seeks to disentangle generalisations in order to fully understand diversity and complexities involved in everyday lives. As such, many studies now show the differential impact of sexuality and intersecting identifications on intimate relationships, on work, on experiences of health and illness and encounters with healthcare, on growing older, and in bereavement and end-of-life care (Fish & Anthony, 2005; Daley, 2006; Fish, 2009; Almack et al, 2010; Lindley et al, 2012).

However, even with such rich and varied scholarship, theorists have remained frustrated with the socially constructed or culturally discursive understandings of the body, as in much of this writing the body still appears dematerialised. This denial of the material is argued to constitute a form of discourse determinism as it renders the biological immaterial and reduced to the social (Williams, 2006). Sharing these concerns over the importance of matter and materiality, many feminists have long retained an interest in the materiality of bodies (Grosz, 1994), but others are now joining in this call for a return to a corporeal realism to rethink the complexity of the material (Bendelow, 2009; Einstein & Shildrick, 2009).

## The return to materialism

Drawing on weaker versions of social constructionism and the biological, but avoiding a retreat to former dualisms of mind over body, there is growing demand for a renewed dialogue concerning biology (Williams,

2006; Fox & Ward, 2006; Barad, 2007; Rose, 2007; Fox, 2012). This shift away from social bodies or constructionism, towards recognition of the ongoing generation of reality in and through sociomaterial practices, constitutes a new materialism that includes conceptualising the 'doing of the body' as a practical accomplishment (Barad, 2007; Coole & Frost, 2010). Both Davis (2007) and Einstein and Shildrick (2009) point to a similar disconnect or misalignment between poststructural, postmodern or postconventional feminist analyses and the women's health movement and feminist health activism. Each insists on the recognition of more complex accounts of corporeality and embodiment.

For Davis, feminist theories of the body need to stop seeing the body as merely a surface or cultural text and re-acknowledge its materiality. This would ensure theory continues to recognise vulnerability and bodies that are ill, infirm, disabled, or in pain or suffering, but this would be a vulnerability that needs to be considered without resorting to biological determinism or essentialism. Understandings of embodied experience also need to continue to account for specificity. This would mean women's different material locations, and how these relate to how they feel, perceive and understand their bodily experiences, can be accounted for. She insists that women be seen as capable of intentional, conscious, practical actions and with an ability to reflect upon, interpret and rework experience, rather than agency being seen as a discursive effect or artefact of shifting cultural discourses (Davis, 2007).

In contrast, Einstein and Shildrick (2009) suggest that the alignment of poststructuralism with the concrete issues of women's health and their bodies is possible and achievable, but only if two continuing modernist assumptions are interrogated. The first is to challenge the way women's health practice and theory continue to operate with unexamined assumptions of the healthy/sick binary, where to make better is to move closer to a universalised notion of normal. The task, as with all poststructural theorising, would be to continue to uncover normative assumptions, but importantly, such theorising would equally need to recognise how the fixity or rigidity of the healthy/sick binary is being destabilised by discoveries in bioscience and medicine itself. Developments in epigenetics and neuroscience further underline and suggest the need to acknowledge specificity, contingency and the rejection of binaries regarding matter, genes, organisms and the environment. Einstein and Shildrick (2009) argue that feminist theories on the body need to engage with the destabilising effects of specificity, of contexts, and the impact of new technological and scientific thinking on corporeality, whereby matter or material mass is now conceived to be constantly emerging, becoming, evolving and changing. Finally, they too argue for revisions to the notion of agency. However, they wish to disrupt the continuing assumption underpinning much feminist health and body theory and practice; that is, of the healthcare consumer as a self-determining subject with unquestionable agency and rights over her body. Rather than focusing on experience or agency and questions of choice or action, Einstein and Shildrick suggest we give full consideration to context. Drawing on relational understandings, the focus is on dynamic and fluid notions of embodiment and the ways bodies interact with space, place, with others, or with discourses, practices or material objects. Einstein and Shildrick (2009) also suggest we focus on how technology or interventions or procedures act on the person and how the person relates back to these interventions, but also to people, contexts, artefacts, experiences, practices, identities, or memories. This would expand the grounds for an analysis and allow for a consideration of the effects and bioethical implications of any interventions and a fuller understanding of what it is to be healthy or ill (Einstein & Shildrick, 2009).

To conclude, there is a wish to retain the criticality involved in interrogating unexamined normativities, simplifications and idealisations, but to combine this with an engagement with the complexities, messiness and misunderstandings that effect choices and actions in the real concrete contexts of health matters (Einstein & Shildrick, 2009). Indeed recent debates theorising health and gender can be found to demand similar relational, intersectional and material understandings and approaches. Gender is conceptualised as systemic: a 'pervasive system of stratification that structures relationships and interactions between and among men and women, shapes access to resources and status, and signifies power' (Springer et al, 2012). These approaches interrogate and problematise rigid binaries of sex and gender and seek to understand the construction of such, paying attention to the situated, contextual or particular differences and sameness between and among women and men.

This demand for a return to the material, alongside rapid developments in biomedicine, science and technology, but in the face of continuing global inequalities, suggests a critical moment in contemporary theorising concerning the body and society. Queer and poststructural feminist theories still hold potential to address this agenda but clearly with the caveats suggested by Einstein and Shildrick (2009). In sum, these two lenses of queer and feminist theory share much together in the priority to interrogate or trouble the material and socially embodied subject. Moving beyond modernist understandings of the body means both feminism and queer theory recognise the body's shared, corporeal vulnerabilities and both work with fluid, relational understandings of gender and sexuality (Butler 1993, 2004; Einstein & Shildrick, 2009). Moreover, each perspective views difference as problematic but creative, as a resource with which to rethink embodied experiences, identities and struggles for equality. This constitutes understandings of bodies as composed of different identities and experiences, as relational, embodied and agential, and linked to contemporary cultural and material worlds. One contemporary issue dominating global public health debates is that of the obesity epidemic or crisis, but it is a topic that provides a clear example of the potential of combining feminist and queer theory scholarship.

## The healthy fat body: Feminist and queer theory critiques

Obesity is considered a significant public health issue worldwide. Its increasing prevalence is described as a global epidemic (World Health Organization, 2000, 2011). This crisis is affecting not only high-income countries, like the USA, Australia, Canada and the United Kingdom (UK), but also middle- and low-income countries, such as those in Asia and Africa, where a 'double burden' of under-nutrition alongside a rapid upsurge in obesity and overweight is now emerging (World Health Organization, 2011). The dominant western classification of obesity is the body mass index (BMI). A BMI of more than 25 to 30 is considered overweight, while a BMI of over 30 is referred to as obese. According to recent estimates in the UK, approximately 25 per cent of men and women are obese and this is set to rapidly increase rather than decline (Department of Health, 2010, 2011).

Both feminist and queer theories have provided substantial critiques of weight, food intake, size and obesity. This scholarship has revealed the politics and sociocultural aspects of eating and body size, and drawn attention to the broader socioeconomic and political context in which these phenomena occur. In neoliberal and neoconservative regimes, where health is recognised as increasingly individualised and commoditised, and where discourses of rights and responsibilities reinforce moralising tendencies, health, identity and notions of the self have become closely correlated with body image and size (Moore, 2010). Increasing individualism and consumerism mean that the pursuit of the healthy body becomes a project:

one of managing risky lifestyles and self-improvement. Health becomes the responsibility of each individual, and what constitutes health expands. This expansion, or ' imperative of health' or 'healthism', is exemplified and critiqued in debates surrounding health promotion in which the fat body is a key object of scrutiny (Lupton, 1995; Crawford, 2006).

Drawing on Foucault's notion of governmentality – understood as modern forms of regulatory power and practices underpinned by new forms of rationality – promoting health or health promotion becomes a project of self-regulation which draws on knowledge and expertise to ensure monitoring, self-management and surveillance of bodily processes (Lupton, 1995; Petersen, 2007; Moore, 2010). This expansion and concealment of power is seen in the extent to which these practices become naturalised or legitimised as technologies of the self or self-care. Health promotion is therefore known to require an active embodied engagement from its subjects in the very techniques and practices designed to normalise or govern their behaviour, selves and bodies (Foucault, 1976, 1988; Annandale, 1998; Lupton, 2003; Rose, 2007; Nettleton et al, 2008). Increasing individualisation, medicalisation and commodification produces what has been called a 'politicisation of the body' (Petersen, 2007). This politicisation of the body, through health and fitness regimes, with a focus on body size, image or appearance and the desire for perfection, has significant consequences in terms of increasing categorisation, regulation and control. Health promotion's conflation of health with healthy bodies, and the body as vulnerable, unstable or susceptible to attack, serves to reproduce traditional ideas about women's bodies. These are bodies seen as uncontrollable, subject to the vagaries of biology, in need of regulation as a matter of personal responsibility and moral virtue. The consequence of this focus and health promotion's attitude to the body means that to do health is to do gender (Moore, 2010).

Framed by these understandings, feminism has shown, for example, how specifically women's embodiment intersects with gendered material and cultural practices related to femininity, size, physical appearance and the disciplines of healthy eating and staying fit (Carryer, 2001; Riley et al, 2008; Cheney, 2011; Woolhouse et al, 2011; Tischner & Malson, 2012). The prevalent and insidious nature of current anti-obesity orthodoxies demands that the gendered, entrepreneurial, neoliberal citizen is one who remains health conscious. This is achieved through constant self-monitoring and maintenance of a normal body size, and through being deemed responsible for making the right choice – the healthy choice regarding food, eating and lifestyle (Tischner & Malson, 2012). For those deemed large or fat and therefore excluded from this normalcy these anti-obesity discourses reinforce moral failure, with feelings of shame and blame ensuring that eating becomes a constant battle or source of guilt (Woolhouse et al, 2011). Many current health promotion orthodoxies are known to fail to consider how cultural norms are gendered and associate contemporary norms of femininity with slenderness, and how these understandings produce and reproduce women as self-regulating subjects (Riley et al, 2008). Moreover, individualised discourses of health and healthy weight only serve to obscure and perpetuate gendered, classed and racialised power relations shaping women's and men's subjectivities over their size, food intake and eating habits (Bell & McNaughton, 2007; Woolhouse et al, 2011).

## Queering the fat body

These progressively critical debates over health promotion and production of the healthy and unhealthy subject overlap with critiques aiming to queer fatness and the obesity crisis (Riley et al, 2008; Lupton, 2013). To accept the obesity discourse is to concede that rapidly rising levels of obesity or fatness are problematic: fat becomes seen as a disease state, as socially undesirable and resulting from faulty individual behaviours and choices (Meleo-Erwin, 2012). Contesting such dominant and seemingly commonsense orthodoxies is to trouble or undo not only fatness but also definitions of health and normalcy indexed to body weight. Queer critiques and scholarship have therefore sought to challenge the medicalisation and pathologising of corpulent or fat bodies and, in so doing, have much resonance with the challenges posed by feminism, black or LGBT activism, and disability rights movements (Lupton, 2013). These areas of scholarship and activism aim to critique and deconstruct or challenge taken-for-granted assumptions circulating in lay, medical and public health discourses surrounding body size, weight and obesity. The aim is to interrogate the moralistic and individualised discourses involved in debates on the obesity epidemic in a bid to fight or disrupt entrenched systemic forms of fat phobia (Lupton, 2013).

Fat activists have therefore attempted to reclaim derogatory labels and understandings of being large and have queered words like fat. This is seen as politically essential as it constitutes a deliberate rejection of concepts like obese or overweight because of their pathologising and normative connotations. There have been efforts to generate collective identities built upon fat as being normal, or in a variation to a norm, or as healthy as any other bodily size. These strategies aim to challenge anti-fat stigma and transgress or resist such denigration by creating positive and affirming identities and fostering cultures and communities of acceptance. In queering fat bodies, notions of normative body size and ideas of normal or normality are revealed to operate as techniques of power, serving to regulate and control. Individuals are shown to be identified and categorised, and they themselves identify and categorise in ways that make them ever more governable (Meleo-Erwin, 2012).

Moreover, queer theorists understand the fat body not as fixed and stable but as performative, fluid and non-essentialising, and so open to challenge and change. There is also recognition that a fat female body challenges cultural expectations of the desirable female form and that anti-fat or obesity discourses affect and target all (Lupton, 2013). Nonetheless, even with these strategies and liberatory politics, dominant derogatory meanings, images and stereotypes of being large or fat persist. Even more importantly, there is an argument that suggests that these transgressive or acceptance strategies may be fundamentally flawed and in need of revision.

Drawing on Foucault and Merleau-Ponty to explore the ambiguities and realities of living with a fat body, Murray (2008) shows that to argue for an identity based on fatness is inherently limited. She suggests this approach perpetuates an often unacknowledged essentialist understanding of identity. Furthermore, it reinforces an individualism and privileging of autonomy and rationale action by asking fat people to change the way they think about themselves. There are also implicit assumptions of a unified, fixed and stable self in that one has to remain consistent in being out and proud as fat. More significantly, she shows how acceptance strategies fail to acknowledge the nature of lived experience and subjective being as experiences that are always, already, constituted intersubjectively through encounters with others. As such, these approaches fail to consider how entrenched and resistant the negative stigmatising response of others might be to any individual efforts to generate self-acceptance (Murray, 2008). This amounts to what she calls a fiction of self-governance, which is, she argues, limiting and flawed in its insistence on individual liberal assertions of identity, as it serves to perpetuate a political intent of 'overcoming the fat body and the response it elicits' (2008, p. 181), but fails to fully acknowledge the embodied politics of lived experience.

In similar ways, Meleo-Erwin (2012) calls for a new politics of embodiment and suggests that attempts to frame fatness as normal are similarly flawed. For Meleo-Erwin (2012), this is in part because such an approach leaves out those unable or unwilling to measure up to normal, and in part, as with all identity politics and strategies based on being different but equal, it implies a valorisation of fatness and fat identity. Instead, she proposes troubling concepts of health, disease, normalcy and treatment underpinning the obesity debates to ensure a more critical politics of embodiment. Drawing on feminist disability studies and queer theory, Meleo-Erwin (2012) suggests that notions of 'ordinary and familiar' replace those of normal and deviant as a way to theorise fatness and resistance. This aims to acknowledge and work with the 'complex, embodied, material reality of being differently bodied' (2012, p. 397). Such an approach allows for a more complex ethos of embodiment that avoids rigid binaries; in part it recognises and positively celebrates differences in body size. Nonetheless, and similar to Murray's (2008) proposition, such an approach acknowledges but does not exclude or silence experiences of illness, pain or impairment, or dislike, shame and/or suffering felt from living with a fat body in contemporary western society. For Lupton (2013), this crucial move acknowledges the ambiguity involved in subjectivity and consequently recognises the unfinished, heterogeneous and dynamic aspects of selfhood and embodiment in relation to fat bodies.

## In conclusion

To consider the body in health and healthcare through the lens of feminism and queer theory suggests a tangled but ongoing creative relationship. This 'braiding together' of queer and feminist interests and priorities might very well constitute a 'queer feminism' (Jagose, 2009; Showden, 2012). This convergence or entanglement and shared conversation can be seen to hold promise, and are, I suggest, potentially productive but also be well timed.

Currently in rich societies, where feminism has commonly become a derogatory term, there is renewed public interest in gender inequality. Responses to the continuing global recession in high-income countries has meant austerity measures manifest mostly as savage cuts in welfare. These cuts are impacting disproportionately upon women. The damaging effects of this will be felt through lives damaged and lost to poverty, disadvantage and injustice. Moreover, the continuing pervasive commodification and violence directed towards female bodies, globally, has sparked outrage, producing a new generation of feminists and novel forms of political activism (Banyard, 2010). Methods reminiscent of queer activism, online organising and direct political action, combined with grassroots movements initiating flash mobs and rallies, have together led to an unprecedented level of visibility for feminism.

At the time of writing, feminist responses and challenges to attacks and attempts to reverse or erode hard-fought-for rights are much in evidence (Baynard, 2010). These are often over issues thought to have been resolved by second-wave feminist campaigns such as sexism, abortion, equal pay, violence, abuse and civil rights – see, for example, networks like UK Feminista and websites such as www.everydaysexism.com. In addition, there are increasing global feminist political movements, demands and calls for action to end gender violence. The international scale and levels of domestic violence, rape, female genital mutilation, sex trafficking and war remain endemic in many parts of the world, and campaigns, such as the 'One Billion Rising' campaign (see http://onebillionrising.org), remind us all of the continuing need to fight and make visible the demand for an end to violence for all.

To conclude, to theorise the body through the lens of feminist and queer theory is critical and conceivable and even fitting to contemporary times. In undoing normative understandings, and in combining attention to the specificities and complexities of embodied experiences, both feminism and queer theory have been shown to share a collective project and common ground. Working with anti-normative understandings of the body, both perspectives now wish to incorporate understandings of difference that refuse rigid binaries and move away from specific prioritising of any one identity. Whilst not wishing to overlook specificities for any given identity, each perspective has been shown to emphasise the intersections of difference rather than valorisation. The recognition of a shift in hetero- or new homonormative relations or practices serves to underscore the importance of analytical links between private, intimate embodied concerns to public, broader sociopolitical agendas, politics and policies. These developments strengthen the creative possibilities for collaboration between the two traditions for rethinking the intersections and ambivalences of the material, cultural, social, relational and affective aspects of the body in health and healthcare. To bring together the politics and theory of feminism and queer suggests valuable, critical and creative possibilities and resources for enriching our understandings of the politics of embodiment in contemporary health and healthcare.

# References

Almack, K, Seymour, J & Bellamy, G (2010) Exploring the impact of sexual orientation on experiences and concerns about end of life care and bereavement for lesbian, gay and bisexual older adults. *Sociology, 44*(5), 908–924.

Annandale, E (1998) *The Sociology Of Health And Medicine: A critical introduction.* Cambridge: Polity Press.

Annandale, E (2009) *Women's Health And Social Change.* London: Routledge.

Banyard, K (2010) *The Equality Illusion: The truth about women and men today.* London: Faber & Faber.

Barad, K (2007) *Meeting the Universe Halfway: Quantum physics and the entanglement of matter and meaning.* Durham, NC and London: Duke University Press.

Bell, K & McNaughton, D (2007) Feminism and the invisible fat man. *Body & Society, 13*(1), 107–131.

Bendelow, G (2009) *Health, Emotion and the Body.* Cambridge: Polity Press.

Bendelow, G, Carpenter, M, Vautier, C & Willimams, S (Eds) (2002) *Gender, Health and Healing: The public/private divide.* London: Routledge.

Bordo, S (1993) *Unbearable Weight: Feminism, western culture and the body.* Berkeley, CA: California University Press.

Browne, K (2010) Selling my queer soul or queerying quantitative research? *Sociological Research Online, 13*(1), *11.* Available from http://www. socresonline.org.uk/13/1/11.html [accessed February 2014].

Burr, V (2003) *An Introduction to Social Contructionism* (2nd ed). London: Routledge.

Bury, M (1982) Chronic illness as biographical disruption. *Sociology of Health & Illness, 4,* 167–182.

Butler, J (1990) *Gender Trouble: Feminism and the subversion of identity.* London: Routledge.

Butler, J (1993) *Bodies That Matter: On the discursive limits of 'sex'.* London Routledge.

Butler, J (2004) *Undoing Gender.* London: Routledge.

Carryer, J (2001) Embodied largeness: A significant women's health issue. *Nursing Inquiry, 8*(2), 90–97.

Casey, M, Hines, S, Richardson, D & Taylor, Y (2010) Editorial foreword: Introduction to a special issue on sexuality. *Sociology, 44*(5), 803–810.

Cheney, A (2011) 'Most girls want to be skinny': Body (dis)satisfaction among clinically diverse women. *Qualitative Health Research, 21*(10), 1347–1359.

Coole, D & Frost, S (Eds) (2010) *New Materialisms: Ontology, agency, and politics.* Durham, NC and London: Duke University Press.

Crawford, R (2006) Health as a meaningful social practice. *Health: An interdisciplinary journal for the social study of health, illness and medicine, 10*(4), 401–420.

Cronin, A & King, A (2010) Power, inequality and identification: Exploring diversity and intersectionality amongst older LGB adults. *Sociology, 44*(5), 876–892.

Daley, A (2006) Lesbian and gay health issues: OUTside of Canada's health policy. *Critical Social Policy, 26*(4), 794–816.

Davis, K (1997) *Embodied Practices: Feminist perspectives on the body.* London: Sage Publications.

Davis, K (2007) Reclaiming women's bodies: Colonialist trope or critical epistemology? *Sociological Review, 55*(1), 50–64.

Davis, K (2008) Intersectionality as buzzword: A sociology of science perspective on what makes feminist theory successful. *Feminist Theory, 9*(1), 67–85.

Department of Health (2010) *Healthy Lives, Healthy People: Our strategy for public health in England.* London. Department of Health.

Department of Health (2011) *Healthy Lives, Healthy People: A call to action on obesity in England.* Available from https://www.gov.uk/government/publications/healthy-lives-healthy-people-a-call-to-action-on-obesity-in-england [accessed 28 January 2012].

Einstein, G & Shildrick, M (2009) The postconventional body: Retheorising women's health. *Social Science and Medicine, 69*(2), 293–300.

Fish, J (2008) Navigating queer street: Researching the intersections of lesbian, gay, bisexual and trans (LGBT) identities in health research. *Sociological Research Online, 13*(1), 12. Available from http://www.socresonline.org.uk/13/1/12.html [accessed February 2014].

Fish, J (2009) Our health, our say: Towards a feminist perspective of lesbian health psychology. *Feminism and Psychology, 19*(4), 437–453.

Fish, J & Anthony, D (2005) UK National Lesbians and Health Care Survey. *Women and Health, 41*(3), 27–45.

Flax, J (1990) Postmodernism and gender relations in feminist theory. In L Nicholson (Ed) *Feminism/Postmodernism* (pp. 36–62). London: Routledge.

Foucault, M (1976) *The Birth of the Clinic.* London: Routledge.

Foucault, M (1988) *The History of Sexuality, Volume 3: The care of the self.* Harmondsworth: Penguin.

Fox, NJ (2012) *The Body.* Cambridge: Polity Press.

Fox, NJ & Ward, K (2006) Health identities: From expert patient to resisting consumer. *Health, 10*(4), 461–479.

Frank, A (1995) *The Wounded Storyteller: Body, illness and ethics.* London: University of Chicago Press.

Grosz, E (1994) *Volatile Bodies: Towards a coporeal feminism.* Bloomington and Indianapolis: Indiana University Press.

Halberstam, J (2013) Transgendered butch: Butch/FTM border wars and the masculine continuum. In DE Hall, A Jagoes, A Bebell & S Potter (Eds) *The Routledge Queer Studies Reader* (pp. 464–487.) London: Routledge.

Hemmings, C (2011) *Why Stories Matter: The political grammar of feminist theory.* Durham, NC: Duke University Press.

Jagose, A (2009) Feminism's queer theory. *Feminism and Psychology, 19*(2), 157–174.

Lindley, LL, Friedman, DB & Struble, C (2012) Becoming visible: Assessing the availability of online sexual health information for lesbians. *Health Promotion Practice, 13*(4), 472–480.

Lloyd, M (2005) *Beyond Identity Politics: Feminism, power and politics.* London: Sage Publications.

Lupton, D (1995) *The Imperative of Health: Public health and the regulated body.* London: Sage Publications.

Lupton, D (2003) *Medicine as Culture: Illness, disease and the body in western cultures* (2nd ed). London: Sage Publications.

Lupton, D (2013) *Fat (Shortcuts: Little books on big issues).* London: Routledge.

McLaughlin, J, Casey, ME & Richardson, D (2012) At the intersections of feminist and queer debates. In D Richardson, J McLaughlin & MA Casey (Eds) *Intersections Between Feminist and Queer Theory.* London: Palgrave.

McNay, L (1992) *Foucault and Feminism: A critical introduction.* Cambridge: Polity Press.

McNay, L (2004) Agency and experience: Gender as a lived relation. In LS Adkins & B Skeggs (Eds) *Feminism After Bourdieu* (pp. 175–190). Oxford: Blackwell.

McRuer, R (2013) Compulsory able-bodiedness and queer/disabled existence. In DE Hall, A Jagoes, A Bebell & S Potter (Eds) *The Routledge Queer Studies Reader* (pp. 488–497). London: Routledge.

Meleo-Erwin, Z (2012) Disrupting normal: Toward the 'ordinary and familiar' in fat politics. *Feminism and Psychology, 22*(3), 388–402.

Moore, S (2010) Is the healthy body gendered? Toward a feminist critique of the new paradigm of health. *Body & Society, 16*(2), 95–118.

Murray, S (2008) *The 'Fat' Female Body.* Basingstoke: Palgrave Macmillan.

Nettleton, S, Burrows, R & Watt, I (2008) Regulating medical bodies? The consequences of the 'modernisation' of the NHS and the disembodiment of clinical knowledge. *Sociology of Health Illness, 30*(3), 333–348.

Nicholson, L (Ed) (1990) *Feminism/Postmodernism.* London: Routledge.

Oliver, K (1993) *Reading Kristeva: Unravelling the double bind.* Bloomington, IN: Indiana University Press.

Oliver, K (Ed) (1997) *The Portable Kirsteva: European perspectives.* Chichester: Colombia University Press.

Petersen, A (2007) *The Body In Question: A socio-cultural approach.* London: Routledge.

Richardson, D & Monro, S (2012) *Sexuality, Equality and Diversity.* Basingstoke: Palgrave Macmillan.

Richardson, D, McLaughlin, J & Casey, M (Eds) (2012) *Intersections Between Feminist And Queer Theory.* Basingstoke: Palgrave Macmillan.

Riley, S, Burns, M, Frith, H, Wiggins, S & Markula, P (Eds) (2008) *Critical Bodies: Representations, identities and practices of weight and body management.* Basingstoke: Palgrave Macmillan.

Rose, N (2007) *The Politics of Life Itself: Biomedicine, power and subjectivity in the twenty-first century.* Oxford: Princeton University Press.

Roseneil, S (2000) Queer frameworks and queer tendencies: Towards an understanding of postmodern transformations of sexuality. *Sociological Research Online, 5*(3). Available from http://www.socresonline.org.uk/5/3/roseneil.html [accessed 28 January 2012].

Sawicki, J (1996) Feminism, Foucault and the 'subjects' of power and freedom. In S Hekman (Ed) *Feminists' Interpretations of Michel Foucault* (pp. 159–178). Pennsylvania: Pennsylvania State Press.

Seidman, S (1995) Deconstructing queer theory, or the undertheorisation of the social and the ethical. In L Nicholson & S Seidman (Eds) *Social Postmodernism* (pp. 116–141). Cambridge: Cambridge University Press.

Shildrick, M (1997) *Leaky Bodies and Boundaries: Feminism, postmodernism and (bio)ethics.* London: Routledge.

Shildrick, M (2002) *Embodying the Monster: Encounters with the vulnerable self.* London: Sage Publications.

Shilling, C (2003) *The Body and Social Theory.* London: Sage Publications.

Showden, C (2012) Theorising maybe: A feminist/queer theory convergence. *Feminist Theory, 13*(1), 3–25.

Stein, A & Plummer, K (1994) 'I can't even think straight': 'Queer' theory and the missing sexual revolution in sociology. *Sociological Theory, 12*(2), 178–187.

Taylor, Y (Ed) (2010) *Classed Intersections: Spaces, selves, knowledges.* Farnham: Ashgate.

Thomas, C (2007) *Sociologies of Disability and Illness: Contested ideas in disability studies and medical sociology.* Basingstoke: Palgrave Macmillan.

Tischner, I & Malson, H (2012) Deconstructing health and un/healthy 'fat' woman. *Journal of Community and Applied Social Psychology, 22*, 50–62.

Turner, BS (2008) *The Body and Society: Explorations in social theory* (3rd ed). Oxford: Blackwell.

Twigg, J (2006) *The Body in Health and Social Care.* Basingstoke: Palgrave Macmillan.

Weedon, C (1999) *Feminism, Theory and the Politics of Difference.* Oxford: Blackwell.

Williams, S (2003) *Medicine and the Body.* London: Sage Publications.

Williams, S (2006) Medical sociology and the biological body: Where are we now and where do we go from here? *Health: An interdisciplinary journal for the social study of health, illness and medicine, 10*(1), 5–30.

Williams, S & Bendelow, G (1998) *The Lived Body: Sociological themes, embodied issues.* London: Routledge.

Woolhouse, M, Day, K, Rickett, B & Milnes, K (2011) 'Cos girls aren't supposed to eat like pigs are they?' Young women negotiating gendered discursive constructions of food and eating. *Journal of Health Psychology, 17*(1), 46–56.

World Health Organization (2000) *Obesity: Preventing and managing the world epidemic. Report of a World Health Organization consultation* (World Health Organization technical report series 894). Geneva: WHO.

World Health Organization (2011) *Obesity and Overweight Factsheet, March 2011.* Available from http://www.who.int/mediacentre/factsheets/fs311/en/index.html [accessed 29 September 2011].

Yeatman, A (1994) *Postmodern Revisionings of the Political.* London: Routledge.

Yeatman, A, Dowsett, G, Fine, M & Guransky, D (Eds) (2009) *Individualization and the Delivery of Welfare Services: Contestation and complexity.* Basingstoke: Palgrave Macmillan.

# 10

# queer teeth

## – olu jenzen –

*There is no political power without control of the archive, if not of
memory. Effective democratization can always be measured by this
essential criterion: the participation in and the access to the archive, its
constitution, and its interpretation.*

(Derrida, 1995,11, n.1)

This chapter brings the methodologies of queer trauma studies (Brown,
2003; Cvetkovich, 2003) and the work coming out of the affective turn
within queer theory (Sedgwick, 2003; Love, 2007; Munt, 2007; Ahmed,
2010) to the debates of a particular section of medical history: the dental
research experiments at the Vipeholm Mental Hospital in Sweden (1945–
1955). In these experiments patients were fed large amounts of sugar to
provoke dental decay in order to generate empirical data. The nature of
trauma in this instance is manifested through bodily pain – toothache and
tooth loss – and the severely compromised wellbeing of the patients, but
it is also significantly bound up with the loss of individual dignity and
autonomy.[1]

The chapter draws on material from the hospital's own archive found
in its attic during a restoration of the buildings in the mid-1990s, in
combination with medical literature emerging from the dental research
and historical research, as well as the very scarce ethnographic sources
available. The archive material comprises mainly official documents, such
as reports from yearly inspections and incident reports, as well as clinical
notes from the experiments, but also some letters, notes, press cuttings
and photographs. The combination of material produced from within the
institution and later subsequent academic engagement and public debates

work together to produce a fuller picture of the experiment as well as everyday life at the hospital.

Queer trauma studies is an emerging field characterised by a critical engagement with evidence, the performative nature of trauma and ideological responses to public traumas. By approaching the archival material and its scholarly commentary from a queer theoretical point of view I will seek to articulate a different understanding of trauma that significantly departs from the dominant and pathologising understanding of trauma. The queerness of the sugar experiment archive material is not a stated tangible fact waiting to be uncovered. It is the structures of affect pervading this material that seem to respond to a queer reading. Working with this archival material, I ask questions about what the queer strategies required to respond to 'the strange archive of feelings' (Cvetkovich, 2003, p. 7) are when revisiting medical and healthcare histories. And how can queer critical engagement with cultures of trauma push beyond customary responses?

In a special issue of the journal *Traumatology* Brown and Pantalone (2011, p. 1) remark on the absence of work situated in the intersection of LGBT studies and trauma studies, stating that 'although often addressing similar concerns [the two fields] have operated in near isolation from another'. However, in the case of cultural theory, and as Cvetkovich (2003, p. 46) observes – commenting on Judith Butler's work – the perceived lack of intersections may be more a question of a separate lexicon. For example, Butler, Cvetkovich writes, 'place[s] trauma at the heart of subject formation', essentially theorising a form of insidious trauma but without using the terminology of trauma studies or clinical psychology. In other words, there is a rich vein of queer cultural critique that speaks to trauma as 'social and cultural discourse' (Cvetkovich, 2003, p. 18).

Correspondingly, there has been a purposeful engagement with the notion of 'the archive' within queer scholarship (Muñoz, 1996; Berlant, 1997; Cvetkovich, 2003, 2012; Morris, 2006; Danbolt, 2010) as well as within queer grassroots activism. Halberstam (2005, pp. 169–170), commenting on transgender lives, notes the political importance of subcultural archives: 'The archive is not simply a repository; it is also a theory of cultural relevance, a construction of collective memory, and a complex record of queer activity.' Furthermore, Rowley and Wolthers (2009, p. 14) highlight the centrality of affect in the queer archive: 'An alternative, queer archive (re)produces not solely knowledge but feeling.' However, queer engagements with the ideologies and contested nature of archives reach beyond LGBTQ-specific public memory work, to include endeavours to trace queer experiences  often 'systemically undocumented' (Cvetkovich, 2003, p. 38) – also in official historical documents and canonised collections of artefacts such as museums; and critical interventions that raise questions about archival heteronormativity and erasures of marginalised lives (Horn et al, 2010; Steorn, 2012). These enquiries fall within broader LGBTQ academic work that queries dominant ways of producing history across disciplines, and that has more recently also turned its attention to our own culture's attachment to a narrative of progression (Love, 2007).

The archive material relating to the dental research projects at Vipeholm has been the subject of a PhD thesis (Bommenel, 2006) and a Swedish radio documentary (Lundqvist, 2010) but beyond that has had very limited national and international critical attention.[2] Bommenel's work (2006), framed within science and technology studies, foregrounds research practice and how the scientists associated with the project had to negotiate pressures from the food industry, research interests and ethical considerations in relation to the contemporary political climate.

The aim in this chapter is different, namely to use this documentation to draw out dynamics of desire and trauma: the desire for and pleasure derived from the sweet candy patients were given in the experiment, and the trauma of the pain (toothache) and invasive oral examinations. This move builds on queer theoretical work that mobilises affect as a mode of doing history (Cvetkovich, 2003; Love, 2007; Freeman, 2010). In addition, this chapter also attempts to illuminate what it means to connect with a traumatic public past, particularly when any registering of its lived experiences is distinctly ephemeral. This particular feature of the archive material is one widely experienced in queer culture and is also in a sense the modus operandi for queer historiography. In the case of the dental experiments at Vipeholm what remains is only the official documentation: the record keeping of the scientists and management, clinical dental photographs, academic publications. In other words, the patients' reality is represented only very indirectly.

The trauma archive, like LGBT history, requires us to attend to the absences, silences and barely tangibly recorded imprints in the documents of dominant culture (Cvetkovich, 2003, p. 8). The significance of absence and silence here thus further reverberates the unrepresentability of trauma. Yet the archive seems to me to be an example of affects permeating public life in all sorts of queer ways. Trauma, as Cvetkovich notes, here 'becomes the hinge between systemic structures of exploitation and oppression and the felt experience of them' (2003, p. 12).

In what follows, I begin by situating the sugar experiment in a historical and cultural context. The chapter then moves on to approach the archive material and its debates from a queer theory of trauma perspective. What is offered here is not an emphatic reading of the cultural trauma of medical experiments. Rather, the will to reach reconciliation will be resisted. Thus the chapter aims to engage with the case of the sugar experiments through a queer theoretical lens as a form of cultural, ethical and political resistance. It draws on knowledge about archives and affect produced within queer scholarship but focusing on trauma, desire and embodiment in a wider sense than directly tied to sexuality.

## The Swedish welfare state and the Vipeholm institution

This section aims to provide some historical background to the archive material discussed in the chapter. The Vipeholm Hospital was founded in 1935. It was a national centre of expertise for the care of people with mental developmental disabilities or brain damage. It was set up in former army quarters and was intended to provide for the most severely disabled. The hospital was identified as the ideal location for the caries experiment as the study required a longitudinal sample from a group where dietary regimes could be implemented and controlled over a significant length of time. For the vast majority of the patients at Vipeholm, rehabilitation was not deemed possible. In other words, if an individual was taken into care at this institution they were likely to live out their life there. The Vipeholm patients were therefore seen as a much better option than prison inmates or soldiers, groups otherwise customarily recruited for medical experiments. Two-thirds of the approximately 1,000 Vipeholm inmates took part in the study, predominantly men but also women and children (Carlén-Nilsson & Holmér, 1998, p. 114).

The dental experiments (1945–1955) took place against a background of intense social and economic reform in Sweden. The mental healthcare system of the time was part legacy of nineteenth-century bourgeoisie philanthropy, part reformist instrument, used as a strategy for social control with the aim to practically as well as discursively shape the modern, productive and well-organised society the country aspired to: the 'Scandinavian model'. In the twentieth century the state had taken on a more active role in the care, control and housing of individuals who were deemed intellectually or mentally weak (Bommenel, 2006, p. 22; Frykman & Löfgren, 1985).[3]

Early twentieth-century discourses of mental disability and illness engage concepts such as otherness, citizenship, and eugenics and as such constitute, as Simonsen points out, a 'category for analyses of power and hierarchies' (2005, p. 138). As Tyden (2010) notes, research on Scandinavian eugenics has for a long time been deprioritised as it challenges the success story of the modern Scandinavian democratic welfare state and opens up debates about historical events that sit awkwardly in relation to Sweden's self-image. It may appear paradoxical that the welfare state, with its aim to develop a more democratic care system, was so ideologically invested in eugenics. However, as Tyden points out, it is not uncommon to find 'links between eugenics and progressive social thought' (2010, p. 37). Good health was regarded as a *national* rather than *individual* asset, and this view required the individual to fulfil their civil duty by maintaining their health in order to put it to the disposal of society (Palmblad & Eriksson, 1995, p. 151). Correspondingly, the intellectually disabled or mentally ill were seen as deprived of the prospect to contribute productively and achieve full citizenship. A project like the Vipeholm experiments was therefore perceived as an opportunity for the patients to approximate citizenship through their contribution to the welfare of greater society. It was seen to enhance their humanity rather than dehumanise. It is within this wider framework of an increasingly medicalised view on health and the body, in combination with ideologies of progress and productivity, that Scandinavian eugenics took form as a dominant discourse, and in 1922 the institute for eugenics was established in Uppsala, Sweden (Frykman & Löfgren, 1985, p. 40).

Historical research (Broberg & Tyden, 1999; Frykman, 1985; Runcis, 1998; Spektorowski & Mizrachi, 2004; Tyden, 2000, 2010) has shown that with emerging discourses of eugenics came a paradigmatic shift in attitudes towards people with intellectual disabilities or mental illness. From having been regarded as a vulnerable group in society, a view reflected in the emerging mental healthcare provision in Sweden during the late nineteenth century, the eugenics-informed view signified the reverse: that society needed protecting from these individuals. These debates have strong overtones of morality and fear of sexuality. In large part it was an imagined sexual deviancy among these groups in combination with pseudoscientific fears about hereditary illnesses spreading in the general population that informed attitudes towards people with mental disabilities and subsequently shaped the care system. Hospitals for the intellectually and mentally disabled became a means to keep these groups of people separate from the rest of society and to restrict their perceived uncontrollable sexuality (see Larsmo, 2010).

Public health constituted a central concern for the Swedish modern welfare state. The welfare state, Hilson notes, 'came during the interwar period to stand above all for modernity ... organised in new ways characterised by efficiency, rationality and hygiene' (2008). The reform employed a range of public health strategies. One was to educate and foster health regimes using scientific and moral rhetoric, often using popular media campaigns (increasingly so in the post-war period) (Palmblad & Eriksson, 1995). Other strategies were more practical, improved housing and the implementation of a pension system for example, but also the development of laws that gave the state increased rights to intervene in people's sexual lives, such as the law of 1934 that allowed the sterilisation of individuals who were branded carriers of genetic defects (Frykman & Löfgren, 1985, p. 51), although the application after an expansion of the law in 1941 was founded on a social as much as biological assessment.[4] Social and sexual otherness was thus policed through a medical discourse within which the legislation was only one, albeit a central, part.

There is an affinity between queer sexual and gender dissidence (and in particular trans folks' experiences) and those subjected to the dehumanising state-sanctioned sterilisation policies at the heart of the modern welfare state's discourse of intellectual and mental health disabilities (Broberg & Tyden, 1991, 1999; Porter, 1999; Runcis, 1998; Zaremba, 1999). My focus in this chapter does not concern reproductive sex per se, but rather takes an interest in the embodied experience of pleasure and trauma; however, the sterilisation debates are important here as they constitute the discursive context of the archive discussed and a field of intense cultural struggle.

The sterilisation policies and practices are revealing in respect of understanding the processes of othering through biopolitics (Foucault, 1997). In 1998 the Swedish government engaged a number of academics to investigate the nation's past sterilisation policies, including an international comparison of the Swedish laws and medical practices to those of other countries. The commission highlighted a number of areas of debate including aspects of medical ethics, the question of coercion/consent, underpinning ideologies of eugenics vis-à-vis practical aspects pertaining to birth control, as well as the overarching question of how our perception of the nature of the welfare state needed to be readjusted in light of an acknowledgement of the integral place of the sterilisation programme (see Broberg & Tyden, 1999).

Although the majority of the sterilisations were voluntary in a strictly legal meaning, the conditions under which consent was given were often imbued by unequal power structures. For socioeconomically disadvantaged women the need to access social benefits put them under pressure to seek voluntary sterilisation. In the case of the other major group of vulnerable members of society that were subject to systemic sterilisation – those classified as 'mentally defected' or 'feebleminded' (people with intellectual disabilities, mental illness and epilepsy) – and regularly institutionalised, 'sterilisation was often made a condition for discharge from institutions ... up until at least the early 1950s' (Broberg & Tyden, 1999, p. 142). Healthcare practitioners and social services thus effected normative structures inherent to the ideologies of the welfare model delineating categories of 'bodies that matter', to use Butler's term.

The 1990s surge in research on the Scandinavian history of sterilisation has posed a host of important and controversial questions about the 'others' of the modern welfare state – questions that have 'cut deeply into the Swedish historical and mental consciousness' (Broberg & Tyden, 1999, p. 143). However, I suggest that the compelling objective to seek closure on the sterilisation issue,[5] evident in the government's involvement, has been made difficult to achieve by the fact that sterilisation remained conditional for the legal recognition of a transgender person's chosen gender identity, and constituted a routine part of sex reassignment treatment in Sweden up until 2013. In other words, there is a distinct connection between queer lives of today and the histories and legacies of the sterilisation campaigns. This connection is, however, remarkably absent in the scholarly body of research and rarely broached in public media debates. A dividing and narcissistic focus on 'our responsibility and guilt to victims of history' (Broberg & Tyden, 1999, p. 141) has overshadowed the experiences of trans people subjected to state-enforced denial of their reproductive lives, as trauma, as well as the ongoing reproduction of marginalising sociomedical policies.[6] In the debates that ensued following the 1998 commission we see how trauma is discursively enlisted in specific ways: foregrounding central affective responses and suppressing other aspects. Therefore I argue that the queer response to both historical and contemporary normative trauma must be one of resisting reconciliation. My argument here is indebted to Heather Love's (2007) work which posits a challenge to LGBT narratives of progress that implicitly requires a disavowal of histories of injury and shame. However, she argues, such desire to detach ourselves from injurious or shameful pasts makes it 'difficult to approach the past as something living – as something dissonant, beyond our control, and capable of touching us in the present' (2007, pp. 9–10).

The residual spectre of eugenics in the enactment of this type of biotechnical control on queer bodies warrants further critical engagement, but the aim in this chapter will be to discursively open up new aspects of the embodiment of trauma through queer models of thinking, by focusing on the nexus of oral sensations of pain and pleasure in the sugar experiments.

## The sugar experiment

The Vipeholm caries experiments, and their central component, the 'sugar experiment', have been deemed highly significant for the development of modern dental health; however, they also caused significant human suffering, a traumatic legacy of the dental health regimes of the contemporary welfare state. It is a 'history of progress' that continues to haunt.

The experiments were commissioned within the dual context of the public health reform at the heart of the emerging welfare state combined with the striving for professionalisation among dentists seeking to give their practice scientific recognition (Bommenel, 2006, p. 19). By the late 1930s caries was endemic and considered the most prevalent health problem in the population. This also had significant financial implications as a national health dental provision had been introduced in 1938, and the scale of the caries endemic threatened to rapidly exhaust its budget. At the point of commissioning the experiment the cause of caries was not scientifically established. The prevailing theory supposed that caries was a symptom of generally poor health. The sugar experiment essentially established the specific correlation between caries and sticky carbohydrates.

The sugar experiment came to an end in 1955. As a result of the findings the dental care provision changed from having mainly provided reactive treatment to an emphasis on proactive or preventive treatment. Its significance for the development of modern odontology is still upheld (see Krasse, 2001, p. 1787). The experiment also resulted in a number of large-scale national public health information campaigns which aimed to instigate behavioural and dietary changes (Petersson, 1991). A further enduring legacy of the experiment that remains thoroughly engrained in Swedish everyday culture and vernacular is the concept of 'Saturday sweets', which essentially means that children are not allowed sweet snacks or candy during the week but are instead rewarded with a generous helping of sweets on the Saturday. This is a direct translation into practice of the scientific findings that had established that slow prolonged exposure to sticky carbohydrates is more damaging than a short, albeit concentrated, exposure (Krasse, 2001).

Initially the experiment was of a benign nature; the principal method involved augmenting the nutrition value of the patients' diet in various ways to study the impact of the dietary composition on the caries process.[7] However, when this didn't produce the results the researchers were looking for, the strategy changed and harm was done by deliberately causing rapid dental decay for the sake of generating data about how caries gradually destroys the teeth. At the end of the experiment 50 or so patients had no remaining teeth at all.

The principal change in strategy was to implement a regime of a very high intake of sugar (Bommenel, 2006, pp. 208–209). A specially made toffee, particularly sticky and large enough not to be swallowed whole, was administered among the patients in the project at intervals throughout the day, every day (some were on a regime of 24 toffees a day, some were on eight toffees a day, some were given chocolate instead of the toffees etc; all were given sugar solution to drink throughout the day)[8]. The type of toffee used in the experiment was not a type of candy available to the general public, but specifically designed, in collaboration with the confectionery industry, to optimise the exposure of the teeth to carbohydrates. In other words, it was designed to cause maximal damage. The extreme phase of the sugar experiment lasted for about two years (1947–1949). During this period the sugar intake was further increased and the damage caused to the patients' teeth went untreated (Bommenel, 2006, p. 209) although at the end of the project damaged teeth were repaired (Petersson, 1991) or removed.

From this short outline it is clear that the project from today's perspective would be deemed unethical.[9] However, the archive material indicates a more complex picture. For example, generally speaking the project was perceived in a positive light at the hospital. It was embraced by the nursing staff who also were invited to be examined as part of the experiment.[10] More importantly, the introduction of sweets and pastries on the wards was in fact regarded by staff (and presumably the inmates too) as a perk – something that made the hospital environment a nice place to work and live. A member of staff narrates:

> … we were offered lots of chocolate bars; 'you should eat a bar of chocolate per day.' … They [staff] were given large boxes of chocolate

to take home that they should eat.

(Cited in Carlén-Nilsson & Holmér, 1998, p. 115, my translation)

The member of nursing staff interviewed here narrates about the experiment in a jovial tone that also reveals a critical distance, expressing doubts about the rigour of the design of the trials:

And then the children [on the wards] had big parties, because there was so much chocolate [left] to finish. So the chocolate study was worth nothing really. It was probably a failure.

(Cited in Carlén-Nilsson & Holmér, 1998, p. 115, my translation)

Patients did not participate on the same voluntary basis. The sugar mixed into their diet could not be avoided and although patients were not formally forced to eat the toffees and pastries in between meals (Carlén-Nilsson & Holmér, 1998, p. 115; Bommenel, 2006, p. 211) it is highly questionable to what extent they were in a position to exercise their right to decline. As Petersson (1991) notes, only practical reasons from the point of view of the research team determined whether a person would be part of the project or not. In other words, if a person was too difficult to handle, they may be excluded from the project. A note from Dr Larson, a physician who was part of the newly arrived research team, to Dr Fröderberg, the senior physician in charge of the whole of the hospital, dated 11 October 1945 gives us some insight into the researchers' perspective:

The [nursing] staff on all wards have done their best to facilitate [our] work with the often rather difficult to handle clientele. … Patients have frequently been resistant and negative, sometimes exceptionally frightened.

(Vipeholmarkivet F3A,[11] my translation)

That people in authority used violence to make the patients comply was probably not uncommon in care institutions at the time, and a range of corporeal restraining tools were also routinely used to handle 'difficult' (violent, destructive, self-harming) patients. For the physician coming into this environment from the outside, the patients' fear of being hit was doubtless a bit startling, as we can tell from the note. It also made it difficult for the researchers to work with patients. Furthermore, Larson remarks on the unexpected nature of persistent resistance where he expected none:

> It has been remarkable how also weak patients of slender build have
> been able to offer very effective resistance to examination.

No physical force was used, but that does not mean that consent was
sought. The 'ideal' scenario from a scientific point of view would be to
create near constant exposure of the teeth to the sugar, so nursing staff were
in all likelihood pressurised to encourage patients to always have a toffee
melting in their mouth. The number of toffees an individual consumed
was monitored and recorded (Carlén-Nilsson & Holmér, 1998, p. 115).
Everyday life on the wards was, however, lacking in clinical precision. A
member of staff describes scenarios very different from what would be
expected in a scientific trial:

> … patients were given pastries and the women who had a big chest,
> they hid these [pieces of pastry] under their breasts. So in the evenings
> when we were undressing them we had to remove the pastries.
>
> (Cited in Carlén-Nilsson & Holmér, 1998, p. 115, my translation)

There are also further accounts of patients' 'unauthorised' interaction with
the toffees: twiddling with them, kneading them into lumps, etc. And
the unceasing snacking meant that patients constantly had sticky fingers.
A member of staff complainingly recalls the increased labour involved in
cleaning the ward:

> … the common room got grubby because the patients had very sticky
> hands. They touched windowsills, beds and tables.
>
> (Cited in Carlén-Nilsson & Holmér, 1998, p. 115, my translation)

So toffees were not just in the mouth, they were all over and bodily
experienced in various tactile ways. The regime enforced upon the persons
involved became their structure of expression, including emotional
expressions and creative responses. The trauma endured is not diminished
by these pieces of information about the embodied and affective relation
to the toffees, but illustrates the complex nexus of trauma and everyday
life that the scholarship of Cvetkovich and others has sought to bring into
critical focus.

## Queer approaches to trauma

Ann Cvetkovich has theorised cultural trauma and public acts of mourning and remembrance from a position of queer critique. Looking at the Swedish debates around sterilisation, discussed above, we can see how they rely on an active repression of contemporary practices of sterilisation of trans people undergoing a sex change in order to construct a narrative of ethical progression.

Another aspect that Cvetkovich emphasises as emblematic of a queer approach to trauma is the recognition of how connected trauma is to 'the textures of everyday experience' (2003, p. 3) as mentioned above. This relates to feminist therapist Laura Brown's theorising of what she calls 'insidious trauma' (1995) attending to types of trauma without an identifiable 'event' that would include duress caused by systemic racism, poverty, heterosexism and homophobia.

The embodiment of trauma – how it manifests as lived experience through affect and resilience – is traceable in the Vipeholm material. The patients' experiences and expressions queerly transfer both desire and resistance to the mouth. In this respect the archive material reflects a queerness that stems from a repudiation of heteronormative understandings of desire and pleasure. The issue of sterilisation, discussed briefly above, did not seem to have been a major agenda at Vipeholm. This was not because the institution management diverted from mainstream consensus in their view on this practice, but rather because the patients were deemed non-sexual beings due to the gravity of their disability, rendering sterilisation redundant in their case (Bommenel, 2006, p. 48);[12] non-sexual, that is, in the heteronormative definition of sexuality as reproductive and exclusively concerning genitalia. So what about the pleasures of the mouth? It is not hard to imagine how the satisfaction of the toffee melting in the mouth may constitute an augmented sensory stimulus in an otherwise extremely austere institutional existence. This point is to show up the often highly complex nature of insidious trauma and does not in any way attempt to condone the practice. It also offers opportunity to think about the queer practice of taking pleasure in situations where none was intended. The purpose of the toffees was clinical, nothing to do with the experience of the participants, yet an embodied 'culture' developed around them, as the archive material shows.

The archive also registers acts of resistance. In this respect, teeth are an agent of anger. The official records reveal how the dentists and other personnel met resistance in the form of patients refusing to open their mouth (Bommenel, 2006, p. 136) or biting them (Lundqvist, 2010). This reality stands in stark contrast to the medical board's confidence in having 'complete control' over the hospital patients, which they expressed in the proposition to use them as investigational subjects.[13] During the first phase of the experiment (1944–1945), which involved a survey of the dental health of the participants, the researchers found it challenging to make the patients comply and conduct examinations without risk of biting. They dealt with this first by administering a sedative (Fenemal) to the participants prior to examination, and second by inserting a block into the patient's mouth to prevent them from biting down during examination (Bommenel in Lundqvist, 2010). Pressure point techniques like pulling the patient's eyelids upwards to make them open their mouth were also used.[14] The patients' reactions often baffled the researchers though, as this account by the physician Dr Larson illustrates:

> Making patients open their mouth has often not worked until one has pulled the eyelids upwards, upon which the patients not uncommonly have opened up their mouth wide open; it has sometimes subsequently been difficult to make them close their mouth again.[15]

So, it was possible to make the patient comply to open their mouth, but no one had thought about a technique for making the patient close their mouth, probably because this act of resistance was unanticipated. It may seem a small or passive act of resistance, to refuse to close your mouth again, but it no doubt disrupted the work schedule and offered a queer or sideways gesture in response to the hyper-rationalised ways of the project and its self-serving aims. I recognise, in this short paragraph, dominant culture's bewilderment when faced with acts of excess that reflects back to this culture its own absurdity, showing up cracks in its assumed rational logic.

In fact, the 'difficulty' of the patients radically reduced the number of participants in the trial – from 1,000 to 660 – as it was stipulated by the medical board that no force of violence was to be used within the project, although this figure also includes patients who for other reasons were excluded.[16] There were also other, less aggressive forms of resistance like avoiding eating the toffees. In a typed document found in the archive a member of staff recalls moving a bedside table, finding it exceptionally heavy, and on closer inspection discovering inside a massive ball of toffees stuck together. 'The lump of toffee weighed no less than seven kilos' (cited in Carlén-Nilsson & Holmér, 1998, p. 115, my translation). The patient, 'Pettersson', had discreetly hidden his portions of toffee inside the bedside table. The artefact speaks of coping strategies developed in response to institutional enforcement of power. It is also a very powerful metaphorical visualisation of the accumulative nature of insidious trauma: a transformation of numerous 'sweeties' into an indigestible lump. And furthermore, the materiality of this ball of toffees – its weight, its sticky surface, its sugar-sweet smell – becomes a testimony of exploitation, an archive of feeling.

Thus, paying attention to the significance of the teeth and oral sensory orders in this material, what the sugar experiment archive of feelings illustrates is exactly the ambivalent status of trauma as pointed out by Mark Seltzer (1997, pp. 4–5) who notes the 'very uncertainties as to the status of the wound in trauma – as physical or psychical, as private or public', and how this produces trauma as cultural text that has 'come to function not merely as a sort of switch point between bodily and psychic orders; it has, beyond that, come to function as a switch point between individual and collective, private and public orders of things'.

## Conclusion

This chapter has sought to highlight the 'messy' nature of trauma, and discuss the potential of queer responses to a medical archive as an archive of feelings. It has focused on the non-pathologising ethos of queer culture and how this may be attuned to the subtleness of the affect of trauma as bound up with a host of other feelings, sometimes including those relating to desire and pleasure.

I also emphasise the need to politicise trauma. This involves moving away from individualising perspectives, insisting instead on the correlation between structural social injustice, discrimination, violence and the individual's lived experience. The layers of discourse within the Vipeholm material – from the construction of the nation, to the structures of the health and dentistry programmes, and the everyday life at the institution – and their interconnectedness help to illuminate this. The chapter has highlighted gestures of resistance that have left an imprint in the archive material, but my reading in itself also offers resistance to regarding the sugar experiments as a contained moment in time which we are now able to mourn. The impetus to do so, to position ourselves as detached from a past that is marked as 'failing' (medically or ethically), I argue, is part of what caused the public trauma of the state-enforced sterilisations to be played out without acknowledging the *ongoing* enforced sterilisations of transgender people. This chapter thus does not directly address the question of LGBTQ visibility in medical history per se but rather focuses on the notion of trauma, as never fully knowable, suggesting that queer political and theoretical engagements may fruitfully insist on a resistance of closure. In this way queer approaches may productively draw on the notion of queer as awkward – continuously insisting on disturbance where mainstream culture wants reconciliation; 'seeking to illuminate the forms of violence that are forgotten or covered over by the amnesiac powers of national culture' (Cvetkovich, 2003, p. 16). The national sense of public health as a success story with its preventive and democratising achievements has demonstrated very strong 'amnesiac powers' and this chapter has sought to illustrate the affective cost involved.

Cvetkovich (2003, p. 3) offers a broadening up of the conception of trauma, not just beyond the canonised discourses of trauma (Holocaust and war narratives), but importantly beyond the individualising and medicalising discourses of physical and psychic trauma, to be 'a name for experiences of socially situated political violence' thus forging 'overt connections between politics and emotion' (2003, p. 12). The approach Cvetkovich suggests is, we could say, a way to let the knowledge of queer sexualities and their histories inform a rethinking of trauma:

> Thinking about trauma from the same depathologizing perspective that has animated queer understandings of sexuality opens up possibilities for understanding traumatic feelings not as a medical problem in search for a cure but as felt experience that can be mobilized in a range of directions.
>
> (2003, p. 47)

Building on Cvetkovich's argument I suggest that part of what queer theoretical methodologies and approaches can contribute to health discourses, policy and practice is to serve as a resource for a 'demedicalised and depathologised model of trauma', but also one that is less bound by mainstream moral values.

The chapter also problematises the taken-for-granted notion that healthcare systems offer to protect vulnerable citizens. This is an issue of continuous relevance. The case of the sugar experiment, as well as the case of enforced sterilisation of transgendered individuals seeking to go through the juridical process of sex reassignment, both offer valuable lessons that the definition of vulnerable, for example, is historically contingent in distinct ways. It is therefore important to try to understand the conditions under which such categories are produced. The processes involved are akin to those described by Judith Butler (2004) as being enacted in the delineation between grievable and non-grievable lives. The healthcare system of the early twentieth century Swedish welfare state designated an idealised – imagined – healthy and productive population as 'vulnerable', in need of protection from the intellectually disabled or mentally ill, and this is evident in the sterilisation policies, regarded essentially as protective actions, not of the individual concerned but of others. Similarly, the aim of the dental research was not to improve or protect the health of the people involved.

Healthcare and its public discourses continue to constitute a key arena in which hierarchies of bodies are formed. As such, it requires continued queer critical engagement, not least in a current political climate that sees the notion of economic crisis being enlisted in discourse and practices that seek to regulate access to healthcare in ways that produce new categories of health loss.

## Endnotes

1. Bo Petersson (1991) points out as particularly humiliating one of the (several) additional side projects that involved the continuous collection of saliva for up to 36 consecutive days, with the extraction of saliva taking place 'more or less the entire time the patient is awake', as the scientific report states (*Tandkaries och Kolhydrater,* 1953, pp. 281–282).

2. See also an article by Bo Petersson (1991) on the Vipeholm dental project and research ethics, where he pointed out that in particular the ethical aspects of the experiment had not been critically discussed in public debate since the mid-1950s.

3. The industrialised and increasingly urbanised welfare society saw a wider trend of centralising and institutionalising different forms of care of children, the elderly and ill people, care that was previously provided by family and the local community.

4. The official figure for sterilisations in Sweden during the period 1935–1975 is in excess of 60,000 people (over 90 per cent of these women).

Among those subjected to this procedure were people deemed mentally ill, alcoholics, criminals, or otherwise antisocial, but race and ethnicity factors also featured and the Roma community was particularly targeted, see Frykman & Löfgren, 1985, p. 52. For an overview of research on other Scandinavian countries see Simonsen, 2005.

5. Approximately 1,600 still-living individuals sterilised against their will were paid compensation from the government as a result of the commission's findings (see Tyden, 2010).

6. Brown and Pantalone (2011, p. 2) note that 'the paucity of research on trauma and transgender individuals is striking'.

7. The trials within the larger study can be divided into two: first, the beneficiary vitamin experiment (supplementing the basic diet with different forms of vitamins); second, the damaging carbohydrate experiment which in turn had subdivided groups (diet high in fat, diet high in sugar and the toffee group).

8. The different groups are outlined in the 1952 project report, *Tandkaries och Kolhydrater: Vipeholms-undersökningarna 1947–1951*. Supplement to the journal *Svensk Tandläkare Tidskrift*, 1953, p. 120.

9. No participants or their next of kin were asked to give consent (see Petersson, 1993). The hospital population had on average less caries than the general population at the beginning of the project, so it is clear that any research undertaken was not primarily for the benefit of the participants but for the rest of society. However, Bommenel (2006) demonstrates how the experiments were very much in line with welfare ideals of the time. The experiments were never considered in relation to the Nüremberg Code (1947) partly because they were initially planned before the code was publicised but it also seems that the Swedish researchers' interpretation of the code was that it gave directives for 'extreme' circumstances, not the regular and reasonable type of research they engaged in, so it was simply not relevant to them (Bommenel, 2006, p. 53). Nevertheless, media attention and a debate in parliament that raised ethical concerns in 1952/3 probably contributed to the closing down of the project in 1955 (Eriksson & Månson, 1991, pp. 31–35); although, as Bommenel concludes, the scientists successfully met the criticism at the time, the criticisms subsided and they secured further funding. She also demonstrates that internal debates around ethics and patient welfare did take place and that the project was not without limitations in this respect (2006, pp. 207–208). I think that the project illustrates the changes in attitudes towards people with intellectual or mental disabilities as well as attitudes towards the role of medical research and accountabilities, in that some of the objections

raised in the 1953 debates were not even considered in the design of the project in the mid-1940s.

10. Such offer of free dental care to those who took part was regarded as an attractive work benefit.

11. Vipeholmarkivet F3A (archive material), my translation.

12. Minutes from the 1942 yearly inspection by an external board mention castration as possible treatment of 'previously sexually unreliable patients' (Vipeholmarkivet F7A, my translation) but I have not found any notes about a follow-up on this.

13. Letter to the King dated 13 October 1944, from Höjer, Björck & Hedborg (of the National Medical Board) (Vipeholmarkivet, F3A).

14. Vipeholmarkivet F3A.

15. Correspondence from Larson to Fröderberg dated 11 October 1945 (Vipeholmarkivet F3A, my translation).

16. For example, a report from 29 December 1945 states that 44 patients were excluded owing to not having any teeth and that patients with TB were excluded as they presented a health risk to the researchers (Vipeholmarkivet, F3A).

# References

Ahmed, S (2010) *The Promise of Happiness*. Durham, NC: Duke University Press.

Berlant, L (1997) *The Queen of America Goes to Washington City: Essays on sex and citizenship*. Durham, NC: Duke University Press.

Bommenel, E (2006) *Sockerförsöket: Kariesexperimenten 1943–1960 på Vipeholms sjukhus för sinneslöa*. Lund: Arkiv.

Broberg, G & Tyden, M (1991) *Oönskade i Folkhemmet: Rashygien och sterilisering i sverige*. Stockholm: Gidlunds.

Broberg, G & Tyden, M (1999) Introduction. *Scandinavian Journal of History, 24*(2), 141–143.

Brown, LS (1995) Not outside the range: One feminist perspective on psychic trauma. In C Caruth (Ed) *Trauma: Explorations in memory* (pp. 100–112). Baltimore, MD: Johns Hopkins University Press.

Brown, LS (2003) Sexuality, lies, and loss: Lesbian, gay, and bisexual perspectives on trauma. *Journal of Trauma Practice, 2*, 55–68.

Brown, LS & Pantalone, D (2011) Lesbian, gay, bisexual and transgender issues in trauma psychology: A topic comes out of the closet. *Traumatology, 17*(2), 1–3.

Butler, J (2004) *Precarious Life: The power of mourning and violence*. London: Verso.

Carlén-Nilsson, C & Holmér, U (Eds) (1998) *Röster från Vipeholm*. Lund: Stiftelsen Medicinhistoriska Museerna i Lund och Helsingborg.

Cvetkovich, A (2003) *An Archive of Feelings: Trauma, sexuality, and lesbian public cultures*. London: Duke University Press.

Cvetkovich, A (2012) Queer archival futures: Case study Los Angeles. *e-misférica, 9*(1–2). Available from http://hemisphericinstitute.org/hemi/en/e-misferica-91/cvetkovich [accessed 1 July 2013].

Danbolt, M (2010) We're here! We're queer? Activist archives and archival activism. *Lambda Nordica, 3–4,* 90–118.

Derrida, J (1995) Archive fever: A Freudian impression. *Diacritics, 25*(2), 9–63.

Eriksson, BE & Månson, P (1991) *Den Goda Tanken: Om etik och moral i forskning med människor*. Stockholm: Allmäna Förlaget.

Foucault, M (1997) The birth of biopolitics. In P Rabinow (Ed) *Ethics: Subjectivity and truth*. London: Allen Lane.

Freeman, E (2010) *Time Binds: Queer temporalities, queer histories*. Durham, NC: Duke University Press.

Frykman, J & Löfgren, O (Eds) (1985) *Modärna Tider: Vision och vardag i folkhemmet*. Malmö: Liber.

Halberstam, J (2005) *In a Queer Time and Place: Transgender bodies, subcultural lives*. New York: New York University Press.

Hilson, M (2008) *The Nordic Model: Scandinavia since 1945*. London: Reaktion.

Horn, A, Winchester, O & Smith, M (2010) *Queering the Museum* [exhibition catalogue]. Available from http://www.bmag.org.uk/uploads/fck/file/Queeringbrochure-web.pdf [accessed 1 July 2013].

Krasse, B (2001) The Vipeholm dental caries study: Recollections and reflections 50 years later. *Journal of Dental Research*, *80*(9), 1785–1788.

Larsmo, O (2010) Agne, ett av alla offer för svensk rasbiologi. *Dagens Nyheter*, 30 March. Available from http://www.dn.se/kultur-noje/kulturdebatt/agne-ett-av-alla-offer-for-svensk-rasbiologi/ [accessed 1 August 2013].

Love, H (2007) *Feeling Backward: Loss and the politics of queer history*. London: Harvard University Press.

Lundqvist, I (2010) *Vipeholmsexperimenten* [radio documentary]. Sveriges Radio P3. Available from http://sverigesradio.se/sida/gruppsida.aspx?programid=2519&grupp=17048&artikel=4217367 [accessed 1 August 2013].

Morris, CE (2006) Archival queer. *Rhetoric and Public Affairs*, *9*(1), 145–151.

Muñoz, JE (1996) Ephemera as evidence: Introductory notes to queer acts. *Women & Performance: A journal of feminist theory*, *8*(2), 5–16.

Munt, SR (2007) *Queer Attachments: The cultural politics of shame*. Aldershot: Ashgate.

Palmblad, E & Eriksson, BE (1995) *Kropp och Politik: Hälsoupplysning som samhällsspegel från 30-tal till 90-tal*. Stockholm: Carlsson.

Petersson, B (1991) Etik och Kolhydrater: En forskningsetisk studie om Vipeholmsundersökningarna 1945–1955. *VEST Tidskrift för Vetenskapsstudier*, *5*(2–3), 3–20. Also in English: Petersson, B (1993) The mentally retarded as research subjects: A research ethics study of the Vipeholm investigations of 1945–1955. *Studies in Research Ethics*, *3*, 1–32.

Porter, D (1999) Eugenics and the sterilization debate in Sweden and Britain before World War II. *Scandinavian Journal of History*, *24*(2), 145–162.

Rowley, J & Wolthers, L (2009) Lost and found: Queerying the archive. In M Danbolt, J Rowley & L Wolthers (Eds) *Lost and Found: Queerying the archive* (pp. 9–23). Copenhagen: Nikolaj Copenhagen Contemporary Art Center.

Runcis, M (1998) *Steriliseringar i Folkhemmet.* Stockholm: Ordfront.

Sedgwick, EK (2003) *Touching Feeling: Affect, pedagogy, performativity.* Durham, NC: Duke University Press.

Seltzer, M (1997) Wound culture: Trauma in the pathological public sphere. *October, 80,* 3–26.

Simonsen, E (2005) Disability history in Scandinavia: Part of an international research field. *Scandinavian Journal of Disability Research, 7*(3–4), 137–154.

Spektorowski, A & Mizrachi, E (2004) Eugenics and the welfare state in Sweden: The politics of social margins and the idea of a productive society. *Journal of Contemporary History, 39,* 333–352.

Steorn, P (2012) Curating queer heritage: Queer knowledge and museum practice. *Curator, 55*(3), 355–365. (1953) Tandkaries och Kolhydrater: Vipeholms-undersökningarna 1947–1951 (Supplement). *Svensk Tandläkare Tidskrift, 45.*

Tyden, N (2000) *Från Politik till Praktik: De Svenska steriliseringslagarna 1935–1975.* SOU.

Tyden, N (2010) The Scandinavian states: Reformed eugenics applied. In A Bashford & P Levine (Eds) *The Oxford Handbook of the History of Eugenics* (pp. 154–172). Oxford: Oxford University Press.

Zaremba, M (1999) *De Rena och de Andra: Om tvångssteriliseringar, rashygien och arvsynd.* Stockholm: Dagens Nyheter. toffee group).

# contributors

**Dr Kay Aranda**

Kay Aranda is a Principal Lecturer in the Faculty of Health and Applied Social Science at the University of Brighton in the UK. She has worked in the NHS and voluntary sector, and in community nursing, primary care and women's health. With an academic background in the social sciences and theoretical interests in feminist theories and practices, her research and interests include gender, health inequalities and questions of difference. She has recently written on the body, embodiment and recognition in healthcare, and is currently interested in how feminist and women's health concerns might be explored through the practice turn in contemporary social theory.

**Leela Bakshi**

Leela Bakshi took part in the Count Me In Too project researching LGBT lives in Brighton and Hove, initially as a participant and subsequently as part of the research team. This has led to a role as an 'activist researcher', working with university researchers in academic fora that offer opportunities for LGBT activism. Leela co-authored with Dr Kath Browne the book *Ordinary in Brighton: LGBT, activisms and the city* (Ashgate, 2013).

**Dr Kath Browne**

Kath Browne is a Reader at the University of Brighton. Her research interests lie in sexualities, genders and spatialities. She was the Lead Researcher on the Count Me In Too research and has worked on LGBT equalities, lesbian geographies, gender transgressions and women's spaces. She has authored a number of journal publications, co-wrote *Ordinary in Brighton: LGBT, activisms and the city* (Ashgate, 2013) and *Queer Spiritual Spaces* (Ashgate, 2010), and co-edited *Queer Methods and Methodologies* (Ashgate, 2010) and *Geographies of Sexualities: Theory, practices and politics* (Ashgate, 2009).

## Dr Alec Grant

Alec Grant is Reader in Narrative Mental Health, School of Health Sciences, University of Brighton. He qualified as a mental health nurse in the mid-1970s and went on to study psychology, social science and psychotherapy. He is widely published in the fields of critical ethnography, autoethnography, clinical supervision, cognitive behavioural psychotherapy, and communication and interpersonal skills. His current and developing research interests and writing coalesce in the areas of narrative inquiry, critical inquiry and autoethnography informed by poststructural representational forms.

## Dr Olu Jenzen

Olu Jenzen is Senior Lecturer in Media Studies at the University of Brighton. Her research spans across a variety of overlapping fields of inquiry within media, cultural studies and literature. She has published on cultures of trauma, the politics of aesthetic form, queer theory and psychoanalysis, as well as social aspects of non-normative epistemologies (the uncanny, the paranormal, etc). She recently co-edited the special double issue of the *Journal of Lesbian Studies,* 'Revolting Bodies, Desiring Lesbians' (Routledge, 2013).

## Dr Helen Leigh-Phippard

Helen Leigh-Phippard has a PhD in international relations and was a university lecturer until she developed mental health problems in the late 1990s and was diagnosed with psychotic depression. In 2004 she joined Brighton and Hove Mind's LiVE (Listening to the Voice of Experience) Project and since then has been actively engaged in local service user participation. She contributes to the development and delivery of training to local mental health service providers, to the training of nurses at the University of Brighton, and to the development of research as a member of Sussex Partnership Trust's Lived Experience Advisory Forum (LEAF).

## Professor Sally R Munt

Sally R Munt is Professor of Gender and Cultural Studies, and Director of the Sussex Centre for Cultural Studies, at the University of Sussex. She has produced many books and articles in queer studies, including *Queer Attachments: The cultural politics of shame* (Ashgate, 2007). Sally is currently writing on refugees and cultural values (funded by the AHRC), and studying for an MSc in Psychiatry.

## Dr Lee Price

Lee is a Principal Lecturer at the University of Brighton. His academic interests are occupational therapy across a range of mental and physical health topics. He has a specific interest in culture and diversity in relation to health and social care. He has presented his work at a number of national and international conferences. He has also conducted research projects concerning older gay men's health and social care needs. He is currently working on a project to explore the socio-historical events in the lives of older gay men and lesbians that helped shape their self-identity.

## Jane Traies

Jane Traies is a postgraduate student at the University of Sussex; her PhD research is an empirical study of the lives and experiences of older lesbians in the UK. Her publications include '"Women like that": Older lesbians in the UK', in R Ward, I Rivers and M Sutherland, *Lesbian, Gay, Bisexual and Transgender Ageing: Biographical approaches for inclusive care and support* (Jessica Kingsley Publishers, 2012).

## Dr Georgina Voss

Georgina Voss is an Associate at the Helen Hamlyn Centre for Design, Royal College of Art. She was awarded her MSc and PhD in Science and Technology Policy from SPRU, University of Sussex; and she also holds a position as an Honorary Research Associate at the Department of Science and Technology Studies, UCL. Voss's research has focused on gender and sexuality; industrial sociology, particularly of the creative and digital sectors; and user-led design practices and ethics. Her work has been published in the *Journal of Homosexuality*, *Oxford Handbook of the Creative Industries* and *Sexualities*.

## Dr Laetitia Zeeman

Laetitia Zeeman has a clinical and academic background in mental health, narrative therapy and clinical governance, gained in South Africa and England. This exposure acts as foundation to her current teaching, scholarly activities and research as a Senior Lecturer in the Faculty of Health and Social Science at the University of Brighton. She is interested in developing knowledge and practices that question dominant discourses of health and recognise the strengths and abilities of people when they face adversity, or have gained experience of mental health problems. Her research explores the interface between gender, sexuality and mental health via critical discourse analysis and narrative inquiry.

# index